MIRRORS
in T I M E

5-2-00

Doria -

    with best wishes for
your journey through time
as you mark the milestone of
your Bat Mitzvah -

Joel Ziff

MIRRORS
in T I M E

A Psycho-Spiritual Journey
through the Jewish Year

Joel Ziff

JASON ARONSON INC.
Northvale, New Jersey
London

This book was set in 12 pt. Garamond by FASTpages of Nanuet, New York.

Copyright © 1996 by Jason Aronson Inc.

10 9 8 7 6 5 4 3 2 1

Acknowledgments of copyright permissions appear in the Credits section at the back of the book.

Library of Congress Cataloging-in-Publication Data

Ziff, Joel David, 1947–
    Mirrors in time : a psycho-spiritual journey through the Jewish
year / Joel D. Ziff.
      p. cm.
    Includes index.
    ISBN 0–7657–5977–2 (alk. paper)
    1. Judaism and psychology.   2. Psychotherapy—Religious aspects—
Judaism.   3. Fasts and feasts—Judaism.   I. Title.
BM538.P68Z54   1996
296.4'3'019—dc20   96–43830
                                         CIP

Manufactured in the United States of America. Jason Aronson Inc. offers books and cassettes. For information and catalog write to Jason Aronson Inc., 230 Livingston Street, Northvale, New Jersey 07647.

לְדוֹר וָדוֹר נַגִּיד גָּדְלֶךָ

To my grandparents
Sara Hene and Tuvia Geffen
Rashe Minna and Nahman Ziff

To my parents
Helen Geffen Ziff and Sam Ziff, ז״ל

To my wife
Elizabeth Rosenzweig

To our children
Max Gershon
Lev Samuel

דוֹר לְדוֹר יְשַׁבַּח מַעֲשֶׂיךָ

CONTENTS

Preface   xvii

Acknowledgments   xxv

1 THE CIRCLE OF THE YEAR: INTEGRATING
  PSYCHOTHERAPEUTIC AND JEWISH
  PERSPECTIVES ON ADULT DEVELOPMENT   1

Holidays: Hollow Days or Holy Days?   3

Habituation and Dehabituation   8
  The Process of Ongoing Growth and
    Development in Adult Life   8
  A Psychological Model of Development: Ego and Self   12
  A Jewish Model of Development: *Nitzotz* and *Kelippah*   15
  Making a Personal Connection   17

The Multifaceted Nature of Consciousness   18
  State-Dependent Learning, Memory, and Behavior   18
  The Implications of State-Dependent Learning,
    Memory, and Behavior for Psychotherapy   19
  A Jewish Theory of State-Dependent Consciousness:
    Kodesh and *Chol*   21

Tools for Change: Ritual, Symbols, Imagery,
  and Stories   24
  Archetypes and Jungian Analysis   25
  Archetypes and the Jewish Tradition   26

The Multi-Dimensional Process of Learning   28
  Treatment Modalities: Behavioral, Interpersonal,
    Emotional, Psycho-Physical, Cognitive, and
    Spiritual Approaches to Psychotherapy   30
  Dimensions of Holy-Day Celebration: Four Worlds
    of *Asiyah, Yetzirah, Briyah,* and *Atzilut*   35
  Unique Focus of Each Holy Day   39

Stages of Development from Dependency
  to Autonomy   43
  Developmental Process in Childhood   44
  Developmental Process in Psychotherapy   45
  Developmental Process in the Holy-Day Cycle   48
  Interdependence: An I-Thou Relationship with God   52

Balancing Structure and Spontaneity:
  Keva and *Kavana*   53

2 PESACH: LIBERATION FROM SLAVERY
   IN EGYPT   59

Turning Crisis into Opportunity: Slavery in Egypt
  as a Positive Transformative Experience   62

Symbols of Transformation   64
  Exodus from Egypt as a Birth   64
  Exodus from Egypt as a Sprouting Seed   66
  Egypt as a Smelting Furnace   67

Stages in the Process of Redemption   68
  The Journey from Israel to Egypt and Settling
    in Egypt   69
  Enslaved in Egypt   70
  Consciousness of Enslavement and Experience
    of Powerlessness   71
  Crying Out   71
  Moses Is Chosen to Lead the Israelites   72
  The Miracle of the Ten Plagues and the Exodus   73
  Splitting of the Sea   74
  Song of the Sea   74

Integrating Qualities of Initiative and Receptivity   75
  Acknowledging Powerlessness as a Basis for Hope   76
  Acting in Spite of Powerlessness   76
  Balancing Powerlessness and Initiative   79

A Clinical Example of Psychotherapeutic Process
Associated with Pesach 80

Applying the Images of Pesach to Our Lives:
An Old Self and New Circumstances 83

Making Personal Connections for Pesach 85

3 SEFIRAT HA'OMER: WANDERING
THROUGH THE DESERT 87

Wandering in the Desert: A Time of Emotional
Turmoil and Dependency 90
Emotional Turmoil 91
Dependency 92

Counting of the Omer: Day-by-Day Learning 93

Infant Development and the Journey
through the Desert 96
From Dependency toward Autonomy 96
From Rules to Reasons 97
Cognitive Development 98
Connection with God as Archetypal Mother 99
Learning to Speak 99

A Psychological Perspective: Left-Brain Learning 100

Personal Application of Principles 102

Journey through the Desert 106

4 SHAVUOT: REVELATION ON MOUNT SINAI 107

Aspects of Revelation 109
Revelation as a Personal Experience 110
The Transcendant Experience of Revelation 110
Nullification: Surrendering Old,
Constricted Knowledge 111

A Transformation of Consciousness   111
Understanding as a Basis for Action   112
Making Commitment   112

Shavuot in Relationship to Sefirat Ha'Omer   **114**
Shavuot: Completing the Fifty Days of the
   Counting of the Omer   115
Offering of Barley and Offering of Wheat   115
Connection with the Archetypal Father   116
Connection with the Twenty-Two Letters   116

A Psychological Perspective: Right-Brain Learning   **117**

**A Psychological Perspective on Making
Commitment**   **120**

Revelation at Mount Sinai   **121**

5 TISHA B'AV: GRIEVING THE LOSSES —
   EXILE AND DESTRUCTION OF THE SANCTUARY   123

**The Process of Grief in Ritual, Story, and Symbols:
Facing Realities and Voicing Feelings**   **129**
Ritual Enactment   130
The Golden Calf   131
The Spies   132
Destruction of the Sanctuary   133

**The Psychological Perspective: A Clinical Example
of the Grieving Process**   **138**

Grief as a Healing Response to Powerlessness   **140**

From Grief to Consolation   **143**

Differentiating Constructive Guilt from
   Self-Abusive Guilt   147
   Constructive Guilt   147
   Jewish Images of Self-Abusive Guilt   150
   A Clinical Example of Working through
      Self-Destructive Guilt   153
   A Psychological Perspective on Working through
      Self-Destructive Guilt   155
   Differentiating Constructive Guilt from
      Destructive Guilt   156

The Healing Process of Grief   159

6 ELUL: A MONTH OF COMPASSION AND
   FORGIVENESS   161

Self-Reflection and Compassion   164

Self-Reflection and Therapeutic Process   167

Compassion and Therapeutic Process   170
   A Clinical Example of Compassion   170
   A Psychological Perspective on Compassion   173

Personal Application: Compassionate Self-Reflection   174

Healing Wounds in Our Relationships:
   Making Amends and Forgiveness   175
   A Clinical Example of Making Amends   176
   A Psychological Perspective on Making Amends
      during Elul   179

Balancing Doing and Nondoing: Compassionate
   Self-Reflection and Active Effort to Achieve
   Forgiveness   179

Practical Application at Elul   181
   The Internal Process of Compassionate
      Self-Reflection   181
   Repairing Interpersonal Relationships   181

7   ROSH HASHANAH: DAY OF JUDGMENT   183

Accountability — Day of Judgment   185
    A Clinical Example of Accountability   187
    A Psychological Perspective on Accountability   191

Responding to God's Challenge: The Process
    of Teshuvah   192

Eetkafya: The Active Principle   195
    Therapeutic Conceptions of the Active Principle   196

Eethafcha: The Receptive Principle   198
    A Clinical Example of the Receptive Principle   201
    God's Response to the Acknowledgment of
        Powerlessness   203

Making Ourselves Accountable   204

8   YOM KIPPUR: DAY OF AT-ONE-MENT   205

Transformation of Evil into Good   207
    A Clinical Example of the Process of Transformation 208
    A Psychotherapeutic Perspective on
        Transformation of Evil   214

Transformation and the Healing of Past Trauma   217

From Essence to Manifestation: Affirmations,
    Intentions and Prayers   219

The Experience of At-One-Ment: The Receptive and
    the Active Process   221
    The Receptive Process   224
    The Active Process   225

Personal Process on Yom Kippur   227

Return to Essence   230

9   SUKKOT: ENJOYING THE HARVEST   231

The Meanings of Sukkot   235
    Acknowledging Changes   236
    Joy and Celebration   236
    Divine Protection and Support   237
    Extending Outward   239

The Journey from Yom Kippur to Sukkot:
    From Essence to Manifestation   239
    Yom Kippur: Fire and the Silver Altar   240
    Sukkot: Water and the Golden Altar   241
    Shemini Atzeret: Collecting the Water   241
    Germination of a Seed as a Metaphor for Inner Work   242
    Daily Prayer   242

Psychological Themes Associated with Sukkot   243
    A Clinical Example of a Psychological Process
        Associated with Sukkot   244
    Behavioral Therapy   245
    Feldenkrais Method   246
    Gestalt Therapy   247

Personal Application of Process for Sukkot   248

Enjoying the Harvest   249

10 CHANUKAH: LIGHTING A CANDLE
    IN THE DARKNESS   251

The Struggle of the Macabees with the Greeks as
    an Archetypal Event   253
    The Spiritual Threat   255
    Primacy of Human Initiative   256

Divine Intervention   256
Step-by-Step Learning   257
Outward Focus   257
Focus on Spiritual Victory   258

The Candle as a Symbol   **258**
The Candle as Symbol of Experiential Learning:
    "Seeing" and "Hearing"   260
The Order of Lighting Candles as a Symbol of
    Step-by-Step Learning   261
The Oil and Wick as a Symbol for Integrating
    Spiritual and Material Dimensions   262
Wick, Oil, Blue Flame, and Yellow Flame as
    Symbols of Four Motivators of Learning   265

**Psychotherapeutic Themes Associated with
    Chanukah**   **266**
A Clinical Example of Therapeutic Process of
    Chanukah   267
Therapeutic Process on Chanukah   272
Lighting a Candle in the Darkness   274

11 TU B'SHEVAT: A NEW YEAR FOR TREES   **275**

The Meanings of the Tu B'Shevat Seder   **278**
Fruit with and Inedible Protective Outside and
    Edible Inside   280
Fruit with an Edible Outside and an Inedible Seed   280
Fruit That Can Be Completely Consumed   281
Incense   282

Psychotherapeutic Process on Tu B'Shevat   **283**

Tu B'Shevat in the Cycle of the Year   **287**

Bearing Fruit: Stages of Growth   **289**

12   PURIM: THE MESSIANIC VISION   **291**

The Developmental Process from Pesach to Purim   294

**Different Paths to At-One-Ment: Yom Kippur
    and Purim**   297

**Integrated Spirituality: Mordecai Riding the
    King's Horse Escorted by Haman**   300

**Esther as a Symbol of Spirituality Expressed
    through the Material World**   303

Ritual Enactment of Archetypal Themes on Purim   307
    At-One-Ment   307
    Celebrating Success   307
    Connectedness with Others   308
    Transformation of Evil   308

Psychological Themes Associated with Purim   309
    Experiencing Satisfaction   313
    Transformation of Negativity   314
    Interdependence and Cocreation   316

Personal Application of Themes from Purim   317

The Messianic Vision   319

13   THE CIRCLE BECOMES A SPIRAL   319

Psychotherapy References   331

Jewish References   337

Index   343

אֲדֹנָי שְׂפָתַי תִּפְתָּח וּפִי יַגִּיד תְּהִלָּתֶךָ

PREFACE

I grew up in an observant Jewish family in Minneapolis, Minnesota. Fortunately, my family communicated the spirit as well as the form of religious practice in daily life. The rituals of daily life— prayer, celebrations, and holidays—provided the foundation for cherished times of family connectedness and warmth. The commitment to religious practice was lived with gentleness and with respect for individual differences. We were motivated more by positive experience than by a sense guilt, shame, and obligation.

I also grew up in the '60s. Our neighborhood in Minneapolis was the old Jewish neighborhood becoming the black ghetto. The public schools I attended were true examples of multicultural education. I attended Columbia University during the era of protest against the war in Vietnam. I lived in California during the time of acid rock, People's Park, and flower children.

In Berkeley, I participated in encounter groups, spent time in meditation centers, and took personal growth workshops at retreat centers including the Esalen Institute. After working with children for several years and teaching elementary school, I returned to graduate school to become a psychologist. In my own therapy and my training, I explored a variety of approaches, including body-oriented psychotherapy, Transactional Analysis, group therapy, Gestalt therapy, family therapy, developmental theory, psychosynthesis, Jungian therapy, and classical and Ericksonian hypnosis. During the last few years, I have focused on integrating these different modalities, clarifying when each approach is most effective in the course of therapeutic treatment. That understanding informs my work with individuals, couples, families, and groups, as well as in training and consultation.

This search for integration also led me to explore the strong connection between spiritual and psychological perspectives. In an effort to understand that connection more completely, I began to study the writings of Jewish mystics whose theories of personal spiritual development seemed to be congruent with contemporary understandings of psychological growth. The psychological view expressed in their interpretations of ritual and of text gave words to describe my own experiences.

The language of the rabbis was different than the language of psychotherapy. They based their work on interpretations of classical texts. They viewed the rituals, the stories, and the symbols of the tradition as tools for understanding and enhancing human growth and development. Despite the difference in their frame of reference, the rabbis' description of this process paralleled many concepts in contemporary psychological theories.

In 1973, I began to study Gestalt therapy. Fritz Perls, who originated this approach, developed a method for resolving internal conflicts. These conflicts might be experienced as two "voices" within one's consciousness. We experimented with identifying these voices within ourselves. We used the psychodramatic technique of externalizing the dialogue so as to better understand the process of interaction between the parts of oneself. Utilizing an empty chair, we conducted a dialogue in which the two parts spoke to each other.

Coincidentally, I found myself exploring the concept of conflict through a Jewish lens. The weekly reading from the Torah told the story of the dispute between Korach and Moses. Korach, a member of the priestly class, initiated a rebellion, challenging the leadership of Moses and Aaron, as they guided the Israelites through the desert from Egypt on their way to the land of Israel. Some of the Israelites sided with Moses and Aaron while others joined Korach. A miracle occurred in which the earth opened, swallowing Korach and all his followers.

To help in understanding the meaning of this story, I turned to the discourses of Yehudah Aryeh Leib Alter, a rabbi who had been the leader of the Gerer sect of Chasidism at the beginning of the twentieth century. He is also known by the name of the book that contains his work, a text entitled *S'fat Emet,* which means "true speech." The *S'fat Emet* notes that the conflict between Moses and Korach ends with the complete destruction of Korach and his followers. He contrasts this outcome with the dispute between the students of two rabbis from the time of the Talmud, the schools of Hillel and Shamai.

On the surface, both disputes involved differences in defining the details of ritual practices. For example, one of Korach's challenges involved a question about the fringes on the ritual garment, the *tallit*. The Torah instructs us to include one blue thread in the *tallit*. Korach wanted to make a *tallit* in which all the fringes were made of blue threads. This dispute seems similar to the conflicts of the rabbis through the generations. For example, the students of Hillel and Shamai disagreed with one another on many details of the law. The *S'fat Emet* wonders why the conflict between Hillel and Shamai was respected as holy and eternal, a dispute "in the name of heaven," while the challenge of Korach ended with his immediate removal from the community in a dramatic manner. According to the *S'fat Emet,* these two types of conflict provide archetypal images to help clarify the nature of conflicts within ourselves and with others.

Korach, in his dispute with Moses, not only disagreed with him but sought to supplant his authority. Korach did not view Moses as having any legitimacy. For this reason, Korach does not survive. In contrast, although Hillel and Shamai disagreed with one another, they respected each other's views and engaged in dialogue. Their dispute is regarded as holy. The *S'fat Emet* suggests that this same principle applies in our relationships:

> In truth, each person has a unique opinion; and, everyone who is engaged in a dispute must acknowledge that his companion also has a unique point of view. One should not stay rigidly attached to his idea, but search for the truth. In this way, God will help their eyes see clearly, and peace will come from conflict. [p. 123B]

This approach can also be used to address conflict within ourselves, as the *S'fat Emet* notes that, "this strife exists within a person, as well. One way of being pulls him in one direction, and another pulls him in a different direction." On the Sabbath, we "have help from Above so that all the attributes of our being are unified, even those which seem to be in opposition" (p. 123A).

The perspective of Gestalt therapy parallels the conclusions of the *S'fat Emet*. Psychological impasses occur when two conflicting voices do not dialogue with one another, hearing each other's views and learning from one another so as to develop a resolution incorporating both perspectives:

> Viewing man as a composition of characteristics rather than merely a resister leads to a picture of man in trouble when he is divided within himself rather than against himself. The war within, frequently either stale or stalemated, is a war of existence waged by each aspect of the person, each with its own energy, its own supports, and its own opponents. Each new synthesis among the populations of differences which is the individual is a fresh alliance, momentarily reflecting the current force of each component. . . . It is this process of developing old, defeated directions and moving into new ones that is the heart of psychotherapy. Through bringing the relevant forces into new contact with each other, one discovers the power of the alienated parts of the self.[1]

As I reflected on the stories of the Torah and the stories of Perls's experiences with clients, I realized that I approached the conflicts within myself as a battle between Korach and Moses. Either one side was right, or the other side was right. Each side tried to discredit and invalidate the other. I needed to approach the conflict with the qualities that were embodied by Hillel and Shamai. Both views were correct. I found integration as I allowed each part to talk to the other and to hear the unique truth of that perspective.

Having grown up in two worlds, the worldview of Jewish tradition could sometimes conflict with contemporary experience. When I found myself in an impasse, I realized that Korach had emerged within me. I needed to challenge that tendency to invalidate one part of myself; I needed to shift to the approach of Hillel and Shamai, an approach in which each side hears and respects the other.

Voices from the past engage us as we elaborate on conversations begun long ago. We live in relationship, not only with the parts of ourselves and with our contemporaries. We are also engaged in a dialogue that extends back through time. We communicate with the teachers from the past, with the patriarchs and matriarchs, Abraham and Sarah, Isaac and Rebecca, Jacob, Leah, and Rachel, with Moses, Aaron and Miriam—our ancestors whose stories are told in the Torah. We speak with the rabbis who interpreted their stories through the generations—the Ba'al Shem Tov, Shneur Zalman of Lyady, Nahman of Bratzlav, Yehudah Aryeh Leib of Gur, and others.

This work is the result of that ongoing dialogue, offering a psychological interpretation of the Jewish Holy-Day cycle. The mystical traditions view the ritual and story as symbolic representations of internal spiritual and psychological development, helping us translate the experience into the language of contemporary psychological theories. Those theories can be applied and refined as we examine our own life experience.

The Jewish mystical tradition includes many different perspectives with a richness of source material from many generations through the centuries. This volume is not intended to be an exhaustive or complete survey of this tradition. In my exploration of Jewish mysticism, I draw primarily from the texts of Shneur Zalman of Lyady. Shneur Zalman, the founder of *Chabad* Chasidism, lived from 1745 to 1813. He was respected as a scholar in traditional talmudic studies, as a kabbalist, and as a mystic. He also had a wide knowledge of science and mathematics. Shneur Zalman was unique in his capacity to systematize and describe clearly the process of mystical experience. For Shneur Zalman, the text of the Torah provides a metaphorical description of the cosmos. It also offers an understanding of personal psychology. I draw from two texts, *Likutei Torah* and *Torah Or,* both commentaries on the *Torah* portion of the week. The commentaries are, for the most part, based on oral discourses that were later edited and transcribed.

The texts of the Jewish tradition describe a process through rituals, images, stories, and symbols that can be difficult to understand because they speak in the language of an ancient, agrarian, hierarchical, and patriarchal culture. Contemporary psychological perspectives sometimes offer a more understandable articulation of concepts than Jewish mystical writings that may be less accessible to us. In my efforts to translate the ideas of the mystics into a framework that makes sense in our culture, I include the theories developed by Freud, Jung, Assagioli, Perls, Erickson, and their students.

The wisdom of the past, both mystical and psychological, informs and guides us in the present. The voices from the past infuse the present as we dialogue with the people with whom we live: mentors, friends, family, colleagues, and clients. The present also speaks to the past. Our experiences allow us to test and refine theoretical principles in the realities of actual life experience. In this spirit, I include descriptions of my work with clients. (To protect privacy, I have changed names, identifying characteristics, and other details of clients' stories.)

Through the generations, commentators have always offered their interpretations of the meaning of ritual, known as *Kavanot*—intentions. The psychological interpretation is only one of many ways of viewing the Holy-Days. It is my intention to add another perspective to the vast storehouse of interpretations in the hope that it will prove useful for others.

As this dialogue continues, we deepen our capacity to hear the voices within ourselves, allowing the parts of the self to speak and be heard. We bring these qualities with us as we face the future. It is my hope and intention that you will join this dialogue, listening with an open heart and a curious mind. In this conversation, the truth of your life experience is a necessary and valuable contribution. Add your own voice to the dialogue. The framework outlined in this manuscript is useful only if it makes sense in the context of your personal journey. You may find particular concepts more valuable than others, or you may need to modify some of this model to better fit your experience. In this way, the Holy-Days become mirrors for seeing ourselves in a new light as we journey through the year. As we do so, we can better manifest the potential of who we may be, healing ourselves, our community, and our planet.

THE INNER JOURNEY THROUGH THE JEWISH YEAR

Holy-Day	Central Images	Ritual Practices	Process of Development	Relationship with God	Focus of Experience
Pesach Passover	Exodus from Egypt; freedom from slavery	*Matza; Seder*	Life transitions; birth; leaving home	Parent/infant	*Asiyah;* behavioral
Sefirat Ha'Omer Counting of the *Omer*	Wandering in the desert; barley offering	Counting of days	Fertile voids; infancy; left-brain learning	Parent/toddler	*Briyah;* mental
Shavuot Pentecost	Revelation; offering of wheat & first fruits	*Tikkun;* study	Insight; reframing; new way of thinking; right-brain learning	Marriage/ union; giving/ receiving	*Briyah;* mental
Tisha B'Av 9th Day of av	Destruction of the Sanctuary; golden calf	Fasting; mourning	Grieving loss; gap between real/ideal	Separateness; alienation	*Yetzirah;* expressive
Month of Elul	The King is in the field; 13 attributes of compassion	*Shofar;* self-reflection	Compassionate acceptance & acknowledg- ment of dysfunctional patterns	Mercifulness; giving/ receiving	*Yetzirah;* expressive
Rosh HaShanah New Year	Day of Judgment	*Shofar;* prayer	Take responsibility for negative aspects of dysfunctional patterns	Judging; discrimination; accountability	*Yetzirah;* expressive
Yom Kippur Day of At- One-Ment	High priest in the Sanctuary; second set of tablets given to Moses	Fasting prayer; *Teshuvah*	Transforma- tion of old pattern; change; forgiveness	Mystical union	*Atzilut;* essence
Sukkot Tabernacles	Living in huts in the desert; bringing harvest to the Sanctuary	*Lulav & etrog sukkah;* ending & begining of Torah cycle	Protected environment to practice new responses	Protector supporting autonomy	*Yetzirah;* expressive
Chanukah	Greeks vs. Macabees; miracle of the lights	Lighting of candles	Working through of changes	Helper supporting autonomy	*Asiyah;* behavioral
Tu B'Shevat New Year for Trees	Day of Judgment for fruit-bearing trees	Eating of fruits; planting trees	Incremental growth	Natural environment for growth	*Asiyah;* behavioral
Purim	Story of Haman, Mordecai, & Esther	Masks; celebration; *Megillah*	Completion of maturation; choice replaces compulsion	Co-creators; silent partner; mystical union	*Asiyah/ Atzilut;* behavioral/ essence

ACKNOWLEDGMENTS

In completing this work, I relied on many people for support, encouragement, and guidance. I appreciate their generosity, wisdom, and persistence, which have nourished and sustained me.

To Rosie Rosenzweig for her timely, detailed, and perceptive literary and stylistic editing; to Moshe Waldoks for helping me see my vision and encouraging my efforts to translate it into a reality; to Jerry Auerbach and Art Green for generously offering their guidance and suggestions; to the many other readers who offered constructive feedback and support including Roberta Apfel, Joan Borysenko, Josef Dellagrotte, Jane Feinberg, Irle Goldman, Avi Hadari, Joan Klagsbrun, Arthur Kurzweil, Susan Nissenbaum, Elizabeth Rosenzweig, Sandy Rosenzweig, Zalman Schachter-Shalomi, Bernie Siegel, Adin Steinsaltz, Charles Verge, Jack Weltner, and Dovid Zeller; to Asaf Hadari for his translations; to Joan Benjamin Farren for artwork that beautifully captures the essence of the conceptual framework; to David Caras and Steve Greenberg for photography; to Ashleigh Brilliant for his generosity and his ability to express profound ideas in a few simple words; to Mitchell Geffen for his timely response to a distant cousin needing help securing copyright permissions; to Tony Rubin for shepherding the manuscript through production.

To teachers and colleagues: Rich Borofsky, David Cheek, Bunny Duhl, Fred Duhl, Irle Goldman, Joan Klagsbrun, Ron Michaud, Mike Miller, Judy Leavitt, Alex MacMillan, Sandy Rosenzweig, Joanna Ross, Ernest Rossi, Ilana Rubenfeld, Emily Ruppert, Tommy Thompson, and Jerry Weinstein. To the clients who have shared their lives and taught me through their example about courage, persistence, and possibility.

To the sources of spiritual understanding: grandparents, parents, siblings, nieces, nephews, aunts, uncles, and cousins; to the communities in which I daven—the Newton Center Minyan, Congregation *Sha'arei Tefillah,* and the Adams Street Synagogue — that ground spirituality in the fabric of daily life; to Joe Polak for introducing me to Chasidic texts and helping me gain fluency in study; to Sandy Rosenzweig for years of *Chevrusa* in studying text and making the personal connections.

To my wife, Liz, for her technical, logistical, and emotional support without which this book would never have been completed.

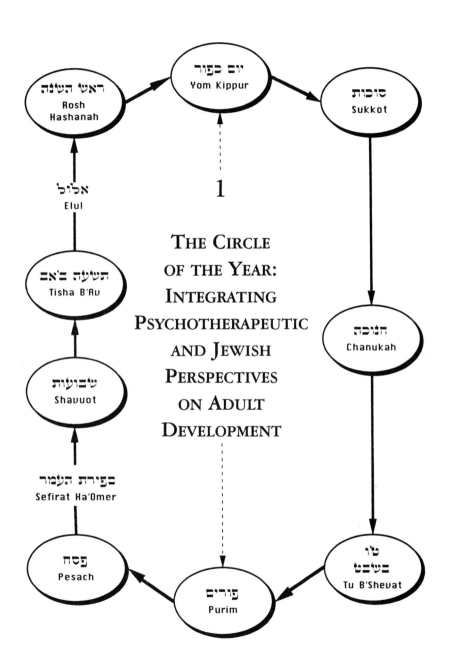

1

THE CIRCLE
OF THE YEAR:
INTEGRATING
PSYCHOTHERAPEUTIC
AND JEWISH
PERSPECTIVES
ON ADULT
DEVELOPMENT

ראש השנה
Rosh
Hashanah

יום כפור
Yom Kippur

סוכות
Sukkot

אלול
Elul

תשעה ב'אב
Tisha B'Av

שבועות
Shavuot

ספירת העמר
Sefirat Ha'Omer

פסח
Pesach

פורים
Purim

ט"ו בשבט
Tu B'Shevat

חנוכה
Chanukah

HOLIDAYS: HOLLOW DAYS OR HOLY DAYS?

To everything there is a season,
And a time to every purpose under the heaven.
A time to be born, and a time to die;
A time to plant, and a time to pluck up what is planted;
A time to break down, and a time to build up;
A time to weep, and a time to laugh;
A time to mourn, and a time to dance;
A time to cast away stones, and a time to gather stones together;
A time to embrace, and a time to refrain from embracing;
A time to seek, and a time to lose;
A time to keep, and a time to cast away;
A time to rend, and a time to sew;
A time to keep silence, and a time to speak;
A time to love, and a time to hate;
A time for war, and a time for peace.

[Ecclesiastes 3:1]

Holidays offer us opportunities for rest and renewal. Celebration of holidays provides quality time with ourselves, our families, and our communities. The rituals and celebrations are designed to give meaning and purpose to our lives, providing a perspective that helps us make sense of our struggles.

However, the pressures of a fast-paced, work-oriented society have led to less time for leisure, relationships, family, and ourselves. In the consumer-oriented world where we live today, we experience our holidays only in the rotation of seasonal displays in supermarkets. At worst, holidays create additional pressures; at best, they allow a temporary respite, time to catch our breath and rest. We have separated ourselves from the rhythms of nature, the yearly cycles of light and dark. We have lost the capacity to use ritual to access transformative experience. The rituals become meaningless exercises, like keys for which we have no doors.

The difficulty is exacerbated because the language used to articulate the theories and practices of the religious tradition is difficult to translate in terms that make sense to us in contemporary culture. We find no immediate connection to stories of the Israelites who lived thousands of years ago, to the rituals and sacrifices of an agrarian and hierarchical society, or to the voluminous and detailed laws that structure celebration of Holy-Days. We find it difficult to talk about or even to conceptualize an experience of divinity, of a personal relationship with God, especially if our image of God is one formed in childhood or based in popular culture, a vision of God as an old man who sits on a throne threatening us with punishment and cajoling us with promises of rewards. Our spiritual understanding is constricted if we rely on primitive and simplistic childhood constructs. Even if we have a more mature and constructive sense of God, we may find ourselves rigidly attached to one image of spiritual Essence, unaware of the rich and varied possibilities for spiritual connection.

Religious ritual and practice includes a psychotherapeutic dimension among its other functions. It serves as a system for self-reflection and personal growth. Psychotherapy offers us a resource for translating the religious traditions and practices into a language that has meaning and significance, allowing us to reconnect with ancient wisdom, to be able to talk about our relationship with God, to speak with God without feeling embarrassed, apologetic, or insincere. Psychotherapeutic perspectives can help us deepen our understanding of the many possibilities for relationship with God.

The yearly cycle of the Holy-Days structures time for reflection and self-transformation. The Holy-Days offer sanctuaries in time, safe havens in which we have support and encouragement to confront challenges. We stop normal daily activity. We locate ourselves in the changes of the seasons, the agricultural cycle, and the sacrificial offerings associated with each Holy-Day. We tell the stories of our ancestors. We enter the experience through rituals that connect us to universal images and symbols. We connect our stories to the stories of our history remembered and reenacted at each Holy-Day. We filter the stories of our own life experience through these lenses. The Holy-Days become mirrors in time, helping us know more of who we are so we may become more of who we may be. The structure of the Jewish Holy-Days offers a framework that can nourish and rejuvenate. These keys—rituals, images, symbols, and stories—can still open the doors to our relationship with God, to the experience of Holiness.

The notion of the Holy-Days as an integrated cycle does not make sense historically because the various festivals were instituted at different times: Tisha B'Av, Chanukah, and Purim were established many generations after the holidays described in the Bible. However, the concept of a developmental process of growth through the year does make sense conceptually and experientially. The Holy-Days are not celebrated as isolated events. The unique character of each Holy-Day is experienced in the context of our journey through the year. Each builds on what came before it; each provides a foundation for what will come after it. The experience of each of the Holy-Days marks the stages in a developmental process. Each year, we give birth to a new aspect of ourselves that matures through the course of the year. Each Holy-Day represents a unique milestone in this process of growth and development. Each Holy-Day provides a different mirror to the self.

The rituals, symbols, and stories associated with each Holy-Day clarify the nature of the particular stage in our own development, helping us identify the challenges of that stage and providing the specific qualities of support we need to respond successfully to those challenges. We enter into relationship with the aspect of Divinity that enables us to resolve the challenge constructively.

The following list provides descriptive summaries of each Holy-Day:

Pesach commemorates the redemption from Egypt, the birth of the Jewish people, and the beginning of the spring. Pesach symbolizes the birth we experience in leaving a particular Egypt each year. Pesach helps us connect with the possibilities and opportunities embedded in the crisis, to acknowledge how overwhelming it can be to make our way in new circumstances, to recognize our vulnerability, to open ourselves to receive guidance and support, and to take concrete actions to address our situation.

Sefirat Ha'Omer marks the counting of the days of the Israelites' journey through the desert from Egypt until receiving the Torah. The counting is also associated with the offering of a measure (omer) of barley in the Sanctuary. Sefirat Ha'Omer is a time for developing understanding of our new situation through step-by-step and day-by-day analysis. Like toddlers who gradually develop cognitive capacities through experience, we begin to make sense of the new environment in which we find ourselves.

Shavuot marks the time of revelation, the giving of the Torah on Mount Sinai. The Holy-Day also commemorates the harvest of first fruits. Shavuot invites us to experience personal revelation, providing a vision of our potential to face the challenge of our situation. Embedded in that vision are the guidelines for how we must live to manifest that ideal. With this understanding, we commit ourselves to make the vision into a reality.

Tisha B'Av, occurring in the sweltering heat of summer, is a fast day that marks the climax of a three week period of mourning. We commemorate the destruction of both the first and second Sanctuaries and the exile of the Jewish people. During this time, we grieve the failures experienced as we work to manifest our dreams and visions.

Elul begins the season of the Yamim Nora'im, the Days of Awe, a time for self-reflection and transformation. During this month, we begin a process of compassionate self-reflection.

Rosh HaShanah celebrates the birthday of the world. It is also the day of judgment, a time to take responsibility for what we create with our lives, for acknowledging the negative consequences of dysfunctional habits of coping.

Yom Kippur is observed as a day of fasting and prayer. On Yom Kippur, we separate ourselves from our material existence, reconnecting with Essence. From this experience, we make commitments to new directions in how we live our lives.

Sukkot commemorates the fall harvest and the temporary shelters in which the Israelites lived during the wanderings in the desert. It is also the time for completion of the yearly cycle of the reading of the Torah. On Sukkot, we nurture, harvest, and enjoy the fruits of our labors, the effort to transform ourselves.

Chanukah, the festival of lights celebrated during the dark days of winter, marks the victory of the Macabees over their Greek captors. Chanukah reminds us of possibilities for creating light in the darkness as we struggle to integrate new commitments into daily experience.

Tu B'Shevat, the new year for trees, offers another more harmonious image of integration: the growth from seed to sprout to plant to fruit suggests the slow development of the new self in contrast to the image of a war associated with the festival of lights.

Purim, a spring festival, honors the victory of the Jews of Persia over their enemies. It is a celebration of the messianic vision, a reconnecting with our Essence as manifest in the material world. On Purim, we celebrate our development, marking our successes in transforming ourselves through the course of the year.

We can access the powerful transformative potential of ritual using psychological theory and practice. Juxtaposing the theories and practices of ritual with those of psychotherapy can reopen the doors to these vital, transformative experiences. Similarly, the ancient traditions enrich and deepen psychotherapeutic understanding. Although a weekly hour of psychotherapy with a trained and focused professional may offer some benefits in providing a place of refuge for reflection, it also compartmentalizes and isolates a vital activity that needs to be integrated into the flow of daily life.

In this chapter, we will integrate Jewish and psychological perspectives, drawing from each approach to understand:

- habituation and dehabituation—how we develop habitual ways of coping with life's stresses and discover new possibilities for responding;

- the nature of consciousness—how we access and integrate learning about ourselves based on multi-faceted consciousness in which self-knowledge can be fragmented and disconnected;

- ritual, symbols, imagery, and stories as tools for change—how indirect, archetypal resources facilitate learning;

- behavioral, emotional, interpersonal, cognitive, physical, and spiritual dimensions of growth and development—how learning includes each different aspect of human experience;

- stages of development—paralleling the child's movement from dependency to autonomy, the process of growth involves a sequence of steps each with a unique challenge and task; and,

- the balance of structure and spontaneity—integrating commitment to ritual practice and responsiveness to the truth of immediate experience.

HABITUATION AND DEHABITUATION

Insanity consists of doing the same thing over and over again and expecting the results to be different.

The Process of Ongoing Growth and Development in Adult Life

There came a messenger unto Job, and said: "the oxen were plowing, and the asses feeding beside them; and the Sabeans

made a raid and took them away; yea, they have slain the ser-
vants with the edge of the sword. . . . While he was yet speak-
ing, there came also another and said: "Thy sons and daughters
were eating and drinking wine in their eldest brother's house;
and, behold, there came a great wind from across the wilder-
ness, and smote the four corners of the house, and it fell upon
the young people, and they are dead. . . . Satan went forth from
the presence of the Lord, and smote Job with sore boils from
the sole of his foot even unto his crown. . . .

[Book of Job 1:14—2:7]

Each year brings change. An intimate relationship begins or ends. A baby is born. We undertake a new project or begin a new job. Disease, chronic illness, or pain disrupts normal routines. Death robs us of someone who is close. A child leaves home. Financial pressures result from loss of a job or unusual expenses. The scars of trauma interfere with our lives. We experience an existential crisis in which we question the meaning of our life. Whether they are positive or as negative, these changes disturb the usual ways in which we live, challenging us to reinvent our identities and our lives.

We mobilize to cope with these changes. We draw from the well of our experience to make sense and give meaning to our situation. This understanding serves as a foundation for beliefs and attitudes about ourselves, others, the world around us, and the nature of our dilemma. These beliefs guide us and shape our feelings. We learn to manage feelings: joy and sadness, fear and excitement, passion and anger, vulnerability and hurt, shame and pride, patience and frustration. We turn to family, friends, and professional care providers, seeking to use people as resources. We translate our understanding into action, making the commitment to do things to resolve difficulties. We take care of our bodies so as to reduce the impact of chronic stress and enhance our capacity to move and respond. Especially in times of serious crisis, we work to reconnect with that inexpressible sense of our own Essence that allows us to face the challenges of the moment with a spiritual perspective.

As we attempt to resolve the challenges of our life, we draw from what we have learned in our past experience. We use coping strategies that have worked before to help us know what to do: how to manage feelings, how to mobilize others in support, how to make sense and meaning, how to relate to our bodies, and how to connect with the divine light within.

Some of these strategies prove to be highly effective; others may obstruct or impede our efforts. Hopefully, we learn from our experience, building on strengths and developing alternative strategies when old methods fail. In this way, the struggle with adversity offers the opportunity to give birth to a new part of ourselves, stimulating a process of ongoing learning and development through the course of life.

Psychotherapy offers a safe environment in which to reflect on the changes in our lives, to gain awareness of these habitual responses, and to develop new strategies. The process of psychotherapy can be understood through an example. Michael decided to meet with me to help him cope with chronic pain. The entire left side of his body hurt all the time. He had been injured as a teenager when he was hit in the back by a baseball. According to the doctors, nothing further could be done medically to alleviate the problem, except to learn to live with it.

When Michael first entered my office, I was struck by the size and apparent weight of his briefcase which he carried in his left hand. He strode briskly into the room, sat down, and told me his story. Michael had always fought his physical distress; he had gone into business for himself and was very successful. He was happily married; his children were doing well as they completed college. He had struggled with his physical condition with the same persistence: he went to every specialist who might be able to help, and he exercised regularly. As an example of his effort, he described how he deliberately carried his heavy briefcase in his left hand so that he could strengthen the weaker side of his body. I asked Michael how he had developed his capacity to fight with so much determination. He explained to me that his father had died when he was 16, just a few months before his injury. He had been angry, and he used that anger to cope with the loss by focusing on succeeding in school and in work.

Michael had developed his capacity to fight against adversity. That quality had been highly effective for him in overcoming many difficulties in his life. However, in coping with his pain, I suspected that the tendency to push himself was counter-productive. I asked Michael to lie down on a massage table. I could see the tension in his body and the discomfort on his face. I placed a pillow under his knees and a rolled-up towel under his head. "Why are you doing that?" he asked. I told him I wanted to reduce the strain on his lower back and neck. "Does that really help?" I removed the pillows, asked him to notice what he felt in his body; then, I put the pillows in place again. He noticed that he felt slightly more relaxed but now felt tension in his left shoulder. I observed that the shoulder was slightly elevated and placed another prop under the shoulder. Again, he noticed some relaxation. We spent the remainder of the session exploring how to provide support so the sense of relaxation could deepen.

This approach did not make sense to Michael. It was the very opposite of fighting to overcome a problem; he experienced himself as giving in to his pain. However, after a few minutes, he noticed that his discomfort had been significantly reduced. We discussed the notion that some of his pain might be due to inflammation that required rest to heal: his efforts to fight his pain interfered with that healing. Michael stood up; he noticed that he felt more comfortable in his movement. He picked up his briefcase with his left hand, hefted it, and started toward the door. Then he paused for a moment, put the briefcase down, and picked it up with his right hand. He discovered that he could listen to his body and find ways to reduce stress even in the course of daily activity.

Over the next few meetings, Michael and I continued to consider the idea that having more support might be helpful in his struggle with pain. Not only did he permit himself physical support, but he also experimented with allowing other people to provide support as well. He asked a colleague to carry his briefcase when they went to meetings together. He even found relief one evening when he shed some tears as he talked with his wife about his pain, receiving her comfort and reassurance.

Michael's strategy of pushing himself made sense in terms of his experience, but he discovered that this approach exacerbated rather than reduced his pain. As Michael took time to reflect on his situation and become aware of previously unconscious coping habits, he was able to develop new strategies that were more effective.

In this same way, each of us makes similar mistakes as we cope with current stresses using old methods. Making changes is sometimes difficult because the approaches we use are unconscious and habitual. Like fish in water, we may not be aware of what we are doing. We need a place and time to reflect and develop more awareness of our previously unconscious coping habits. Becoming more aware of who we are and of how we live, we begin to discover new possibilities.

A Psychological Model of Development: Ego and Self

When you reach the end of the road, there's only one thing to do: build more road.

© Ashleigh Brilliant

The dilemma and opportunity of unconscious habitual coping patterns is described in Carl Jung's model of psychological development. According to Jung, the psyche includes two parts: the Self and the Ego. The Self refers to the essence of the person, the central inexpressible core, the unique individuality, the potential that includes all of who we may be. The Ego is defined as the particular identity we develop as an expression of the Self during a specific time in our lives. Jung took issue with Freud in the notion that the unconscious is solely the repository of negative aspects of the personality: primitive impulses, conflicts, memories, and learning. Jung believed that the unconscious was also the repository of the positive, which he called the collective unconscious.

The Ego includes the habitual ways in which we think, feel, and act. The Self guides and informs the process of developing our personality. The Ego represents the best we can do to manifest our uniqueness and potential in the current circumstances of our lives. The relationship between Self and Ego can be compared to the relationship between the DNA and the actual human body. The DNA encodes our biological structure, which is then manifested into material form. If the DNA is like the Self, the actual physical body is equivalent to the Ego

The manifestation of the Self in the Ego is always flawed and incomplete. Identifying ourselves with the Ego, we lose connection with the Self. We are unable to create what we imagine. We imagine that some identity will be satisfying, but the conceptualization is mistaken. Even if we succeed, our needs and environment change, making obsolete a particular identity that previously served us well.

The Ego identity is challenged when we experience crises and transitions in our lives. In response to these difficulties, the old identity is shattered. The Ego, which once served us, no longer helps us manifest our potential. The circumstances of life challenge us to sur-

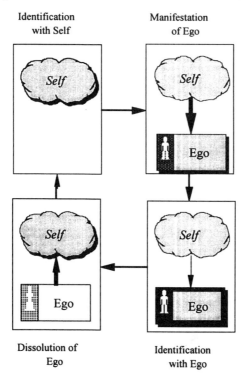

Identification with Self

Manifestation of Ego

Dissolution of Ego

Identification with Ego

render the old Ego, to reconnect with the Self, the core sense of our being. We then begin to create a new identity, a new Ego, that enables us to respond more effectively.

For Michael, the capacity to push himself developed as a way to overcome the trauma of his father's death. That capacity served him well in many respects. However, in so doing, he lost connection with his Essence, the Self, and identified himself only with the Ego—the ability to ignore pain and focus on achievement. This strategy failed him as he attempted to overcome his physical difficulties, challenging him to dis-identify with his Ego, reconnect with the Self, and discover new potentials.

Roberto Assagioli (1976) was a student of Jung who developed his own method of therapy known as psychosynthesis. Although we do not know the extent of Assagioli's fluency with Jewish practice, he identified himself as a Jew. Assagioli elaborated on Jung's notion of Ego and Self. Assagioli described a Higher Self, paralleling the Self, and a Lower Self, correlating to the Ego. The habitual responses are associated with the Lower Self. Assagioli emphasized the notion that habitual

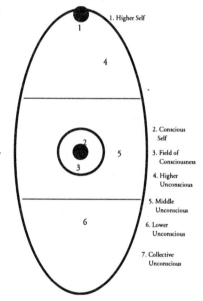

1. Higher Self
2. Conscious Self
3. Field of Consciousness
4. Higher Unconscious
5. Middle Unconscious
6. Lower Unconscious
7. Collective Unconscious

responses are not intrinsically destructive but become dysfunctional when a person responds rigidly.

In psychotherapeutic process, a person works to clarify the parts of the Self and to integrate all those parts, each of which becomes a valid and useful way of being when it is integrated so as to work in concert with other parts. The task in therapy is to develop new possibilities and be able to choose responses that are most constructive at a particular time. For example, Michael's ability to ignore pain and work hard to achieve a goal was positive. However, when it became his only coping strategy, it proved to be ineffective in reducing his pain. As he developed the capacity to ask for and receive support, he no longer identified himself exclusively as someone who can "push" himself. He could use each skill appropriately, when it would be most effective.

A Jewish Model of Development: *Nitzotz* and *Kelippah*

Inside every older person, there's a younger person, wondering what happened.

©Ashleigh Brilliant

The Jungian description of the Ego developing from the Self and Assagioli's concept of Higher Self and Lower Self are striking in their similarity to the Chasidic notion of a universal Spirit to which each of us is connected through a spark of Divinity present within each person. There are two aspects of the soul: the higher, Divine soul and a lower, Corporeal soul. These two qualities are also described using the metaphor of the spark, the *Nitzotz,* and the protective covering or shell, the *Kelippah.* The spark symbolizes the inner Essence of a person; the shell represents the outer identity that protects the spark. When a seed is planted, the shell rots, dissolving into the earth and allowing the seed to sprout, grow, and blossom. For the seed to grow, the shell must dissolve. In the same way, the spark manifests itself only when we are able to remove the shell.

The higher soul, the *Nitzotz,* like the Self, is viewed both as the unique individuality of the person and a larger oneness that unifies all life. In the same way as the Self manifests into a particular Ego, the spark of Divinity is clothed in a material form, the animal soul. The *Kelippah* includes the physical body and the personality that expresses the life force. The *Nitzotz* is associated with the Essence of God's presence, *Ayin*—literally translated as "no-thing-ness." The *Kelippah* is associated with God manifest in the world, *Yesh*—literally translated as "some-thing-ness."

The rabbis in the Middle Ages described the relationship between the Divine soul and the Corporeal soul using the analogy of a blind man and a lame man who are lost in the woods. The lame man represents the *Nitzotz,* the Higher Self that can see where to go but is unable to move in the world. The blind man is like the Corporeal soul which can act but cannot see where to go. Each needs the other. They find their way by having the lame man climb onto the shoulders of the blind man; the lame man guides the blind man who can then follow the proper path.

Shneur Zalman draws from the story of the patriarch Jacob in describing the relationship between the Corporeal soul and the Divine soul:

> *When the time came for her to give birth, there were twins in her womb. The first one came out reddish, as hairy as a fur coat. They named him Esau. His brother then emerged, and his hand was grasping Esau's heel. Isaac named him Jacob.*
>
> [Genesis 25:24–26]

Jacob represents the Divine soul; his brother Esau, known for his skill as a hunter and referred to as a man of the fields, symbolizes the Corporeal soul. In the Torah story, Jacob pretends to be his brother so as to receive the blessing from his father Isaac. Jacob appears before his father dressed in the clothes of his brother Esau. For Shneur Zalman, Jacob's deception provides an archetypal image of the relationship between the Corporeal soul and the Divine soul. The Divine soul, similar to Nahman's description, cannot act in the material plane. Spirit must act through the garment of the Corporeal soul that operates in the material world. If there is a disconnection between the Divine soul and the Corporeal soul, the Corporeal soul acts independently, lacking the vision and guidance of Spirit. The blind man cannot find his way out of the woods. Esau's power and energy expresses itself destructively. Reconnection is necessary for us to live in harmony with our true Essence.

The Jewish understanding of the human situation resembles the psychological perspective, although each uses a different language: both approaches focus on the notion of an unconscious that must give way to awareness. According to the *midrash,* each of us is all-knowing and fully conscious before we enter our bodies. Before birth, an angel touches us on our upper lip, leaving the indentation that remains with us through our lives. At that moment, we lose consciousness. This archetypal moment symbolizes all of what we no longer know, paralleled in psychological language as rigid, habitual, unconscious responses that interfere with our ability to manifest our potentials fully. As in therapy, the task is to heighten awareness, to regain the knowledge that we once had, to realize we have other choices, and to develop new ways of manifesting our Essence in the world. The habitual, coping strategies are not rejected as useless and destructive but are no longer viewed as the only possibility.

Paralleling the Jungian theory, we identify with the outer shell of material existence. We then work to reconnect with the spiritual Essence. In the same way as the Ego is shattered in response to changing circumstances of life, the material form of our lives is constantly developing. In response to the circumstances of life, we discover ways to more fully express our Divine potential.

The Jewish perspective, like Assagioli's image of development, does not regard the Corporeal self as intrinsically negative; dysfunction occurs when we lose connection with our Essence, becoming identified with a rigid response pattern. In this spirit, Rabbi Nahman tells the story of a garden as an allegorical description of how the personality can be reorganized. There is a garden that is in great disarray, overgrown and out of control. No one knows how to repair the garden until a wise man enters the garden and discovers a statue of a person and a throne that have been misplaced. He restores them to their rightful location, and the garden is transformed, once again becoming a place of beauty and nourishment.

MAKING A PERSONAL CONNECTION

- Recall a moment of crisis when a habitual, unconscious way of coping with stress was ineffective. What was the turning point when you became aware of the habit and the need to change?

- Recall moments when you experienced connection with your Essence. How did that experience transform you?

THE MULTIFACETED NATURE OF CONSCIOUSNESS

State-Dependent Learning, Memory, and Behavior

My picture of the world keeps changing before I can get it into focus.

© Ashleigh Brilliant

What we know and who we are is constantly changing. We have many states of consciousness, each with unique awareness, memory, and intelligence. Ernest Rossi (1993), a student of Milton Erickson who has written extensively on the psychobiology of consciousness, calls this phenomenon state-dependent learning, memory, and behavior (SDLMB). We all experience this phenomenon of shifting mental states at times of momentary forgetfulness. For example, I walk from the kitchen to the bedroom in search of scissors. When I arrive in the bedroom, I suddenly cannot remember what I want. I walk back into the kitchen and then remember my original intention.

The momentary lapse in memory is a result of a change in the state of consciousness. At any moment, various parts of the brain are "turned on" and others are "turned off." We are connected with whatever is stored in those parts of the brain that are activated and disconnected from the parts that are not activated. We have access to experiences, memories, feelings, understanding, beliefs, physical responses, and biochemical reactions stored in the activated parts of the brain while other information is unavailable to us. In the example of forgetfulness, my need for the scissors is associated with the visual environment of the kitchen. When I leave that room, a change occurs in the state of consciousness. Disconnected from the part of the brain containing that information, I forget my original purpose. When I return to the kitchen, the visual cues reconnect me with the initial state of consciousness, allowing me to remember that I wanted scissors.

Rossi (1993) explains the experience of trance induced through hypnosis as a particular type of state-dependent consciousness in which a person suspends ordinary logical, analytic processes focused

on activity. In trance, consciousness is associative, nonlinear, and synergistic, focused on being rather than doing. The trance state allows
time for withdrawal, reflection, and self-discovery, creating possibilities for new understanding.

This shift in consciousness is associated with changes in brain
activity. Ordinary consciousness is usually accompanied by higher
levels of activity in the left hemisphere of the cerebral cortex of the
brain; the trance state is characterized by higher levels of activity in
the right hemisphere of the cerebral cortex. Rossi suggests that our
bodies are neurologically programmed to alternate between ordinary consciousness and a spontaneous trance state in a regular
ongoing daily cycle known as the ultradian rhythm. In the ultradian cycle, our brains tend to shift hemispheric dominance approxi-
mately every ninety minutes, giving us the opportunity to shift
states of consciousness and access different sources of intelligence
within ourselves.

The Implications of State-Dependent Learning, Memory, and Behavior for Psychotherapy

Life has been very confusing because I've been different ages at different times.

© Ashleigh Brilliant

The Ego and Self can also be understood as two different states of
consciousness. When the Ego is activated, the person is connected to
all the memories, feelings, beliefs, behaviors, and physical responses
that have been learned in that state. For this reason, the person has
no awareness of other possibilities, but only the habitual patterns.
When we access the Self, the Essence of our being, we make connection with a different quality of consciousness, attuned to the purpose, goal, and meaning of our lives.

The fragmented nature of consciousness must be taken into
account as we work to transform dysfunctional habitual responses to
crisis. Our habitual responses to stress are associated with particular
states of consciousness. A stimulus in the present reminds us of other
experiences in our life that are similar, accessing the consciousness

that includes memories, feelings, behavioral impulses, and attitudes. Other possibilities are not available to us in that moment. When the stimuli are emotionally charged, it can be very difficult to shift consciousness. I cannot access other information simply by walking to a different room.

Rossi (1993) cites the placebo effect to illustrate the power of state-dependent consciousness. He describes a cancer patient who goes into remission when he learns that a research study has validated the effectiveness of a drug he has been taking. A short time later, another study concludes that the drug is completely ineffective. His cancer immediately returns. The patient's changing beliefs impact his immune system's ability to fight his disease.

In this same way, our habitual responses are often encoded in state-dependent consciousness and are activated by an evocative stimulus. In order to become aware of habits that operate outside conscious awareness, we need to enter the particular state of consciousness in which the difficulty occurs. For example, a person who wants to deepen understanding of panic attacks may speculate and theorize about the causes and reasons: he or she may have many valuable insights. However, in the actual moment of experiencing an episode of panic, there is an additional potential for learning as one explores the richness and detail of physical sensations, feelings, associations, actions, and attitudes. In that moment, there is also a possibility of discovering new choices. This quality was an important aspect of the work with Michael: he did not simply theorize about his coping patterns—he experienced, in the moment, how he coped with his pain, clarified the effects of that approach, and experimented with a more constructive approach.

Similarly, if we want to reconnect to the Self, we need to access that state of consciousness in which we experience the Essence of our being so we gain information about the purpose, goal, and meaning of our lives. We can then work to allow that consciousness to inform daily life. For example, if I ask you to relax, you may be unable to do so. If you feel tense and harried, you may not believe you can relax, or you might react negatively in being told what to do by someone else. The part of the brain that stores information on relaxation may be inaccessible. However, the outcome might be different if I approach the task of relaxation in a different way. I might ask you to recall a time, perhaps, at the beach, or somewhere else where you experienced a very satisfying sense of relaxation. I might ask you to see the place vividly, in your mind's eye, remembering the sand, the sky, and the water, in all their colors. I might ask you to recall the sounds of the ocean and the birds. I might ask you to remember the feeling in your body, the warmth of the sun, the sand that molded itself to the contours of each limb. As you recall that image vividly, relaxation usually occurs.

Hypnosis uses various techniques to access both the state of consciousness in which we are locked into a habitual response as well as the state of consciousness in which we have resources for finding solutions. In psychosynthesis, guided meditations are used for the same purpose. In Gestalt therapy, these states are activated by enacting the inner dialogues to make them more accessible.

A Jewish Theory of State-Dependent Consciousness: *Kodesh* and *Chol*

Is life better understood by looking at it more closely or by stepping back farther from it?
© Ashleigh Brilliant

In Jewish practice, the notion of different states of consciousness also provides a foundation for understanding how we learn. We differentiate a special state of spiritual consciousness from ordinary consciousness: the concepts of *Kodesh* and *Chol*, "Holy" and "Everyday."

This state of higher consciousness known as *Kodesh* is usually translated as "Holy." *Kodesh* is more accurately translated as "separate" or "different," a quality of consciousness in which we separate ourselves from identifying with our material existence. The root of the word is also associated with prostrating ourselves, bowing down in response to the experience of God's presence in which our own particular individual self is nullified. In this altered state of consciousness, we are not dissociated from ourselves but connected to our true Essence in which the particular ego identity is no longer our focus. In the state of *Chol,* we are connected to the material world, engaged in everyday activity. In this state, we may not have access to the beliefs, behaviors, feelings, and perceptions associated with the state of *Kodesh.*

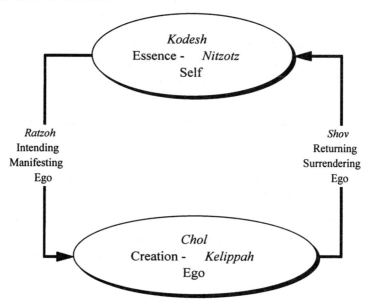

Jewish ritual structures time to ensure we have moments for shifting consciousness. Each day is punctuated by times for prayer and by blessings associated with the activities of daily life. Six days of the week are followed by the day of rest, *Shabbat.* These rituals encourage a movement back and forth between *Kodesh* and *Chol,* between being and doing, a movement from Essence into manifestation, and from manifestation surrendering back into Essence. The movement from Essence into manifestation is known as *Ratzoh,* which is associated with the root word for "will," "desire," and "intention"; in this process, we manifest our intention into actuality in the material world. The movement from manifestation back to Essence is known as *Shov,* associated with the root word for "turning," "returning," and "repentance"; in this phase, we surrender the old identity, turn our focus to Essence, and reconnect with our being.

Shneur Zalman interprets the biblical vision of the patriarch Jacob as the archetypal image of this process:

> *He had a vision in a dream. A ladder was standing on the ground, and its top reached up toward heaven. God's angels were going up and down on it.*
>
> [Genesis 28:12]

The top of the ladder extends up into the heavens, symbolizing *Kodesh,* the dwelling place of God's Essence, the Self. The foot of the ladder rests on the earth, the material reality, *Chol,* created by God, the Ego. Angels making their way up and down the ladder suggest the movement of life from Essence to manifestation, and from manifestation back to Essence, *Kodesh* to *Chol,* and *Chol* to *Kodesh.* It is no accident that Jacob has the dream at a dramatic moment, a turning point in his life. It is the time when he has left home, carrying his father's blessing but fleeing from his brother's wrath. He journeys toward an uncertain destination. His future is unknown. It is one of those moments of transformation in which an old identity dissolves to make way for a new way of being to fit the changes in life.

This cycle is macrocosmic and microcosmic. God's creation of the universe represents the movement, *Ratzoh* and *Shov,* from Essence - *Kodesh,* into manifestation—*Chol;* that phase will be followed by a return back to Essence. For each person, the process of life involves a similar movement back and forth. The day is punctuated with times for prayer morning, afternoon, and evening, as well as blessings associated with the various activities of daily life. Time is also devoted to study of religious text. Each of these activities allows for time to disconnect from material existence and reconnect with spirit, after which one moves back to reconnect with daily life with renewed clarity. The week similarly involves a cycle of six days of work punctuated with a day of rest, the Sabbath.

The Holy-Day cycle of the year provides a similar mechanism of *Ratzoh* and *Shov.* We stop ordinary activity, immerse ourselves in ritual that allows us to experience *Kodesh,* a different trancelike quality of time in which we encounter the archetypal images, stories, and symbols experientially. Each provides time for withdrawal, reconnection with Essence, and manifestation of a new way of being into everyday life.

TOOLS FOR CHANGE:
RITUAL, SYMBOLS, IMAGERY, AND STORIES

A Jewish man remembers the Sukkah in his grandfather's home
and Sukkah remembers for him
the wandering in the desert that remembers
the grace of youth and the Tablets of the Ten Commandments
and the gold of the Golden Calf and the thirst and the hunger
that remember Egypt.

Yehudah Amichai[1]

Ritual, symbols, imagery, and stories are tools for change in the context of both psychotherapy and Jewish practice. They help us make our way through the difficult process of self-transformation at each stage. They are concrete anchors, providing a language that communicates the complexity simply and memorably. They are also ambiguous enough to allow us to shape their meaning in a way that best addresses the particular conditions of our lives at a given time. They are simple but not simplistic. They allow people to learn indirectly, using right-brain consciousness, which bypasses everyday critical functions.

For example, projective tests are often used to access material from the unconscious. A person looks at a complex and undifferentiated image such as an inkblot and describes what is seen. Since the image can be interpreted in many different ways, a person is likely to project his or her own unconscious associations on the drawing. One person who has experienced trauma around death might see a coffin; someone else who has recently become a parent might see an image of birth.

Archetypes and Jungian Analysis

Jung believed that imagery, story, myth, and symbol could serve as a focus for reflection, allowing us to access the collective unconscious. Over the course of a lifetime, a person might interpret images in different ways, finding new meaning, new perspectives, and new understanding. Each encounter with archetypal, universal symbols provide an opportunity to rediscover and reinvent ourselves.

For example, our identity as sexual beings is part of the Self, a masculine and feminine quality known as the *Animus* and *Anima.* This essence is unconscious and inexpressible; however, we conceptualize it on the basis of particular understanding at a particular time. What does it mean to be a man? A woman? Who are our role models? How do we act, feel, and think? We create our sexual identity on the basis of these images. The particular identity is always incomplete. We may be unable to act on the basis of our understanding, the understanding may be flawed, or the images may change at different times of our lives or as a result of larger changes in the culture. Through the course of our lives, our identity evolves and develops. Archetypes mediate the movement between Self and Ego. As we experience the archetype, we reconnect with our Essence and re-create the new Ego identity based on new insights.

Jung's interest in symbols led to an appreciation of the richness of symbols and imagery in many religious traditions. He looked to those traditions as a resource for us in our journey through life. More recently, Joseph Campbell (1988) applied these principles, viewing myth and story as rich sources of archetypal images that can allow us to see ourselves in new ways:

> *People say that what we're all seeking is a meaning for life. I don't think that's what we're really seeking. I think that what we're seeking is an experience of being alive so that our life experiences on the purely physical plane will have resonances within our own innermost being and reality, so that we actually feel the rapture of being alive. . . . Myths are clues to the optimal potentialities of the human life.*[2]

Archetypes and the Jewish Tradition

The Chasidic masters also understood ritual, story, and images of the tradition as archetypal images that were keys to the experience of *Kodesh,* practical tools designed to teach, inform, and guide us in our lives. They help us reconnect with our purpose, reminding us why we are here and where we are headed. When we use them as mirrors to reflect on our own lives, they enable us to see ourselves in new ways.

Shneur Zalman describes how images from the material world allow us to know God in ways that can be even more powerful than the direct experience of revelation. He interprets the text of the Torah describing creation in which God says, "There shall be lights in the heavenly sky." Shneur Zalman explains that "lights" refer to two different ways to experience God:

> The word, me'orot, has many different meanings. In addition to its literal translation as "lights," marot are "mirrors" or "glasses." The word can also be translated as "visions." When the Torah says that God created lights, the text refers not only to the sun and the moon but to two kinds of glass, to two ways of seeing, symbolic of two ways of perceiving the Infinite.
>
> One kind of glass, Aspaklaria Ha'may-ira, is a transparent glass like that in a telescope. We see through the telescope in a straight line. This glass is symbolic of the vision of Moses who directly perceived the infinite. . . . In the same way as we experience the light of the sun as it shines, we directly experience the light of God's Presence as it flows from the Garden of Eden to the material plane of existence.
>
> The other kind of glass is a mirror, Aspaklaria She'ayna Mai-ira, a transparent glass which has a thin barrier or covering of silver. This covering prevents us from seeing an object directly, but we can see an image of the object. There is an advantage as well as a disadvantage to this type of glass. A mirror allows us to see ourselves and to see what is behind us. In the same way as the light of the moon, like a mirror, comes from its capacity to reflect the light from the sun, the later prophets experienced God indirectly. Moses operated at a higher plane than the prophets: they were unable to directly perceive God, and they only experienced God through images. Nonetheless, this indirect experience enabled them to perceive God in ways that Moses could not. God says to Moses, "No one can see my face and live," because

it is not possible to live and experience God's Presence directly. However, the prophet Isaiah says "And I see God" because he is able to perceive more through indirect means.

That which appears to be a barrier to the light paradoxically allows us to perceive the light. [An example of this phenomenon in the natural world occurs when we try to view the sun during an eclipse. If we attempted to stare directly at the sun, we run the risk of damaging our eyes. We can see the sun by looking through a barrier such as a card with only a pinhole.]

Our bodies, our animal self, our material existence serve as a similar thin covering like the silver on a mirror, allowing us to perceive a new light, mirrors for our souls.

Torah Or 29A

In this spirit, the Torah provides us with stories, symbols, images, and rituals. Through the generations, commentators, scholars, and rabbis contribute their understandings and interpretations, adding to the storehouse of possibilities from which we can nourish ourselves.

The archetypes do not change. The *Torah* is immutable, regarded as the word of God, the embodiment of Truth. According to the mystics, God creates the world with the letters and words. Not only each word, but each letter is viewed as significant and meaningful. Interpretations are also made on the basis of numerology. Since each Hebrew letter has a numerical value, connections can be made between words that are mathematically equivalent, a process known as *gematria*. For example, the Hebrew word for "lion," אריה , equals 216, which is equivalent to the sum of the letters in the word for strength, גבורה . The rabbis relied on four different approaches in their interpretation of the text. *P'shat* refers to the literal obvious

א	= 1
ר	=200
י	= 10
ה	= 5
	= 216

ג	= 3
ב	= 2
ו	= 6
ר	=200
ה	= 5
	= 216

explication based on the explicit reading of the text. *Remez* is translated as "hint," interpretation inferred or suggested, albeit indirectly. *Drash* is an elaboration of the text in which missing details are expanded. *Sod* is the secret, hidden significance derived through numerology or other kabbalistic techniques. Taking the first letter of each of these approaches makes the word *PaRDeS,* the word for "garden" and also for "the Garden of Eden," the resting place for souls who have passed from this world to the next.

Since the Torah is the word of God, every phrase, every word, and every letter are significant. There can be no mistakes. Any seeming error, inconsistency, redundancy, or other discrepancy cannot be dismissed but instead is regarded as having some purpose or meaning that we do not, in our limited intelligence, yet understand. Often, the style of rabbinic discourse involves identifying some apparent difficulty in the text that is then interpreted so as to deepen one's understanding. Each serves as a rich source for discovering new meanings that speak to the unique and universal character of our particular life situation. Paralleling the Jungian notion of work with archetypes, the understanding of that truth does change and develop.

THE MULTIDIMENSIONAL PROCESS OF LEARNING

I could while away the hours
Conferring with the flowers
Consulting with the rain;
And my head I'd be scratching
While my thoughts were busy hatching
If I only had a brain.

I'd unravel every riddle
For any individ'l
In trouble or in pain;
With the thoughts I'd be thinking
I could be another Lincoln
If I only had a brain.

Oh, I could tell you why
The ocean's near the shore;
I could think of things
I'd never thunk before;
And then I'd sit and think some more.
I would not be just a nothing

My head all full of stuffing
My heart all full of pain;
And perhaps I'd deserve you
And be even worthier of you
If I only had a brain.

When a man's a lucky fellow
He should be on his meddle
And get'em toward a part'
Just because I'm presumin'
That I could be kind of human
If I only had a heart.

I'd be tender, I'd be gentle
And awfully sentimental
Regarding love and art;
I'd be friends with the sparrows
And the boy that shoots the arrows
If I only had a heart.

Picture me a balcony
Above a voice sings low
Wherefore are thou Romeo;
I hear a beat, how sweet.

Just to register emotion,
Jealousy, devotion
And really feel the part;
I would stay young and chipper
And I'd lock it with a zipper
If I only had a heart.

Life is sad, believe me missy
When you're born to be a sissy
Without the vim and verve;
But I could change my habits
Never more be scared of rabbits
If I only had the nerve.
Well, I guess there's no denyin'

I'm just a dandelion,
A fate I don't deserve.
But I could show my prowess,
Be a lion, not a mou-ess,
If I only had the nerve.

Oh, I'd be in my stride
A kingdom to the core;
I could roar the way I never roared before;
And then I'd ruff and roar some more.

I would show the dinosaurus
Who's king around the forest
The kind he'd better serve;
Why, with my regal geezer
I could be another Caesar
If I only had the nerve.

E.Y. Harburg

Treatment Modalities: Behavioral, Interpersonal, Emotional, Psychophysical, Cognitive, and Spiritual Approaches to Psychotherapy

In psychotherapy and the Jewish tradition, there are many dimensions to the process of transformation. How we cope with the challenges of life involves a complex set of responses that includes what we do, how we feel, what we believe, how we relate with others, and how we organize ourselves physically. Each of these dimensions operate interdependently and synergistically. In making changes, we can focus on each of these aspects as we seek to heighten awareness of our habits and develop new capacities. We can focus on (1) behavioral patterns—how we structure time, eat, rest, work, and live our lives; (2) inter-personal patterns—how we relate to others; (3) emotional patterns—how we express and cope with our feelings; (4) psycho-physical patterns—how we sit, stand, and move; (5) cognitive patterns—how we organize, understand, and give meaning to our perceptions and experience; and (6) spiritual patterns—our experiences of transcendence.

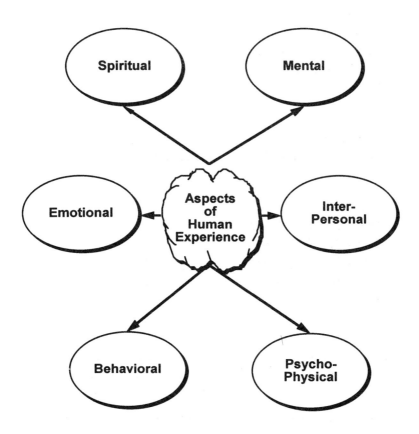

Behavioral

Our ability to cope is also a function of what we do, of our behaviors. If we maintain a lifestyle that is overly hectic and does not allow time for rest, taking action to have a better balance of activity and rest can help us to avoid overwork, reduce tension, and improve our health. Michael had learned to cope by ignoring pain, not permitting himself time for rest, and staying active. In behavioral therapies, the clinician focuses on resolving difficulties by identifying behaviors that need to be eliminated, changed, enhanced, or increased. For changes in his capacity to work with his body to be effective, Michael needed to take control of his schedule, to make specific, practical commitments to allocate time for self-care.

Interpersonal

Our relationships with others also play a role in exacerbating or healing the symptom. Michael was forced by circumstance to rely only on himself. Having lost his father, he survived by making sure that he did not depend on others. He never leaned on anyone. He never asked for help. Without thinking about it, he tended to carry a load himself rather than allow someone to assist him. He put up with an uncomfortable chair rather than inconvenience someone else by making a special request. His interpersonal habits interfered with the healing process. As Michael learned to reach out to others, he reduced stress that had previously exacerbated his condition. In approaches such as family therapy, transactional analysis, and group process, the therapist works with the network of relationships, clarifying ways in which relationship patterns affect one's ability to cope with difficulty.

Emotional

Our emotional responses also need to be considered as we work to improve our health. Michael survived by learning to ignore his sadness, fear, and hurt. Most of the time, he did not even notice those feelings. When he did, he was quite critical of himself. He tended to devalue the legitimacy of such emotions, shaming himself as a way to control his feelings. In so doing, he exacerbated physical tension because it often required physical effort to stop himself from crying, shaking, or otherwise expressing himself. Michael worked to sense more clearly when he felt sad, afraid, or hurt, and to allow himself time to express the feelings in ways that felt safe and relieving. This shift further reduced the buildup of tension during the course of the day. The habitual ways in which he managed feelings were abandoned in favor of new, more effective strategies. In expressive and experientially based therapies such as psychodrama, Gestalt therapy, transactional analysis, bioenergetics, primal therapy, and abreactive hypnosis, work focuses on contacting and expressing emotions safely and fully so as to free and mobilize our energetic potentials.

Psychophysical

The most direct, obvious approach to resolving a physical dysfunction is to work with body process. Michael unconsciously and habitually tensed his body, moved inefficiently, and maintained poor posture, all of which exacerbated his physical condition and increased the tissue damage to muscles, ligaments, nerves, or bones. His methods of trying to heal himself actually resulted in further damage. In body-centered approaches such as the Feldenkrais method or the Alexander technique, the practitioner works with the client using focused awareness, imagery, intention, and gentle movement to help facilitate changes. By learning to heighten his kinesthetic awareness, Michael was able to assess more accurately the results of his actions, to develop effective ways to relax chronically tense muscles, and to learn to move with better alignment and more ease, reducing pressure that exacerbated pain and injury.

Cognitive

Our beliefs are also an important factor. What we believe affects how we feel and how we respond. Beliefs and attitudes are habits. We develop our mental habits as a result of what we learn from our life experience. Michael believed, as a result of his father's death, that problems were overcome by ignoring pain and forcing oneself to focus on achieving goals. Asking for help was a sign of weakness. These beliefs helped Michael survive the crisis of his father's death, but they did not help him heal his body. As he became more aware of the nature of these beliefs, he was able to question the extent to which they served him and to experiment with new mental images and frameworks that proved more helpful.

Cognitive behavioral therapists facilitate change by working with the beliefs, images, and ideas that unconsciously help us organize, understand, and make sense of our experiences. These beliefs are not objective, hard facts; they are subjective constructs. Depending on the current situation, the beliefs may be helpful or destructive. For example, if I am rejected by a potential employer, I try to make sense of that experience. Why did it happen? What is the cause? If I decide that I was rejected because I am a stupid, incompetent person, I will become depressed, withdraw, and make no further efforts to find work. If I believe that I was not suited for that particular job, or that I lacked needed skills that I could learn, or that the decision was incorrect, I will remain optimistic, active, and continue my search. The belief becomes a self-fulfilling prophecy. In psychotherapy, I can work to clarify my beliefs and develop ones that are more helpful to me in my life. This process is also known as re-framing.

Spiritual

Ultimately, significant problems create spiritual dilemmas. We develop spiritual habits in the same ways we develop other kinds of habits. These habits have to do with our beliefs: What is the meaning and purpose of our lives? How do we confront death and evil in a way that makes sense of life? Is there a God or some transcendent power in the universe? What is the nature of that Presence and our relationship with it? How does it play a role in our lives? How do we make connection with that Presence? Especially when we face extreme challenges, our spiritual habits affect how we respond. For Michael, there was no God, no transcendent sense of life. He had learned to focus on material survival as an ultimate goal and test of life. Was there more to life than making money and providing for his family? Was there intrinsic value in being compassionate with himself in pain, or was that simply a method for reducing stress? In transpersonal psychotherapy, psychosynthesis, and Jungian therapy, there is a recognition that the problems of life are often resolved by making connection with a spiritual experience that gives us perspective, meaning, and direction with which to face the challenges.

Each type of habit—behavioral, interpersonal, emotional, psychophysical, mental, and spiritual—contributed to Michael's difficulty in resolving his problem. In each aspect of his coping, as he heightened awareness of his patterns, he could define new, more helpful ways to respond. Changes in one area helped build confidence and create momentum for changes in other areas. They also provided a foundation for further work, seeding possibilities that could be elaborated. For example, when Michael created a change in his body by allowing himself to be physically supported, he established an experiential point of reference which he was able to use as he focused on habitual beliefs, on interpersonal rigidities, and on emotional imbalances.

At different times in the healing process, it is helpful to concentrate on one or another aspect of our habits as we attempt to address difficulties. For Michael, it was helpful to begin by working with his physical process because it offered a direct, immediate, and logical approach to address his explicit concerns. However, if we had only addressed the physical level, he would not have made changes in related patterns that indirectly but significantly affected his condition. For each person there is a particular sequence of movement between approaches depending on what proves to be most helpful.

Each different type of psychotherapy offers unique understanding and tools with which to address various aspects of a person's dysfunction. Although practitioners sometimes make the mistake of narrowing their focus and work only with one dimension, the most effective therapy utilizes a multi-modality approach, working with different aspects of the habitual patterns of coping.

Dimensions of Holy-Day Celebration: Four Worlds of *Asiyah, Yetzirah, Briyah,* and *Atzilut*

Healing can happen in many ways: through touch, through thought, and through the word. Reb Shimon from Yaroslav, a disciple of the Belzer *Rebbe,* visited the Radziner *Rebbe.* The Radziner said he had heard of the great healings performed by the *Rebbe* of Belz and asked how the *Rebbe* accomplished them. The *Chasid* said that his *Rebbe* was able to heal a sick person by touch. "What is the basis for this method in the *Torah?*" asked the *Rebbe.* The *Chasid* responded by citing the verse in the *Torah,* "God sends forth the word and they are healed." The verse in Hebrew is *YeeShLaCh DeVaRO VeYeeRPaAiM".* Taking the first letters of each word—*yud, daled,* and *vav*—one constructs the word for "His hand"—*yado.* According to this mystical interpretation of the letters,

י שלח ה

ד בר ו

וירפאם

we can conclude that the *Torah* validates the concept of healing through touch.

The disciple noted that he had heard that the Radziner also had the power to heal and asked how he practiced his work. The Radziner replied, "I heal through the mind, through the power of intention." "What is the basis for your method in the *Torah*?" asked the *Chasid*. The Radziner replied, citing the same verse, "If you take the last letters of the verse—*YeeShLaCh DeVaRO VeYeeRPaAiM*—you obtain the letters *chuf, vav,* and *mem.* Reversing the order makes the word for "brain," *MOaCH.* According to this method, we conclude that the *Torah* validates the concept of healing with the mind."

Jewish mysticism also uses a multidimensional framework for understanding human experience and the process of development. According to the mystics, spirit manifests into material existence as a chain of emanation through four worlds: (1) the world of Essence—*Atzilut;* (2) the world of Creation—*Briyah;* (3) the world of Formation—*Yetzirah;* and (4) the world of Action—*Asiyah.* Each of these worlds has a particular quality. *Atzilut* is associated with the word for "close" or "near." In the world of Essence, we are connected to Spirit, the nonverbal experience of oneness. The world of Creation is the world of mind, thought, and idea. The first step in the creation of the world is God's idea and intention. The world of Formation is associated with the translation of ideas into feelings and the neurological programming of our movement. In the story of creation, God translates idea into words. In the world of Action, the words create the material universe—what we do and how we relate to others.

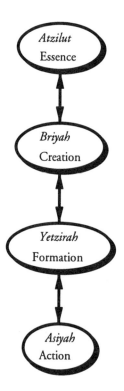

In the process of *Ratzoh* and *Shov,* as we journey from *Kodesh* to *Chol* and then return from *Chol* to *Kodesh,* we also recapitulate the process of creation, experiencing each of the four worlds. As we do, we access resources for growth and healing in each of these areas: in the world of *Asiyah* through our behavior and our interpersonal responses, in the world of *Yetzirah* through our psychophysical process and our emotions, in the world of *Briyah* through our cognitive and perceptual organization, and in the world of *Atzilut* through our spiritual experience. Each of the Holy-Days allows us to experience the four worlds.

Asiyah—Behavioral

Celebration of each Holy-Day requires that we make behavioral changes, structuring our time in particular ways. For major Holy-Days, we stop ordinary working activity, abstain from tasks devoted to our economic survival, and refrain even from handling money. We perform rituals that help us turn inward and focus on the quality of life in the present moment. We mark the beginnings and endings with specific ritual acts that help separate these days from ordinary days. We occupy ourselves with particular rituals, traditions, and prayers that shape the unique quality of each Holy-Day. According to custom, each Holy-Day involves a unique diet, excluding some foods and encouraging others. The behavioral changes ensure that we interrupt our habitual routines. They provide us with time to withdraw from a focus on activity in the world and turn inward.

Asiyah—Inter-Personal

The Holy-Days do not take place in isolation, but in relationship with others. Our sense of connectedness is reinforced as we are asked to join together in our families and communities as part of our ritual celebration. The rituals encourage a variety of ways of being with others: giving and receiving, playing together, teaching and learning, grieving and comforting, challenging and being challenged, and facing vulnerability. As we travel through the cycle of the year, the Holy-Days offer opportunities to make connections with others that nourish us in our efforts to develop and grow.

Yetzirah—Emotional

The focus of emotional expression in the ritual of the Holy-Days is through the structure of prayers. Some of the prayers are common to all days; some are unique to each of the Holy-Days. Prayer is not an intellectual but an expressive activity in which we open our hearts and speak to God from the depth of our being. Various prayers focus on different feelings, allowing us to find connection and a vehicle for expression of a wide range of emotions: love, awe, joy, appreciation, grief, regret, fear, anger, frustration, determination, and others.

Yetzirah—Psychophysical

The growth process of the Holy-Days is grounded in the body. The experience of spirituality and Essence does not result from disconnecting and disidentifying with the body but rather from heightening our awareness of moment-to-moment experience in activity. Although traditional Jewish practice does not explicitly focus on body process, the ritual and liturgy are grounded in activity; spirit is experienced through the body. Cessation of ordinary work offers an opportunity for rest and rejuvenation. Rituals are linked to primary human activities such as eating, drinking, and other bodily functions. The rituals invite us to become conscious of body experiences that are usually performed unconsciously. For Kabbalists, immersing oneself in the *mikveh,* the ritual bath, served as preparation to help access the experience of holiness. In prayer and singing, we work indirectly with the breath and with movement.

Briyah—Mental

The rituals, stories, and symbols of each Holy-Day also provide a framework for working to develop more constructive beliefs, attitudes, and images about ourselves, others, and the nature of the challenges that face us. Each Holy-Day is associated with particular historic events. There are rituals associated with changes in the seasons and with the sacrificial services in the Sanctuary. The various prayers and customs present us with unique images. We are invited to view our lives through these lenses. For example, on Pesach, I experience myself as coming out of Egypt, finding understanding and guidance from particular aspects of the biblical story that are helpful in gaining a new perspective on my situation.

We develop our understanding in two ways: theoretical and experiential. We use logical, analytic processes associated with left-brain functioning as we study the laws and rituals. We access right-brain synergistic and associative learning as we immerse ourselves in the experience of rituals and prayers. All of these elements are experienced, not as theoretical concepts but as archetypal images that help us define ourselves in new ways.

Atzilut—Spiritual

As we add the focus on behavior, relationship, emotions, the body, and mind, the changes we experience interact synergistically. Each is nourished by and reinforces the others, creating a powerful process for transformation that is more than the sum of the parts. At the level of Essence, the Holy-Days facilitate a spiritual experience, a quality of being that cannot be reduced to words.

Unique Focus of Each Holy-Day

It was six men of Indostan To learning much inclined
Who went to see the Elephant
  (Though all of them were blind),
That each by observation
  Might satisfy his mind.

The First approached the Elephant
  And happening to fall
Against his broad and sturdy side,
  At once began to bawl:
"God bless me, but the Elephant
  Is very like a wall!"

The Second, feeling the tusk,
  Cried, "Ho! What have we here
So very round and smooth and sharp?
  To me 'tis very clear
This wonder of an Elephant
  Is very like a spear!"
The Third approached the animal

And, happening to take
The squirming trunk within his hands,
*   Thus boldly up he spake:*
"I see," quoth he, "The Elephant
*   Is very like a snake!"*

The Fourth reached out an eager hand,
*   And felt about the knee:*
"What most the wondrous beast is like
*   Is very plain," quoth he, "*
"'Tis clear enough the Elephant
*   Is very like a tree!"*

The Fifth, who chanced to touch the ear,
*   Said, "E'en the blindest man*
Can tell what this resembles most;
*   Deny the fact who can:*
This marvel of an Elephant
*   Is very like a fan!"*

The Sixth no sooner had begun
*   About the beast to grope*
Then, seizing on the swinging tail
*   That fell within his scope,*
"I see," quoth he, " the Elephant
*   Is very like a rope!"*

And so these men of Indostan
*   Disputed loud and long,*
Each in his own opinion
*   exceeding stiff and strong.*
Though each was partly in the right,
*   They all were in the wrong!*

John Godfrey Saxe

Each Holy-Day operates on all levels, on behavior and relationship in the world of *Asiyah,* on emotion and psychophysical process
in the world of *Yetzirah,* on cognitive process in the world of *Briyah,*
and on spirit in the world of *Atzilut.* Each Holy-Day also has a par-

ticular emphasis, inviting us to focus on that dimension in our own lives. As we celebrate the Holy-Days through the cycle of the year, we also journey through the worlds. On Pesach, the focus is on the material world of *Asiyah* with rituals of cleaning and changing our diet. During the counting of the *omer* and our commemoration of the wandering in the desert, we work to translate our experience of the world into understanding, shifting from the world of *Asiyah* to the world of *Briyah* and cognitive process. Shavuot also emphasizes the cognitive dimension. Immersing ourselves in study and celebrating revelation on Mount Sinai, we access new understanding. During the period of mourning that climaxes with the Tisha B'Av, we begin to make connection with the world of *Yetzirah* and our emotions, especially our feelings of grief in realizing the extent to which our understanding does not translate into reality.

The focus on emotional process continues during the Days of Awe. During the month of Elul, we compassionately examine our responses. On Rosh HaShanah, we make ourselves accountable in acknowledging dysfunctional aspects of our coping strategies. On Yom Kippur, we reconnect with *Atzilut,* disconnecting from the material world through prayer and fasting. As a result, we can shift our focus to manifesting our Spirit into the world. We begin emotionally in the world of *Yetzirah,* as we celebrate the harvest of Sukkot. We are then return to work behaviorally to translate our understanding and feeling into action. The next Holy-Days take us into the world of *Asiyah* as we celebrate our struggle to create a light in the darkness on Chanukah and as we commemorate Tu B'Shevat, the new year for trees with its images of growth. We end the year with Purim, when we again connect with *Atzilut* but through integration of spirit into the material world.

Each of the Holy-Days focuses on a particular aspect; at the same time, each Holy-Day also includes elements of all levels—behavioral, physical, emotional, mental, inter-personal, and spiritual. In the same way as we shift modalities in psychotherapy depending on what is most efficient and effective, the richness and texture allows each of us to focus on the particular dimensions of experience that are most constructive for us in our unique situation and moment in time. We benefit from a structure that encourages us to focus on one element of our being while also maintaining the flexibility to adjust that focus as necessary.

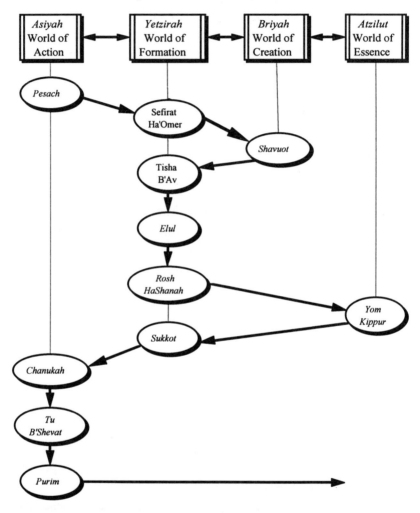

STAGES OF DEVELOPMENT
FROM DEPENDENCY TO AUTONOMY

Yesterday a child came out to wonder
Caught a dragonfly inside a jar
Fearful when the sky was full of thunder
And tearful at the falling of a star.

Then the child moved ten times round the seasons
Skated over ten clear frozen streams.
Words like "when you're older" must appease him
And promises of someday make his dreams.

Sixteen springs and sixteen summers gone now
Cartwheels turn to carwheels through the town
And they tell him "Take your time it won't be long now
Til you drag your feet to slow the circles down."

Years spin by and now the child is twenty
Tho' his dreams have lost some grandeur coming true
There'll be new dreams, maybe better dreams and plenty
Before the last revolving year is thru.

And the seasons they go round and round
And the painted ponies go up and down.
We're captives on a carousel of time
We can't return, we can only look
Behind from where we came
And go round and round and round in the circle game.

Joni Mitchell

The process of growth and development in childhood involves a series of stages. In the same way as a child requires a different quality of parenting at each stage of development, the therapist needs to respond differently at each stage of the learning process. Similarly, the Holy-Day cycle involves a series of stages in which we make connection with a different aspect of God's Presence appropriate for our particular stage of development.

Developmental Process in Childhood

The infant begins life helpless and dependent, unable to satisfy or even to verbalize his or her needs. The infant needs a parent who watches over the child, who works to understand the child's experience and provides the particular nourishment or support that the child needs. The baby must be fed, clothed, moved, and supported by others. Gradually the infant begins to develop some competence and skill in movement, speech, and understanding. At this stage, the parent still takes care of the toddler's basic needs but also helps the child develop increasing autonomy. The parent balances freedom and encouragement to explore with guidance, limits, and rules to ensure safety and well-being. The parent helps the child understand and talk about his or her experience. The toddler can ask for what she or he wants, can say yes and no, can follow his or her curiosity in exploring the world, crawling, walking, grabbing, and manipulating.

As the child develops more competence, he or she is able to take more responsibility and to begin to act more autonomously, able to take care of more of his or her own needs. The child learns to dress, use the toilet, and enact a vivid fantasy life, exploring every imaginable role and character. At this stage, the parent offers a different kind of support. No longer is it helpful to take care of all needs. The parent attempts to find a balance between taking care of the child when necessary and also helping the child learn by expecting more self-reliance.

This period can also be a time of frustration as the child becomes more aware of both possibilities and difficulties. The child realizes that she can learn to pour her own drink but discovers that balancing a heavy bottle of juice may present unforeseen problems, leaving a mess on the floor and nothing in the glass. At this stage, the child needs a patient, empathic parent who knows when to provide nurturance and understanding, or when simply to hold the child through her tears. The child who falls off a bike needs time to cry and receive a hug rather than being encouraged too quickly to try again or to be asked to examine the mistakes that led to the fall.

Hopefully, the child is able to move from frustration to commitment and patience, realizing that he or she can develop skills and competence. At this stage, the child needs a parent who helps the child understand the challenges, cope with the range of feelings, and develop the capacity and persistence to learn from mistakes.

In adolescence, the child is more able to operate independently. The teenager needs opportunities to make decisions, experience the consequences, and learn from his or her own actions. At this stage, a parent supports this exploration in two ways: separating so as to allow space and freedom for self-discovery while also providing encouragement, intervening when necessary and helping in making sense of life.

In time, the child develops into adulthood, able to function autonomously and interdependently. Autonomy does not mean rigid separateness or an end to self-development. Autonomy requires that the person takes charge of his or her own life, facing the challenges and dilemmas, able to reflect on his or her responses to those challenges, and committed to an ongoing process of learning.

Developmental Process in Psychotherapy

In order to reach where I am now, I had to pass though everywhere I've ever been.

© Ashleigh Brilliant

A similar process often occurs in psychotherapy as a person moves from dependency to autonomy. The client faces a different challenge at each stage, and the therapist responds in a particular way to address the needs at each stage.

We initiate therapy because we reach an impasse. Old methods for coping have somehow failed. We do not know what to do. Initially, we may rely on the therapist for guidance and direction to achieve a sense of basic safety and control. For example, when I began with Michael, he knew he was in pain, but he did not know what to do to help himself. I guided him through a process that allowed him to relax his tension, thereby reducing his pain. Initially, Michael could not replicate what he did with me; he was not even able to make sense of what happened.

As we continued to work, Michael focused on trying to understand what I was doing that proved helpful. At this stage, it was not sufficient for me to "fix" the problem. I assisted him by asking questions that allowed him to reflect on his situation and gain insight about how he responded. I offered my own thoughts and ideas for him to consider. I supported him in the trial-and-error process of learning. In this way, Michael developed a cognitive basis for being able to make changes on his own.

This task became increasingly frustrating for Michael as he began to realize how he reacted unconsciously and habitually. Moreover, he became painfully aware of the suffering he had created for himself over many years as a result of these habits. He also grasped the extent to which the trauma of childhood left him wounded and handicapped. His tendency to push himself had been helpful at the time of his father's death, but that same tendency also resulted in irreversible damage to his body. Michael realized he had never cried after his father died because no one provided emotional support. Some of his tension stemmed from the effort required to contain his sadness. This inhibition was activated at other times in his life when losses had occurred. At this stage, Michael needed support from me to grieve, to express the sadness, rage, and fear. He needed me to listen, not to try to fix the problem or make the pain go away but simply to give space and time to express his feelings. He told me the story of his father's death, allowing himself to feel the sadness and even shed some tears. He recalled also how he had lost his first child at the age of 3 months. He had never shed a tear about that loss, but now he felt that pain as well.

In truly feeling his pain, Michael also strengthened his commitment to do everything possible to ensure that he not continue to repeat old patterns; he became more disciplined in self-observation, identified dysfunctional responses, and experimented with new alternatives. At this stage, my role again shifted. Michael needed compassion, empathy, and understanding as he gained awareness of dysfunctional aspects of his own habits of coping. He opened himself to challenge and confrontation from me. My perceptions, albeit difficult to hear, provided more information that he was able to add to his own discoveries. I also challenged him to make changes. When one of his sons suffered some economic difficulties, Michael's initial response was to make plans for the future and work hard to implement them. I questioned the wisdom of Michael's timing; perhaps his son also needed time to grieve. Michael agreed and shifted his approach. He spent time with his son, listening and empathizing, sharing some of his own experiences.

As Michael appreciated his growing ability to support others when they experienced losses, he also realized that he needed to develop the capacity to express vulnerability and receive support in coping with his own difficulties. He made the commitment to stop when he was too "pushy" with himself, either physically or emotionally. He worked through this same process time after time. As he practiced, his skill developed. He became conscious of the automatic response sooner: he was able to shift to the new response more and more easily. At this stage, Michael again needed me to shift in my role. He did not need me to guide or interpret; he already understood what he needed to do. He was able, on his own, to identify when he regressed into his old habit of deadening himself, using that feeling as a signal to turn inward, clarify his feelings, and reach out to others. He did need me to listen; he also needed me to provide encouragement and some reassurance that he was making progress when he became frustrated or impatient. Occasionally, I offered a suggestion or an insight of my own.

In time, Michael found that he no longer automatically and unconsciously fell into the habit of pushing himself inappropriately. He was able to allow himself to feel sadness and vulnerability as well as to reach out to others for support most of the time. He continued to value his ability to work hard to achieve goals, but that quality was now balanced with his new way of being. He found humor in occasional moments when he responded unconsciously. He was now free to choose when to work hard and when to allow time for sitting with his pain. We took time to appreciate the work he had done and what we had accomplished together. There continued to be difficulties with which he had to struggle: his son continued to contend with issues of work; he still experienced discomfort physically. However, he was more able to deal with the difficulties. At this stage, the sense of mutuality in our relationship became more important. We could celebrate together what we had accomplished and commiserate about the difficulties of life that had no easy solutions. I was not so much guide or facilitator as fellow traveler on life's journey.

This description of the psychotherapeutic process is somewhat oversimplified. Although there were distinct stages in the work, the movement was not always distinct and smooth. There were moments when Michael jumped ahead or shifted back to previous stages. Not every aspect of the work fit into this model. Nor would work with other clients necessarily follow the same process. However, in the same way that a map is not a completely true representation of the territory it depicts, this model can offer us a way to understand what happens in the therapeutic work even though it is not completely accurate.

Developmental Process in the Holy-Day Cycle

The Holy-Days provide a context that offers similar opportunities to those experienced in psychotherapy, creating time to reflect on the nature of challenges we face and to consider how we might best respond. The progression of development through the course of the year parallels the process of growth in childhood. We begin the year as infants at the time of Pesach; we end the year as adults at the time of Purim. The parent responds differently to the child at different stages and ages; the therapist also responds differently to the client at different stages in therapy. In the same manner, God also responds differently at each Holy-Day, reflecting different needs in the process of development:

I speak of You, with words of praise
I honor Your name with songs of love.
I speak of Your glory, and I do not see You,
I describe visions of You, and I know You not.

Through hands of Your prophets, the mysteries of Your ser-
vants,
You have revealed images of Your honor and glory.
Your power and Your greatness,
They described what is manifest in Your acts.
They described images of You, but not Your Essence,
They found likeness of You in Your works.

They imaged You in many visions,
But You are one beneath all the images.
They saw You as old and as young,
Your hair as gray with age, and black with youth.
Aged on the day of judgment,
Youth in battle, like a warrior, fighting hand-to-hand.
Dew of light upon Your head,
Your locks of hair, darkness like the night.

I glorify You, You want me,
You are for me a crown of beauty.
Your head, like pure fine gold,
Upon Your forehead inscribed Your Holy Name.
Your glory shines upon me, and my glory upon You,
You are close to me when I call You.
May my meditation be pleasing to You,
For my soul longs for You.

Anim Zemirot
Shabbat morning liturgy

On Pesach, we experience ourselves like the Israelites enslaved in Egypt; we are powerless and vulnerable. Just as the Israelites were liberated only with the leadership of Moses and God's miracles, we require external support to free ourselves from that which constricts us. The mystics make a connection between Egypt and the womb. The exodus from Egypt is compared to the journey through the birth canal. Pesach invites us to make a connection with the aspect of ourselves that is newly emerging, experienced, perhaps, as suffering in a situation that had once felt nourishing and then became constricting. We may identify as well with ways in which we find ourselves taken out of this enslaved environment and thrust into a new situation that is liberating but also challenging and frightening.

The time of the counting of the *omer* is connected with the wandering in the desert, a time when the Israelites still needed God's protection and guidance but also a time when they gradually gained understanding. In the tradition, the Israelites are compared to toddlers in their wandering through the desert, taking steps on their own but still in need of guidance and nurturance. This time symbolizes our own wanderings as we gain understanding of our new situation, a time when we take our own first steps but require support and guidance.

The Holy-Day of Shavuot marks the moment at Mount Sinai when the Israelites received the Torah, a time of revelation and commitment. This Holy-Day is associated with the child's ability to develop insight independently. It is also viewed as a marriage between God and the Israelites. Shavuot symbolizes the experience of revelation as we make sense of our new situation and make commitment to a new path and direction.

On Tisha-B'Av, we grieve the destruction of the Sanctuary. It also marks the time when the Israelites, while awaiting Moses' return from Mount Sinai, made the Golden Calf. Revelation cannot easily be brought into manifestation. It is not always easy to translate insight into action. Our new understanding makes us painfully aware of the discrepancy between our dreams and the reality. In the developmental process, this stage corresponds to the loss of innocence in childhood; we understand enough to feel both the potentials and the limits of our lives. This Holy-Day offers an archetypal image of grief that occurs after we develop sufficient understanding to appreciate the depth of our losses and failures.

The Days of Awe offer us time to develop our awareness of how we respond, make judgments regarding the consequences of our actions, and make commitment to necessary changes. From this point in the

Holy-Day cycle of the year, we function as adults in the developmental process. We begin during the month of Elul, a time for compassionate self-reflection. On Rosh HaShanah, the day of judgment, we hold ourselves accountable for ways in which our responses are dysfunctional. On Yom Kippur, we experience the moment of transformation in which we make a commitment to change.

Through the rest of the year, we work to integrate those changes, to fully translate a commitment into manifestation. We begin on Sukkot, a harvest festival that we commemorate by living in the temporary shelter, the *Sukkah*. Moving into a new living environment enacts the internal commitment to change our habitual response. The new environment offers protection but is also fragile. Chanukah commemorates the Macabees' victory over the Greeks in spite of their lesser numbers. Their victory is symbolized by the miracle of the lights in which the oil sufficient for one day lasted for eight days. Chanukah offers the image of our potential. We can struggle against the darkness of our situation. We can change habits that have been with us for many years even though they appear to be impossible to change. Tu B'Shevat, the new year for trees, immerses us in an image of change that is less adversarial, a gradual, organic, and natural development.

On Purim, we experience the culmination of the learning process through the year. The victory of the Jews over Haman occurs without direct, divine intervention. Purim is taken as a symbol of the Messianic era in which God's will is fully manifested in the material world. The process of change that began at Pesach is completed. We have fully integrated the new way of being, freed from the rigid habitual patterns and able to choose the response that is most appropriate for any situation.

Pesach through Tisha B'av	Unconscious dysfunctional responses	Identification with old Ego structure
Elul through Yom Kippur	Conscious dysfunctional responses	Disidentification with old Ego structure
Sukkot through Chanukah	Conscious effective responses	Manifestation of new Ego structure
Purim	Unconscious effective responses	Identification with new Ego structure

The model of development in the Jewish Holy-Day cycle, like the model of development in childhood and in psychotherapy, is not intended to be applied rigidly. The wealth of the tradition — the variety of images, stories, interpretations, and rituals that have developed through the generations—allows us to select those aspects that are appropriate for us in our unique growth process, which cannot be reduced to inflexible categories.

Inter-Dependence: An I-Thou Relationship with God

That must be the answer—God is a committee.

© Ashleigh Brilliant

In Jewish religious practice, the material world is not regarded as a diversion or an obstacle to spirituality. The focus is on manifesting our spiritual potential on earth. For the mystics, all of creation is constructed on a common foundation. This theme is expressed succinctly in the aphorism "As above, so below." The form of the human body is viewed not only as the structure of a particular creature but also as a map that describes the structure of the universe. Creation can be compared to a hologram. Each element of the hologram contains the whole. If one cuts a section of a holographic photograph, it is still possible to reconstruct the entire image. For this reason, when we understand ourselves and the world around us, we can also understand the world of spirit. In the same manner, as we develop our spirituality, we deepen our understanding of how to live.

As we journey through the year, a cosmic evolution occurs as well. We not only draw from the well of tradition and the generations before us who have enriched us with their stories, images, symbols, rituals, and archetypes, we also add to the storehouse of the tradition, contributing our own stories and our unique perspective. We add to the understanding of spirit. As we grow, God also develops in relationship with us, bringing the cosmos closer to the moment of complete integration, the time when the Name of God and the Essence of the Divine Presence shall be one.

BALANCING STRUCTURE AND SPONTANEITY
KEVA AND KAVANAH

Each man has a name, given him by God, and given him by his
father and mother.
Each man has a name given him by his stature and his way of
smiling, and given him by his clothes.
Each man has a name given him by the mountains and given
him by his walls.
Each man has a name given him by the planets and given him
by his neighbors.
Each man has a name given him by his sins and given him by
his longing.
Each man has a name given him by his enemies and given him
by his love.
Each man has a name given him by his feast days and given
him by his craft.
Each man has a name given him by the seasons of the year and
given him by his blindness.
Each man has a name given him by the sea and given him by
his death.

Zelda[3]

In the Jewish tradition, the practice of ritual is based on two principles that exist in dynamic tension, referred to in Hebrew as *Keva* and *Kavanah*. *Keva* refers to something that is permanent, regular, constant, or fixed. *Kavanah* is associated with the word meaning

"direction." On the one hand, we need *Keva,* the structure of a regular practice that requires discipline, a commitment to undertake
required religious practices. We fulfill that commitment regardless
of our feelings in the moment: we practice the ritual even when we
feel disconnected, skeptical, or pressured. On the other hand, each
of us has a unique name, a particular way of making connection with
God at each moment. We need *Kavanah,* the quality of intention
that helps us make that connection, guiding our practice in the
proper direction, evoking the feeling and the experience that the ritual is designed to access. *Keva* provides the possibility for moments
of *Kavanah.* Without *Keva,* we do not create time, space, and
opportunity for spiritual experience. Without *Kavanah,* the ritual
practice is empty and serves no purpose, becoming a meaningless
routine.

The Holy-Day cycle establishes a dynamic balance between *Keva*
and *Kavanah,* between external structure and inner experience. The
Holy-Days offer oases in time. We build moments for retreat, reflection, and rejuvenation into the cycle of the year. The particular ritual practices of each Holy-Day bring us into contact with specific
themes and issues that challenge us in the process of adult growth
and development.

At the same time, the ritual offers opportunity for individual differences because the variety, depth, and ambiguity make it possible
to select the specific aspects of the ritual that are most appropriate
and nourishing for each person and each life situation. The ritual is
multi-layered and multi-dimensional. Even though a particular
Holy-Day may emphasize one aspect of experience, we still have the
opportunity to focus selectively on a dimension that is more in tune
with our needs: on behavior, on emotion, on relationship, on physical process, on mental process, or on cognitive process.

The Holy-Day cycle cannot be reduced to a linear process. The
cycle might be compared to a hologram. In a hologram, each part
contains the whole. Similarly, each Holy-Day is embedded with the
themes and symbols of other Holy-Days, allowing us to selectively
make connection. For example, even though Pesach celebrates the

redemption from slavery in Egypt, and Shavuot is concerned with revelation at Mount Sinai, the prayers and rituals of all Holy-Days make reference to these events. If we find ourselves in conflict with the tradition, disconnected from the obvious focus or opposing its message, we can look to the tradition for support. For example, we can make connection with Abraham and Moses who argue with God. Similarly, Levi Yitzchak of Berditchev asked God to repent on Yom Kippur, confronting God for causing so much suffering.

In this same spirit, the cycle of development outlined in this book should be viewed as one of many possible approaches rather than as a definitive, exclusive, monolithic, and authoritative description. Through the centuries, commentators in each generation add their unique images and views, adding to the richness of choices and expanding possibilities for each of us making unique connections.

For example, there is not only one new year in the Jewish calendar. There are four new years. We need not think only of the cycle beginning at Pesach; we can also consider the beginning from Rosh HaShanah, the head of the year when we echo creation by making judgments as to what we need to manifest during the coming twelve months. We can consider the beginning of the year from Tu B'Shevat, the new year for trees that marks the sprouting of a new seasons vegetation. We can mark the new year from the beginning of the fiscal year associated with determination of tithing, the biblically prescribed taxes. We can also view the Holy-Days as a cycle divorced from the sequence of time; the Kabbalists associated each Holy-Day with the emanation of Divine energy from Essence into material form through the archetypal entities of the *Sefirot.*

Living with this complexity and diversity, we can find the particular dynamic balance for ourselves as we connect to each Holy-Day. Perhaps, on Pesach, I make connection with the exodus from Egypt and am able to experience the freedom from constriction that has occurred in my own life. However, I can select the particular focus that is most energizing for me. I might identify with the miracles, the experience of a positive force outside myself that provides unexpected support; or, I may focus on how the Israelites did not want to leave Egypt, connecting with my own resistance to changes that occur despite my own wishes. I might relate to the image of Nachshon who took the first steps into the sea, trusting that God would help. Perhaps his action helps me take steps toward the future in spite of apparent risks. I may find myself at odds with the explicit themes, arguing with the text and its message, knowing myself better as I struggle with the tradition in the spirit of Jacob wrestling with the angel and receiving the name Yisrael, which means "the one who wrestles with God."

It is in this spirit that I invite you to approach this perspective on the Holy-Days. Rather than viewing it as the only truth or rejecting it as incorrect, allow yourself to find your particular connection, to be in an I-Thou relationship with the ideas. What speaks to you? What parts fit your experience? Which do not connect? How would you modify this framework for yourself?

This process requires effort. Although the Holy-Days are a time for nurturance and relaxation, they require preparation. When we decide to develop our skill in something, it takes work. If I want to ski or windsurf, I get the right equipment and invest time and energy in learning. As a novice, I fall down innumerable times until I develop my skill. As I learn, I can take on more difficult challenges. In the same way, the capacity to access the special state of consciousness known as *Kodesh* takes time and energy. We must make a commitment to take the time, have the right equipment, and learn how to use it. We must feel as well as think, relate to others as well as to our inner self. We are connected not only to the present moment but to our roots through our parents, grandparents, and ancestors. Joined to our history, we connect to our future as well.

In the following chapters, we explore each of the Holy-Days through the cycle of the year, describing the themes embedded in the particular images, stories, rituals, and customs associated with the celebration of that Holy-Day. The psychological themes are clarified through the stories of my clients. You may find it helpful first to read the entire book to gain an overall appreciation of the developmental process through the course of the year. With this foundation, you may then find it useful to review particular chapters at the time of each Holy-Day to help make a personal connection in the mirror offered by that day.

I hope that you will be able to use the precious time of the Holy-Days to see yourself more clearly and become more of who you may be.

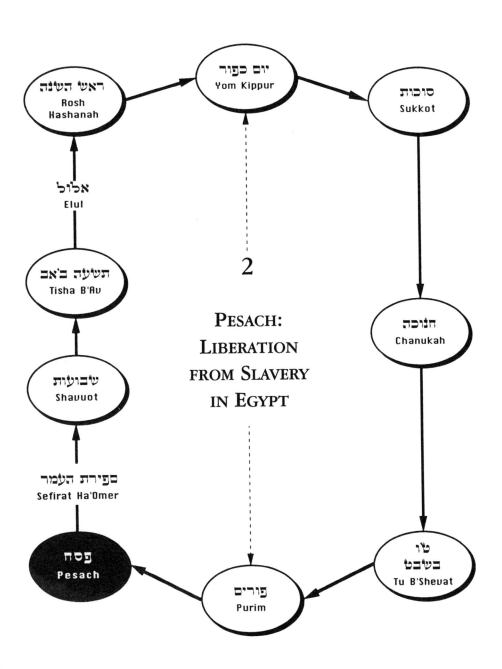

2

Pesach:
Liberation
from Slavery
in Egypt

In the first month, on the evening of the fourteenth day is Pesach. And on the fifteenth day of that month is the holy day of God, the holy day of the matzot *which you shall eat for seven days. On the first day is a holy day and you shall do no manner of work. And you shall make a sacrifice to God for seven days; on the seventh day is also a holy day and you shall do no manner of work then.*

[Leviticus 23:5-8]

We commemorate the experience in Egypt not only during Pesach; we are asked to remember the exodus from Egypt every day. We refer to our servitude and the subsequent liberation in our daily prayers and the liturgy of every Holy-Day. Why do we give such a central place to this story in our liturgy and ritual practice?

The liberation from slavery in Egypt marks the birth of the Jewish nation; it also serves as a symbol for all the periods of exile and redemption in Jewish history. The exodus represents deliverance, not just from oppression in Egypt but from all exiles in the past, present, and future. It speaks both to the inevitability of oppression throughout history, as well as to the trust in an equally inescapable liberation. The event serves not only as a marker of turning points in the development of the Jewish people; it is also symbolic of critical moments in our own lives. For this reason, we read in the *Hagaddah* that "each of us is obligated to consider ourselves as coming out of Egypt." The coming out of Egypt is an archetypal image of life transitions. It embodies every narrow passage we traverse as we give birth to ourselves: leaving home, career changes, marriage, divorce, birth, sickness, death, addiction, and recovery from trauma.

TURNING CRISIS INTO OPPORTUNITY: SLAVERY IN EGYPT AS A POSITIVE TRANSFORMATIVE EXPERIENCE

While unconscious creation—animals, plants, crystals—functions satisfactorily as far as we know, things are constantly going wrong with man.

Carl Jung

The inevitable difficulties of life can overwhelm us, leaving us defeated, hopeless, and depressed. If we view these experiences solely as oppressive events, we find ourselves also enslaved in Egypt and unable to escape. The stress can destroy our will, energy, and capacity to respond constructively. The story of slavery in Egypt offers us a different possibility: the Israelites not only overcome the adversity; they develop into a nation. Viewing our lives through the mirror of the Israelites' experience, we may be able to envision a similar outcome for ourselves in which we not only overcome difficulties but also develop new capacities in the process.

The biblical story of slavery and redemption validates the notion that such experiences in our lives are inevitable and ultimately constructive events. The period of slavery in Egypt was not an accident, nor was it an interruption to God's plan. At the same time that God pledged to Abraham and Sarah that their children would become a holy nation, God also announced that their progeny would fall into servitude before inheriting the land promised to them. Slavery in Egypt, as well as the redemption, occurred inevitably and in accordance with God's plan:

> *Know that your progeny shall be a stranger in a land that is not theirs, and shall serve them; and they shall afflict them four hundred years; and also that nation, whom they shall serve,*

will I judge; and afterward they shall come out with great
wealth.

[Genesis 15:13-14]

This theme of opportunity in adversity is repeated again in the
story of the Israelites' initial migration to Egypt. Jacob's sons became
jealous of their brother Joseph and sold him into slavery. Joseph was
taken to Egypt. He predicted a famine and developed a plan to store
grain and avoid disaster. When the famine struck, Jacob's sons came
to Egypt and were saved by Joseph. Joseph did not resent his brothers or punish them. Instead, he reminded them that their misdeed
ultimately produced a positive outcome, saving the Israelites from the
famine: "Do not be angry with yourselves that you sold me, for God
sent me before you to preserve life." (Genesis 45:5).

A similar theme is expressed in the reading from the prophets on
the Sabbath that occurs during Pesach, about Ezekiel's vision of the
valley of dry bones which are miraculously brought back to life:
"Behold, I will cause breath to enter into you, and you shall live. I
will lay sinews upon you, and will bring up flesh upon you, and cover
you with skin, and put breath in you" (Ezekiel 27:5–6). This image
of resurrection of the dead offers hope in face of the ultimate vulnerability of death.

These stories not only reassure us that powers outside ourselves can
sometimes provide salvation; they also suggest that sometimes birth
does not occur willingly. We are freed despite ourselves. Perhaps current resistances can be understood as resistance to freedom, viewed as
birth pains rather than ordinary suffering and misery.

SYMBOLS OF TRANSFORMATION

My life might be easier to put together, if I could find the instructions.

© Ashleigh Brilliant

A variety of images and symbols are associated with the historical events that help us understand this experience in a positive way. Egypt is associated with the womb, with the soil in which a seed is planted, and a smelting furnace. The exodus from Egypt is seen as the journey through the birth canal, the sprouting of a seed, and the creation of a strong metal in the smelting furnace. The mirrors provided by these images and symbols allow us to see ourselves in a new way. We may experience the circumstances of our lives as an oppressive slavery, a birth, a germinating seed, or the heat of a furnace. These images also serve as metaphoric analogs of the Jungian theory regarding formation and dissolution of the Ego. The wealth of images and their variety allow us to select those images and themes that may be most useful to us at the particular time in our lives. The change in perspective and image changes how we feel, the meaning we give the events, and how we respond.

Biblical story	Egypt for sustenance	Slavery	Exodus	Entry into the desert
Birth	Pregnancy	Labor	Delivery	Birth
Seed	Seed before planting	Putting seed into the ground	Rotting of shell	Germination
Smelting	Unprocessed metal	Fire	Melting	New alloy
Psychothera-peutic analog	Formation of ego	Changed circumstances	Dissolution of Ego	Chaos before reconnection with Self

Exodus from Egypt as a Birth

The Hebrew word for Egypt, *Mitzrayim,* means "narrow place." Shneur Zalman suggests an association with the narrowness of the womb. Just as Egypt offered sanctuary to the seventy souls of Jacob's family who fled the famine in Canaan, so the womb offers sustenance, warmth, and protection to the fetus. As the fetus reaches full term, the once nurturing womb becomes oppressive. In the same way, as Jacob's family prospered and grew, Egypt was transformed into a place of servitude. The image of the splitting of the sea is suggestive of the breaking of the waters that occurs just before birth. The exodus becomes the passage through the birth canal.

The journey through these straits cannot be accomplished without outside intervention. The Israelites cannot mobilize to fight their oppressors: they can only cry out in their suffering. They are reluctant even to support Moses as he begins his struggle. The God of the exodus is all-knowing, an omniscient God who hears the cries of the Israelites ascending to heaven and descends to earth to see their plight. The God of the exodus is all-powerful, an omnipotent God who calls Moses from the burning bush, brings ten plagues upon the Egyptians, and leads the people out of Egypt with an outstretched arm.

Similarly, the growing fetus, pushing the limits of the womb, initiates the birth process but must rely on external forces to make the journey through the birth canal, a process that takes great effort. The newborn infant is dependent and powerless; a baby cannot survive independently. The infant needs a parent who accepts the powerlessness and vulnerability, who offers unconditional support and nurturance.

As we view our lives through the mirror of this image, we can validate our ability to recognize and express our pain. We can also acknowledge our powerlessness. We learn to accept our resistance to the birth of a new aspect of self. We focus on sources of unconditional support, both spiritual and material, that help us through the crisis.

Exodus from Egypt as a Sprouting Seed

Some say love, it is a river
That drowns the tender reed;
Some say love, it is a razor
That leads your soul to bleed;
Some say love, it is a hunger
An endless aching need;
I say love, it is a flower
And you its only seed.

It's the heart, afraid of breaking,
That never learns to dance;
It's the dream, afraid of waking,
That never takes the chance;
It's the one who won't be taken,
Who cannot seem to hear;
And the soul, afraid of dying,
That never learns to live.

When the night has been too lonely,
And the road has been too long,
And you think that love is only
For the lucky and the strong,
Just remember in the winter
Far beneath the bitter snows
Lies the seed that with the sun's love
In the spring becomes the rose.
                                        Amanda McBroom

Pesach is known as *Chag Ha'Aviv,* the festival of spring. In the agricultural cycle, Pesach marks the beginning of the first harvest, the harvest of barley. Shneur Zalman also associates Pesach with an image appropriate to the spring, the image of germination. Shneur Zalman cites the text "And I planted her for me in the land" as referring to the time of slavery in Egypt. In planting, the seed is covered with dirt, hidden in the ground. Then, for the seed to sprout, the outer shell must rot and dissolve before growth may occur. A little seed produces a plentiful harvest.

Similarly, Jacob journeys with his family into the darkness of the slavery in Egypt, hiding the potential of the unborn Israelite nation. The oppression and suffering of slavery breaks down the old identity, allowing for the germination of a new nation. The image of a seed offers another image that we can apply to our own life experience; the crises of our lives are the soil that temporarily hide our Essence. The old Ego structure rots in response to the external conditions. From the essence of Self, a new, more appropriate Ego sprouts, making its way out of the earth.

Egypt as a Smelting Furnace

In the Torah, Egypt is also described through analogy to a smelting furnace: "But God has taken you out of the iron furnace, out of Egypt to be a people of inheritance, as you are this day" (Deuteronomy 4:20). In a smelting furnace, raw metal is exposed to extreme heat. As it melts, impurities are separated and the now liquid metal can be mixed with other materials to create a new, stronger substance. It can be shaped and molded for a variety of purposes. Correspondingly, the heat and fire of oppression produces a transformation: impurities are separated and removed, so that the remaining essence can be mixed to shape the Israelites for their higher work, the task of manifesting spirit in the material world.

The image of the smelting furnace offers another mirror for making sense of our experience. The fire of crisis is no longer a destructive force. In the heat of the fire of crisis, the old Ego melts, the impurities within ourselves can similarly be removed, and the Essence can be reshaped, allowing for creation of a new material, a new Ego that is suited to the new conditions we face.

Each of these images—the birth, the seed, and the smelting furnace—not only suggest an external change, they also provide an image of internal transformation: a baby is born, the seed germinates, and a new substance is created. The changes that bring us out of slavery are similarly not only external; the forces in the environment around us motivate us to make changes in how we respond.

Matzah as a Symbol

The central focus for ritual on Pesach is the unleavened bread, *matzah*. Leavened bread has had time to rise; the *matzah* is not allowed to rise. No inflation is permitted. The

 *matzah* symbolizes the uninflated Essence of ourselves, the Self, the *Nitzotz. Chametz,* the yeasted, inflated bread, represents the inflated *Kelippah,* Ego, with which we have become overly identified and with which we rigidly respond to the difficulties in our lives. To overcome adversity, we must first rid ourselves of any inflation, returning to the Essence of our being.

Shneur Zalman notes that this principle is also echoed in the ways in which *chametz* and *matzah* are written in Hebrew. The words use almost the same letters: both have a *mem* and a *tzadik.* Even the differing letters are written almost identically: the *heh* and the *chet* differ only in the broken line of the *heh* compared to the solid line of the *chet.* In the same way as *chametz* symbolizes our tendency to inflate the importance of our Ego, the letter

חמץ
חמץ
מצה
מצה

chet with its solid line offers a graphic image of this concept. The uinflated Ego is similarly represented by the contacted line of the *heh.*

The *matzah* reminds us to reconnect with our Essence in the face of momentous changes, not to credit ourselves overly much or to focus on temporary exhilaration that is not yet grounded. The emphasis placed on the painstaking search for and removal of *chametz* is designed to bring the need for return to Essence into the foreground.

STAGES IN THE PROCESS OF REDEMPTION

One commentator asks why God, who is omnipotent, did not simply take the Jews immediately from Egypt. What was the need for responding to the resistance by Pharaoh with plagues and other miracles? Why bother with all of these intermediary steps instead of resolving the issue quickly and directly? If the only issue was oppression, God could have acted more efficiently. However, the material oppression left its mark spiritually and emotionally, scarring the souls of the Israelites. They needed to confront the introjected slave mentality, not just leave the land of oppression. The plagues and the various stages in the journey to freedom are important insofar as the Israelites are transformed in the process. The events in the story of redemption serve as symbolic representations of the beginning of the process of *Shov,* the surrender of material existence and the return to Essence. They also fit with the psychotherapeutic process of beginning to separate from one's Ego and return to connection with the Self. The stages include the following:

Biblical Story	Psychotherapeutic Meaning
1. The journey from Israel to Egypt and settling in Egypt	1. Emergence of Ego identity
2. Enslavement in Egypt	2. Rigid, unconscious, dysfunctional identification with Ego
3. Consciousness of slavery and experience of powerlessness	3. Awareness of dysfunction
4. Crying out	4. Expression of pain
5. Selection of Moses as leader	5. Emergence of intuitive inner guide
6. Ten plagues and exodus from Egypt	6. Initial disconnection from Ego identification
7. Splitting of the sea	7. Struggle against the pull of the Ego identity
8. Song of the sea	8. Gratitude and appreciation in reconnecting with Self

The Journey from Israel to Egypt and Settling in Egypt

The children of Jacob journeyed to Egypt to escape a famine in the land of Israel:

> There was famine in all the other lands, but in Egypt there was
> bread. . . . Jacob learned there were provisions in Egypt and he
> said to his sons, "Why are you afraid? I have heard there are

*supplies in Egypt. You can go there and buy food. Let us live
and not die."*

[Genesis 41:56-42:1]

This image is important insofar as we tend to view ourselves negatively: we may judge ourselves unduly harshly for coping with situations in a dysfunctional manner. The Israelites' journey from the
land of promise in Israel to Egypt invites us to view ourselves more
compassionately. Each of us journeys to our own Egypt, as a way to
respond to a threat or address a need—the original manifestation of
Self into Ego, the process of *Ratzoh,* the creation of the outer shell of
our being, the *Kelippah.*

The Children of Jacob continue to reside in Egypt even after the
famine has passed in the land of Israel. The Israelites' experience
helps us remember that we can fail to recognize changes in our circumstances and make parallel changes in our responses. Instead, we
continue to act as if our situation is unchanged; we become compulsive, habituated, rigid, and unconscious. In the Jewish framework,
we identify with the outer shell of our being, the *Kelippah* . In psychotherapeutic terminology, we disconnect from the Self and our
Essence, identifying ourselves with the Ego.

Enslaved in Egypt

*There is a period when it is clear you have gone wrong but you
continue. Sometimes there is a luxurious amount of time before
anything bad happens.*

Jenny Holzer

When a new pharaoh takes the throne, the Israelites lose their
special privileges:

*A new king, who did not know of Joseph, came into power
over Egypt. He announced to his people, "The Israelites are
becoming too numerous and strong for us.". . . The Egyptians
appointed conscription officers over the Israelites to crush their
spirits with hard labor.*

[Shemot 1:8–11]

Egypt is transformed from a land that sustains and nourishes, becoming instead the land in which the Israelites are enslaved. However, the Israelites are not initially aware of their condition and its effects on them. The Israelites' blindness reminds us that we may also be enslaved by forces that we do not notice and whose effects on us are unrecognized.

Consciousness of Enslavement and Experience of Powerlessness

Having the courage to admit defeat can sometimes be a kind of victory.

© Ashleigh Brilliant

The process of redemption begins with awareness. The awareness that one is enslaved and suffering fuels the determination and the wish to change. When did the Israelites notice? Was it when their working conditions deteriorated? Was it when the decree was made to kill all male infants? We remind ourselves of this suffering when we eat *maror,* the bitter herbs at the *Seder.* As we identify with the pain of our ancestors, we become more aware of our own condition, of how we are also enslaved and powerless. Like the Israelites, we may not be able to escape, but we can acknowledge that our habitual coping method is ineffective. We acknowledge that we exacerbate our suffering rather than help ourselves when we rigidly cope with our situation in dysfunctional ways.

Crying Out

I may not have many other talents, but you should hear me groan.

© Ashleigh Brilliant

The capacity and willingness to experience pain is central to the story of the Israelites. According to tradition, God made a decision to intervene after hearing the cries of the people:

I have indeed seen the suffering of my people in Egypt. I have heard how they cry out because of what their slave-drivers do,

and I am aware of their pain. I have come down to rescue them
from Egypt's power.

[Exodus 2:7]

Although the Israelites were unable to mobilize to free themselves, their ability to know they were enslaved and their willingness
to cry out literally moved the heavens, bringing God to earth. Their
cries were so powerful that God initiated the redemption, even
though the slavery had not continued for the 400 year period originally established by God in the promise to Abraham.

As we experience the suffering of our condition and our inability
to make changes in it, we begin to cry out for help. Often, we may
criticize ourselves for breaking down or failing to act more independently. The crying out of the Israelites provides a more constructive
image. When we feel buffeted by circumstances beyond our control
and find ourselves unable to act effectively, we can identify with the
powerlessness of the Israelites in their slavery and find our own pain
reflected in the mirror of the story. The expression of our pain is not
a negative quality: it marks the end of denial and illusion, it
acknowledges the reality of our powerlessness, and it implies hope
that help is possible.

When we cry out for help, we are beginning to reconnect with the
Essence of life, with the Self, with the *Nitzotz* within ourselves,
opening ourselves to receiving support. We reconnect with the
Essence of our being even while we remain trapped in the old Ego
identity.

Moses is Chosen to Lead the Israelites

Moses recognized and fought against the slavery, but he was
unable to save the Israelites on his own. According to the *midrash,*
Moses killed an Egyptian taskmaster who was beating an Israelite.
After this confrontation, he fled into the desert. Moses' difficulty in
functioning in the material world is also symbolized by his speech
impediment. Nonetheless, God selects Moses to confront Pharaoh
and lead the Israelites out of slavery. Indeed, Moses' most celebrated
attribute is his humility. Moses' humility is significant because a

humble person does not become self-inflated and overly identified with the Ego identity.

Moses symbolizes the inner aspect of our being that recognizes oppression and fights against it. This aspect of our being is not powerful enough, on its own, to facilitate a complete transformation, nor is it able to articulate its perceptions clearly. We may tend to devalue this part of ourselves because of its limits. Just as Moses is the one who speaks directly with God, the parallel inner quality of Moses is the aspect of our being that is in dialogue with the Self and leads us toward that connection. This aspect of our being recognizes the truth of our situation and struggles to make changes.

The Miracle of the Ten Plagues and the Exodus

But if I shout for help, somebody might hear me.
© Ashleigh Brilliant

With Moses as an intermediary, God brought ten plagues upon the Egyptians: blood, frogs, lice, wild animals, illness, boils, hail, locusts, darkness, and death of the firstborn. These plagues affect every aspect of material existence: earth, air, and water as well as vegetable, animal, and human. Even though Pharaoh resisted Moses, even though the Israelites were powerless, external forces brought an end to the slavery. Pharaoh allowed the Israelites to leave after the last plague in which the firstborn sons of the Egyptians die. God takes the Israelites out of Egypt.

The miracle of the ten plagues is an important image because it reminds us that external forces in the universe can help us even when we are unable to help ourselves. Our experience, unfortunately, may teach us not to trust that the universe will be a positive force in our lives. We do not have experiences of being helped and do not believe anyone will be there. These miracles help us trust that the universe can be powerful, compassionate, and supportive. External forces can miraculously break the power of the old Ego identity and our attachment to the *Kelippah,* the material form with which we have identified.

Splitting of the Sea

After the Israelites leave Egypt, Pharaoh regrets his decision and pursues them. The Israelites stop at the edge of the sea, which they are unable to cross. The Israelites are also ambivalent. In spite of the miracles they have seen, they feel hopeless. They complain to Moses. God responds:

> God said to Moses, "Why are you crying out to Me? Speak to the Israelites, and let them start moving. Raise your staff and extend your hand over the sea. You will split the sea, and the Israelites will be able to cross over on dry land.
>
> [Exodus 14:15]

God causes the sea to split, and the Israelites cross safely. When the Egyptians follow them, the waters return and they are all destroyed. We can easily make the mistake of imagining that the experience of liberation is one of joy and relief. However, liberation is often stressful and filled with uncertainty. The Israelites' struggles, their anxiety, and the need for continued intervention from God remind us that our own liberation also may be stressful and that we may be ambivalent about change. The story of the splitting of the sea provides an archetypal image of the struggle we experience as we disconnect from the *Kelippah,* the old Ego identity.

Song of the Sea

After the miracle of the splitting of the sea, Moses, Miriam, and the children of Israel, for the first time, sing praises of gratitude to God: "I will sing to God for His great victory. Horse and rider He threw in the sea" (Exodus 15:1).

Until this moment, the Israelites were skeptical. They did not believe they could escape Pharaoh's oppression. With the miracle of the sea, they realize that liberation is possible. In this same way, we experience joy as we are freed from the oppression of the *Kelippah,* the old Ego identity; we experience the freedom of choice rather than compulsion.

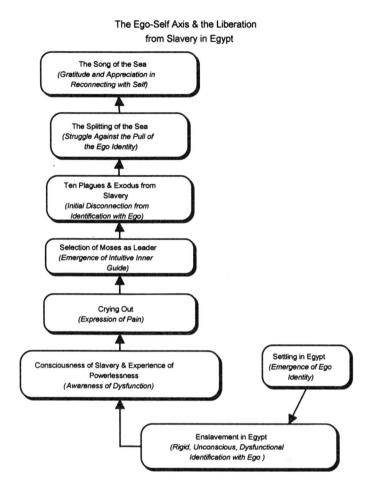

The Ego-Self Axis & the Liberation
from Slavery in Egypt

The Song of the Sea
*(Gratitude and Appreciation in
Reconnecting with Self)*

The Splitting of the Sea
*(Struggle Against the Pull of
the Ego Identity)*

Ten Plagues & Exodus from
Slavery
*(Initial Disconnection from
Identification with Ego)*

Selection of Moses as Leader
*(Emergence of Intuitive Inner
Guide)*

Crying Out
(Expression of Pain)

Consciousness of Slavery & Experience of
Powerlessness
(Awareness of Dysfunction)

Settling in Egypt
*(Emergence of Ego
Identity)*

Enslavement in Egypt
*(Rigid, Unconscious, Dysfunctional
Identification with Ego)*

INTEGRATING QUALITIES OF INITIATIVE
AND RECEPTIVITY

There's nothing to do, and leave nothing undone.

The liberation from slavery involved two seemingly contradictory qualities: (1) acknowledging powerlessness as a basis for hope and (2) a commitment to act in spite of powerlessness. Both qualities are needed in this phase of self-development. We need to trust we will receive help even though we are powerless; we also need encouragement to be self-reliant and take initiative to change our situation.

Acknowledging Powerlessness as a Basis for Hope

At least I have the courage to admit that I'm a coward.
                                                        © Ashleigh Brilliant

The story of the liberation from slavery is permeated by the theme of hope. Paradoxically, the more we acknowledge our powerlessness, the more our hope is reinforced. The acknowledgment of powerlessness serves as a foundation for building hope. The oppression of slavery inevitably gives way to liberation. The Israelites' ability to acknowledge and express their pain causes God to come down from the heavens and intervene. Moses is selected as the leader even though he is a refugee who was forced to flee from Egypt, a man who cannot speak well. His humility qualifies him to lead the Israelites out of Egypt. The notion of acknowledging powerlessness as a positive quality is also expressed in the image of the fetus that is born only with the help of the mother's contractions, of the seed that cannot sprout until the shell rots, and of the new alloy that is forged by the heat of the furnace.

In acknowledging our powerlessness, we no longer live in denial and illusion. We open ourselves to ask for and accept help. The acknowledgment of powerlessness and the quality of receptivity offers a foundation for overcoming adversity and freeing ourselves from rigid patterns of coping. For example, an alcoholic who lies to himself does not regard the drinking as a problem, does nothing to change the situation, and is not open to receiving support. The first step in making change occurs in acknowledging the addiction, allowing oneself to feel the pain, being honest about how difficult it is to stop, and having the courage to ask for help.

Acting in Spite of Powerlessness

Morris was a God-fearing man. When the warning was sounded that a flood was coming, he had complete trust that God would protect him. So, he remained in his home even while others fled. The local police came to his door and offered to help him evacuate, but he assured them that he was safe. The

*rains came and the waters began to rise. The emergency rescue
team came to his house in a boat and urged him to leave, but
Morris refused to go with them. As the flood worsened, Morris
finally moved onto the roof of his house to escape the water. A
military helicopter flew over to him; but Morris was persistent
and trusted that God would protect him. Unfortunately, the
storm continued unabated. Morris was carried off and
drowned. When he arrived in heaven, Morris was enraged.
How could God have abandoned him when he had such great
trust? Quickly a response came, "Morris, I tried to help you. I
sent the police in a car. Then, I sent the rescue workers in a
boat. And, then I sent the army in a helicopter."*

The liberation from slavery requires active intervention from God,
but human initiative and action are also required in the process.
Only when the Israelites cry out does God respond with miracles of
the plagues. At the time of the last plague, the Israelites are asked
to slaughter a lamb, which was worshipped as a God by the
Egyptians, and to mark their doorways with its blood. When
Pharaoh finally allows them to leave, the Israelites immediately act
to escape from their slavery: they leave in the middle of the night,
not even waiting for their bread to rise. At the sea, when the
Israelites are unable to cross, Moses turns to God. God promises to
respond, but the Israelites must take the first step. Nachshon, one of
the Israelites, acting on faith, enters the water. When the water
reaches his nostrils, the sea splits.

The importance of action as a basis for growth can be understood
by reflecting on the learning process. Initially, the baby is virtually
helpless, unable even to move. Gradually the infant learns to move
on its own, first crawling and then walking. The toddler learns by
doing; only later does the child make sense of the world. The toddler has more capacity for becoming independent and taking some
responsibility. The parent begins to make demands; the word "no"
becomes part of the conversation.

In the same way, the archetypal Parent begins to make demands
on us at this stage, to take small steps on our own. For this reason,
the Torah focuses on action in the world. The commandments, the

Mitzvot, are all concerned with actions in the material world: to wear fringes on our garments, prepare food in particular ways, and so forth. This notion is especially expressed in the rituals of Pesach. This focus on material concerns is unparalleled by any other Holy-Day in its dramatic and powerful effects on daily life. In preparation for the Holy-Day, one is commanded to thoroughly clean the house, to remove all vestiges of *chametz*. In contrast to the time before Rosh HaShanah when we are asked to take time to focus directly on self-reflection and self-evaluation, on Pesach, we emphasize the physical work of cleaning. Although the task carries symbolic meaning, we do not focus on that meaning directly.

The focus on action is analogous to what happens in psychotherapeutic approaches to crisis management. During a time of trauma, a person needs guidance that is practical, specific, and action oriented. It is not the time for insight and reflection; a focus on behavioral management is most helpful in stabilizing the situation. This principle is illustrated in a biblical story: the Israelites took small steps that resulted in effects that miraculously exceeded the results one might logically expect. Small steps create momentum that activates and energizes; they lead to affective changes as well as enhancing self-confidence and self-image. For example, when someone is depressed, the tendency may be to withdraw from activity and social contact. If the depressed person can take a few steps to improve social contact and structure activity into daily life, major changes can sometimes result in feeling and attitude, changes that serve as a foundation for taking even more initiative to reach out.

For each of us at this time of year, it is similarly helpful to focus on the specific, practical actions we need to take to cope with the crisis. As we do, we must be aware of tendencies to act on the basis of our old identity. We challenge ourselves to resist the pull of that habit and to act in a constructive way even if it feels awkward, unfamiliar, and uncomfortable. This difficulty of this task is symbolized by the example of Nachshon who took the step of walking into the sea, trusting, in spite of reason, that he would somehow reach the other shore.

This same effort is required of a person who is depressed. It is difficult to believe that effort will produce success. There appears to be no reason to force oneself to get out of bed or call a friend. In reaching out, the person gives up comfort and security, risking anxiety and disappointment. In this respect, inhibiting the dysfunctional coping response requires that we relinquish our trusted, familiar means of nurturance, equivalent to the Israelites sacrifice of the lamb, worshipped as a God by the Egyptians.

Balancing Powerlessness and Initiative

Obsessed by a desire to win the lottery, Yankel decides to immerse himself in the study of kabbalistic magic. He fills his days with meditations, incantations, and the writing of amulets designed to force the divine will. Finally, after a long night of meditation, the skies are filled with thunder and lightning. The heavens open, and God appears before Yankel. Yankel looks up at God, and says, "So, what about the lottery?" God responds, "OK, OK, I'll see what I can do. But Yankel, do me a favor, will you? Please, meet me halfway! Buy a ticket!"

Moses provides a role model for balancing the acknowledgment of powerlessness with the commitment to action. Moses knows his limits, but he also responds to the calling from God to lead the Israelites. He dialogues with God to clarify the time for action and the time for receptivity. At the burning bush, he protests to God that he is unfit for leadership. God offers him reassurance and allows him to share the task with Aaron. When Moses continues to protest, God rebukes him, and Moses stops resisting. At each moment in our own journey, we similarly need to stay in dialogue, to acknowledge our limits and reach out while also doing whatever we can to make changes.

A CLINICAL EXAMPLE OF PSYCHOTHERAPEUTIC
PROCESS ASSOCIATED WITH PESACH

Even normal people have problems, and sometimes those problems can be solved only by becoming less normal.

© Ashleigh Brilliant

The process of self-development embedded in the Pesach story is illustrated by Mark's work to free himself from panic attacks. The first incident occurred while cutting up salad for dinner when he suddenly, vividly, and spontaneously imagined slitting his wrists. Heart pounding and sweating profusely, he put down the knife. He was unable to get the thought out of his consciousness. Many hours passed before he was finally able to sleep. After this incident, the panic attacks came without warning several times a week. There seemed to be no reason for the problem. There were no precipitating factors; there was no pattern that could be identified. Mark did not experience any major crisis in his life. He thought his childhood had been a normal one, he felt satisfied in his marriage, and he was successful in his work.

Although Mark claimed there were no real problems in his life, I noticed that he spent some time in each session voicing complaints about work. Mark worked as a financial analyst in a large investment company. Initially, he taught economics in a business school, but he was frustrated with a limited salary. He was hurt when he failed to receive tenure. He had successfully switched to the corporate environment five years previously. In the beginning, the work had been challenging, but now he was bored. He felt isolated from his colleagues. His expertise was in a specialized field; he missed the sense of collegial dialogue. He also found himself isolated because his interest in social issues, especially environmental concerns, was not shared by others in the company. Mark tended not to voice his frustrations. Instead, he withdrew more and more from contact with others in his office.

In the same way as the Israelites journeyed to a foreign land to escape a famine, Mark chose a career that did not quite suit him as a result of his material concerns. In both situations, the choice solved one problem but contained the seeds of oppression. For each of us, likewise, material concerns may motivate us to make choices that address those needs but that also enslave us.

As he talked about work, I realized that Mark was enslaved but did not fully sense the depth of his pain. I asked Mark to tell me more about his family and childhood. His father had grown up in poverty, the son of immigrants. He never finished school, but he worked hard to build a successful retail business. His father had worked long hours during Mark's childhood. He was rarely at home on evenings and weekends. Mark had learned from his father's example to view life as a struggle for survival in which there was little room for play, joy, or satisfaction.

As we talked, I wondered aloud to Mark, "Is there a connection between the panic attacks and your frustration with work?" He did not see any logical, immediate connection. Using hypnosis, I asked Mark if his unconscious might be willing to provide us with some understanding of any connection between the frustration with work and the panic attacks. We waited in silence for a few moments. Then, I saw Mark's face change: a tear ran down his left cheek. "What did you discover?" I asked. "All these images of suicide," he replied. "I'm killing myself at work!"

From that moment, something changed. His panic attacks did not disappear, but they occurred much less frequently. Mark showed more feeling when he talked. He complained about his dissatisfaction with work. He felt trapped because he did not want to return to academia, nor did he want to make do with less money. His lifestyle required that he earn a good salary. He felt helpless and hopeless. I did not see any solution either, but I felt we were making progress. In the same way as the Israelites' awareness and expression of their suffering brought God to earth, Mark's awareness and expression meant he could begin to work to solve it.

In the same way as the Israelites were propelled out of Egypt by external events, help came from an outside source: Mark's firm merged with another, even larger, investment company. In the ensuing reorganization, Mark was given an opportunity to leave with a generous severance package, enough to allow him to live for almost a year before having to return to work. He responded immediately and decisively: he preferred an uncertain future filled with possibility to the security that enslaved him.

Mark experienced a mixture of feelings. On the one hand, he felt relieved to leave a job he hated, working with people he disliked and forced to ignore values that were important to him. On the other hand, Mark felt terrified and hopeless about finding anything else.

In the same way as the Israelites took small steps toward a distant goal, Mark needed to take action to achieve his dream. As Mark struggled with his situation, we established priorities about how to cope with his dilemma. He focused on two themes: clarifying what kind of work he really wanted to do, and developing strategies for reducing the stress while he searched. He realized he needed to sample a variety of areas that might interest him. He also needed some structure in his day. To address both concerns, he decided to take a course at the local university. He obtained a catalogue, and he selected three courses; however, he found himself unable to complete the process by registering for the classes he had chosen.

In discussing the difficulty, he became aware of feeling afraid he might fail in his efforts. So long as he did not really make the commitment to his new path, he protected himself from experiencing shame that would come if he was unsuccessful. Moreover, he felt a lack of self-confidence. Taking a class seemed inconsequential in relationship to all he would need to do in order to make a career change. Why bother even starting? Having identified the source of his resistance, he felt some relief. He renewed an agreement with me to take action. At the next session, he showed up at his session with a big grin on his face, waving the receipts for three courses. Appreciating himself and appreciating my work with him, Mark felt hopeful for the first time in many months. The journey was far from complete, but he had taken an important step in the same way as the Israelites felt relieved when their journey into the sea saved them from their enemies.

Mark had been unaware of his frustration and boredom. The pressure from his panic attacks and the loss of his job disrupted old habits; Mark now had an opportunity to turn inward to understand his feelings and how to cope with them. The crisis proved to be an opportunity.

APPLYING THE IMAGES OF PESACH TO OUR LIVES:
AN OLD SELF AND NEW CIRCUMSTANCES

Liberty is not the power to do what one wants, but it is the desire to do what one can.

Jean-Paul Sartre

The journey of the children of Israel to Egypt began as an effort to escape the famine in the land of Israel. Egypt provided nurturance for many years. But then, a new pharaoh came to power, one who "did not know Joseph." The circumstances changed. What had been a place of nurturance became a place of slavery. The children of Israel suffered but were unable to extricate themselves. Only with divine intervention could they free themselves. Once they left Egypt, they found themselves in the desert, a new environment with different circumstances. Although they were free, they had no sources of food and water; they lacked the structure that shaped their lives. The mentality of the slave no longer provided a useful identity that could enable them to survive and grow.

We see ourselves in the mirror of the story of the redemption from slavery in Egypt. We identify how we may be trapped and enslaved in our lives so as to begin our own process of liberation. As we grow and develop, our needs change. We find ourselves constricted in some way. Initially, we may fail to notice that a problem exists. We may not be aware of other possibilities; we may deaden ourselves to our dissatisfaction; we may not understand the true cause of difficulties we do experience; we may be afraid that change is not possible. We may cry out in our pain but not know the cause or the solution. We begin to address the problem only when something happens to push us out of the old structure of our lives, forcing us into a new environment.

The changed circumstance requires a different coping response; however, when we are habitually patterned in our responses, we may be unable to respond differently. Enmeshed in the pursuit of material concerns for survival and attempting to make a living to provide ourselves with basics of food, clothing and shelter, we are forced to turn our attention away from the spiritual sense of purpose of who we are and to focus instead on material concerns. That which is supposed to be a means becomes the sole focus of our experience. During Pesach, we clarify how our search for material sustenance has enslaved us and caused us to lose connections with our true spirit and purpose.

The celebration of Pesach immerses us in the images of slavery and redemption. As the circumstances change, we find ourselves attracted to different elements in the tradition. Perhaps we identify our personal experience of "Egypt," a once nurturing environment that now enslaves us. We may discover some of the habitual coping responses that served us well in "Egypt" but no longer help us as we face a different environment. We may find support for expressing our pain. We may focus on the possibility that forces outside ourselves can provide support even when we are powerless. We may clarify particular actions we need to take to help us in coping with the crisis.

According to tradition, when the Jews are in exile, the divine Spirit, the spark of divinity hidden within each person, goes into exile with them. That spark symbolizes the hope that the positive forces in the universe are always there to provide ultimate support. That sense of trust and optimism is vital if we are to survive adversity. We can then be open to see and receive the help that may be available. We are encouraged to hope that forces outside ourselves will support and nurture us.

MAKING PERSONAL CONNECTIONS FOR PESACH

- What circumstances in my life do I experience as "Egypt" this year?

- In what ways has my "Egypt" served as a womb to nurture and protect me? As the soil for germinating a seed within me? As a smelting furnace whose fire produces a new alloy?

- How does my "Egypt" now constrict and oppress me?

- What habitual coping responses served me well in "Egypt," but no longer are effective after liberation?

- How can I face and express my powerlessness? What is my prayer for help?

- What events—outside my control—can I trust to liberate me from this constriction and oppression?

- What feelings do I experience in this process—positive and negative?

- What do I need to do—specific, practical, actions—to respond to the crises?

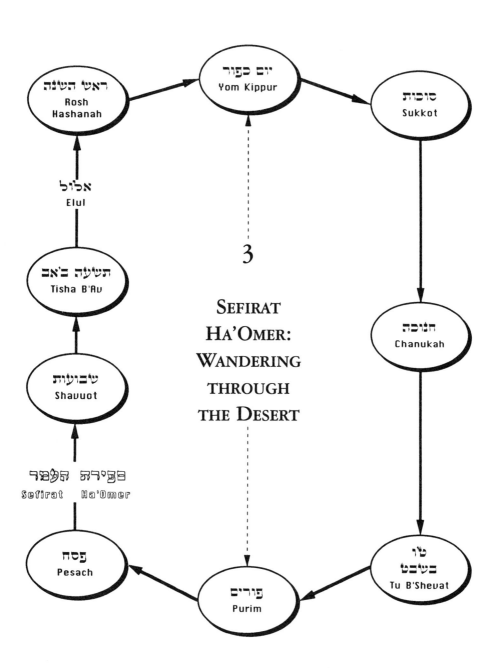

ראש השנה
Rosh
Hashanah

יום כפור
Yom Kippur

סוכות
Sukkot

אלול
Elul

3

חנוכה
Chanukah

תשעה ב'אב
Tisha B'Av

SEFIRAT
HA'OMER:
WANDERING
THROUGH
THE DESERT

שבועות
Shavuot

ספירת העמר
Sefirat Ha'Omer

פסח
Pesach

פורים
Purim

טו
בשבט
Tu B'Shevat

You shall then count seven complete weeks after the day following the Passover holiday when you brought the Omer *as a wave offering.*

[Leviticus 23:15]

Sefirat Ha'Omer refers to the forty-nine days of counting beginning on the second day of Pesach. It also corresponds to the forty-nine-day journey of the Israelites from Egypt to Mount Sinai. In the agricultural cycle, it marked the time of the barley harvest and the barley offering in the Sanctuary. The archetypal experience associated with these days is that of a toddler exploring and gaining understanding of the nature of his or her environment with the supervision and guidance of a nurturing, firm parent who provides structure and rules. For Shneur Zalman, Sefirat Ha'Omer is associated with step-by-step, concrete development of understanding symbolized in the step-by-step journey through the desert and the daily counting of the *Omer.* In contemporary culture, this learning is associated with the left hemisphere of the cerebral cortex.

The liberation from slavery in Egypt symbolizes life transitions, especially external events that free us by transforming the universe in which we live, an environment that has shaped and constrained us. Wandering in the desert symbolizes the confusion and the emotional turmoil we experience as we explore the new world around us. In the same way as the Israelites learn to survive in new circumstances, we gradually develop understanding of our situation in our new environment. In reflecting on the current issues of our lives through the mirror of Sefirat Ha'Omer, we focus on developing understanding of our situation, clarifying how to cope most effectively.

Historic antecedent	Fifty-day journey
Mythic experience	Wandering and learning
Ritual	Sefirat Ha'Omer; counting of days
Agricultural cycle	Barley harvest
Sanctuary service	Barley offering
Image of God	Archetypal mother
Speech	Breath differentiated into five vowels
Learning	Analytic study
Psychology	Left-brain analysis

WANDERING IN THE DESERT:
A TIME OF EMOTIONAL TURMOIL AND DEPENDENCY

When Pharaoh let the people leave, God did not lead them along the road of the Philistines, even though it was the shorter route. God's conclusion was that if the people encountered armed resistance, they would lose heart and return to Egypt.
[Exodus 13:17]

After the Israelites left Egypt, God did not take them through the land of the Philistines directly to Israel. Instead they went by way of the sea and then into the desert, a more difficult and challenging journey. At one moment, they were terrified as they faced the sea with the Egyptians chasing them; at the next moment, they were filled with gratitude as the sea split. The gratitude soon gave way again to fear when they did not have water or food. According to Shneur Zalman, the Philistines are associated with a focus on material pleasure. The decision to avoid the land of the Philistines suggests that material pleasure is not to be expected at this stage.

The initial joy of liberation is fragile and impermanent, like the infatuation that marks the beginning of a romantic relationship. An infatuation becomes strained as differences and conflicts emerge. Pleasure that is complete and trustworthy comes only after a working through of those differences. In this spirit, we read the love song of Solomon, *Shir HaShirim,* during Pesach. We must struggle to achieve a spiritual and psychological transformation before true freedom occurs.

This theme is also reflected in the other archetypal symbols associated with this time of year: the fetus must emerge through the constriction of the birth canal, the seed is covered by the dirt and the shell must rot before it can sprout, and the metal is melted in the fire of the furnace before it can be purified.

Liberation for each of us is a complex, lengthy process. We might initially feel exhilarated, as our ancestors did when they left Egypt; however, at this stage, life can be an emotional roller coaster. The liberation is not complete. New challenges and new difficulties are encountered. We must work through these problems. We need to identify and change old habits of coping that no longer serve us before we can stabilize ourselves in the new environment. This is a painful process. We are forced to give up what seems to be our very Essence. Only later do we discover that we have surrendered the outer shell.

Emotional Turmoil

I asked for roses, but I wasn't expecting thorns.
© Ashleigh Brilliant

The journey was a difficult one: at one moment, the Israelites celebrated their freedom, grateful to God for their liberation; at the next moment, they were frustrated and overcome by difficulties real and imagined, wanting desperately to return to the comfort and stability of slavery in Egypt:

> *There in the desert, the entire Israelite community began to complain against Moses and Aaron. The Israelites said to them, "If only we had died by God's hand in Egypt! There at least we could sit by pots of meat and eat our fill of bread! But you had*

*to bring us out to the desert, to kill the entire community by
starvation."*

[Exodus 16:2]

The perspective reflected in these images helps us prepare for the
emotional turmoil. As we realize that our exhilaration may be fragile and short-lived, we are not surprised when we find ourselves suddenly frightened or confused. We shift our expectations, not hoping
for ease and pleasure but realizing that this stage of transformation
is difficult. As we encounter a new situation and respond in new
ways, we are likely to experience more stress and anxiety. Only as the
changes are solidified do we begin to experience the satisfaction. For
example, when a person who suffers from alcoholism stops drinking,
he gives up a crucial tool for managing stress and reducing anxiety.
Even though he may be relieved to give up his addiction, he experiences more stress without the usual method for coping. Only after
developing other substitutes for managing stress is there an experience of satisfaction and pleasure.

In this spirit, according to one *midrash,* the Israelites eagerly antic-
ipated revelation. Each day they arrived at their destination, they
were overjoyed, expecting they had come to the place were God's
Presence would be manifested. In the morning, when they learned
they had to continue on their journey, they were disappointed.

Dependency

The Israelites had no capacity for self-sufficiency. When the newly
freed slaves left Egypt, God provided a pillar of smoke by day to
guide their journey and a pillar of fire to guide them by night: "God
went before them by day with a pillar of cloud to guide them along
the way. By night it appeared as a pillar of fire, providing them with
light" (Exodus 13:22).

God also provided the manna to sustain them in the desert, a
miraculous food that fell from heaven each day. Water came from a
well that sprang up wherever they camped, a miracle attributed to
the merit of Miriam, Moses' sister. The Israelites were helpless
against their enemies without divine intervention. When they

encountered difficulties, they were filled with complaints. Through all the turmoil, God provided for them.

As we struggle to cope with changes in our lives, we may be impatient with our confusion, with our inability to take care of ourselves, with our emotional volatility. The story of the Israelites in the desert validates our own experience, reminding us that we can legitimately expect ourselves to be confused, dependent, emotionally volatile, and lacking in understanding. We can respect our need for nurturance, support, and guidance. We can clarify the need to learn from our experience, gradually developing understanding of our situation and how to cope with it.

COUNTING OF THE *OMER:* DAY-BY-DAY LEARNING

Sefirat Ha'Omer is also associated with the sacrificial service in the Sanctuary. Beginning on the second day of Pesach, the sixteenth day of the month of Nissan, an offering was brought to the Sanctuary known as the *Omer,* a sheaf of barley. It was permissible to eat grain from the new harvest only after this offering had been made. The barley was harvested by three different farmers, each with his own scythe and basket. The grain was then brought to the Sanctuary where it was ground into a coarse flour. The flour was sifted through thirteen sieves. One-tenth was mixed with oil and frankincense and used for the offering in which the priest "waved" the grain on the altar, moving it up and down and side to side, asking God to protect the harvest from winds and other potential calamities. After the waving, a handful was burnt on the altar; the rest was eaten by the priests.

Although the offering of the *omer* is no longer required since the Sanctuary was destroyed, we still mark this time. We are asked to count the days, making a special benediction and using a particular formula in which both the number of days and number of weeks are mentioned. For example, the standard formula on the eighth day is "Today is the eighth day of the *Omer,* making one week and one day of the *Omer.*" Since the counting is the core of the ritual, we are asked to avoid mentioning the number inadvertently before the ritual: if I have not yet counted and you ask what the number of the day is, I reply by giving the number of the previous day rather than prematurely speaking the current day. In addition to the counting, it is customary to refrain from weddings and cutting one's hair to further emphasize the seriousness of this time.

According to Shneur Zalman, each day of the barley offering has a unique spiritual quality paralleling the learning of the Israelites day-by-day on their journey from Egypt to Mount Sinai. Although God's Essence is unified, one can differentiate various types of spiritual energy, each with unique and separate qualities. In the kabbalistic system, God's Presence is experienced through archetypal energies known as the *Sefirot.* There are ten *Sefirot:* Wisdom *(Chochma),* Understanding *(Binah),* Knowledge *(Da'at),* Loving-kindness *(Chesed),* Containing Strength *(Gevurah),* Mercifulness/Beauty *(Tiferet),* Power/Victory *(Netzach),* Presence/Glory *(Hod),* Energy/ Foundation *(Yesod),* and Manifestation/Kingdom *(Malchut).* In some mystical frameworks, *Da'at* is replaced by *Keter* (Crown). The first three *Sefirot* cannot directly be experienced.

Shneur Zalman connects the barely offering to the *Sefirot* by referring to Ezekiel's vision, which is included in the reading from the Prophets on Shavuot. In this vision, the prophet experiences God's Presence with the appearance of a human figure riding on a chariot. On the sides of the chariot are four faces: a lion, an ox, an eagle, and a human:

> *And I looked, and, behold, a whirlwind came out of the north, a great cloud, and a fire enfolding itself, and a brightness was about it, and out of the midst thereof as the color of amber, out of the midst of the fire. Also out of the mist thereof came the*

likeness of four living creatures. And this was their appearance;
they had the likeness of a man. And every one had four faces,
and every one had four wings. . . . As for the likeness of their
faces, they four had the face of a man, and the face of a lion, on
the right side: and they four had the face of an ox on the left
side; they four also had the face of an eagle.

[Ezekiel 1:4-10]

Since barley is the grain eaten traditionally by animals, the offering symbolizes nourishment of the "animals" of the chariot, the
"animal soul" that is the material part of the self. Each of the figures
symbolizes one of the *Sefirot*. The face of the lion symbolizes *Chesed;*
the face of the ox represents *Gevurah;* the eagle symbolizes *Tiferet.*

During the forty-nine days of counting, we focus each week on
one of the seven lower *Sefirot*. Each day we focus on a particular
aspect of that *Sefira*. Each of the seven *Sefirot* incorporates within
itself an aspect of all the others. We can therefore meditate on the
quality of *Chesed* in *Chesed, Gevurah* in *Chesed, Tiferet* in *Chesed,*
and so forth. For this reason, we refer to the number of the weeks
each time we count, for example, "Today is thirty days, which is four
weeks and two days."

In the same way as a child comes to understand the abstract concept of number only through repeated counting of actual objects, we
make sense of the abstract, archetypal spiritual energies in terms of
our daily experience. Theoretical concepts can be understood only
when they are grounded in real life. Step-by-step, we build understanding. Spirit that is, by definition, incomprehensible and infinite
becomes understandable by clarifying the various different parts.
Each day, as we count, we consider one quality of spirit, separating
and differentiating into comprehensible pieces. Each day, we focus
on a different aspect of God's Essence and clarify how to make a personal connection to that quality.

For Shneur Zalman, this process was known as *Tikkun*—repair of
the *Sefirot*. Through the days of counting, we meditate each day on
our understanding of the definition and meaning of each attribute
and how to integrate that learning into our lives.

Our learning is cumulative: each day builds on the foundation we
have previously established. This notion is suggested by the ritual formula for counting. Rather than declaring, "Today is the third day" or
"Today is the seventeenth day," we are instructed to say, "Today are
three days" or "Today are seventeen days, which are two weeks and
three days." Each day, we add to our count. Although each day's
offering is separate, each day adds to the cumulative effect.

INFANT DEVELOPMENT AND THE JOURNEY
THROUGH THE DESERT

Shneur Zalman understands the process of development at this
time of year through analogy to growth and development in childhood. He follows the logical progression of his imagery from Pesach.
The liberation from the "constriction" of Egypt is analogous to the
journey through the narrowness of the birth canal; the journey
through the desert is associated with the process of growth during
early childhood. The themes associated with this time of the process
of development are discussed in the following sections.

From Dependency toward Autonomy

Like infants, the Israelites are helpless and dependent on God for
nourishment from the manna and for water from Miriam's well.
They rely on the pillars of smoke and fire to guide their journey.
They are inarticulate and ineffective, able only to cry out in their
pain, relying on Moses and Aaron to intercede on their behalf. In the
same way, the young child is helpless and dependent, unable to care
for him or herself. The toddler cannot satisfy his or her own needs;
there is no ability to define needs or comprehension of how to interact with the environment to meet those needs. The infant relies on
others for basic needs of food, water, warmth, shelter, and protection. When uncomfortable, the only recourse is to cry as a way to
make needs known.

The Israelites gradually make sense of their situation through
their experiences. Shneur Zalman notes that the infant is nourished

by milk, a food that requires no effort from the child to be digested. As a result of this nourishment, the infant grows, developing teeth and the capacity to chew. With teeth, the young child is now able to take in solid food, taking a step toward autonomy and self-sufficiency. The custom of eating dairy foods and the wheat offering on Shavuot offer us a way to experientially connect with this developmental process.

In this same way, each of us is dependent and confused requiring outside support and nourishment to help us as we try to make sense of our situation and explore how to cope with it effectively.

From Rules to Reasons

I think my life is trying to tell me something, but I don't have time to listen.

© Ashleigh Brilliant

A child is unable to comprehend abstract notions of cause and effect separate from actual experience. Lawrence Kohlberg (1964), a psychologist who studied children's moral development, notes that children initially conceptualize values as rules to be obeyed and applied to concrete situations; there is no capacity to understand the reasons. At this stage, God relates similarly to the Israelites: If you do what God asks, life will go well for you; if you fail to heed God's commands, you will have difficulty:

> *If you obey God your Lord and do what is upright in God's eyes, carefully heeding all the commandments and keeping all the decrees, then I will not strike you with any of the sicknesses that I brought on Egypt. I am God who heals you.*
> {Exodus 15:25}

Similarly, in our initial struggles with new circumstances, we have difficulty in conceptualizing and understanding our situation. We may need to rely on simple guidelines.

Cognitive Development

Initially, the child lacks conceptual faculties. As the child interacts with the environment, the capacity for cognitive understanding develops. Jean Piaget (1962), a psychologist who studied child development, notes that the child develops the capacity for abstract reasoning through hands-on experience of the universe. For example, a child may be able to count from one to ten but fails to comprehend the abstract concept of number. Only through repeated counting of actual objects does the child eventually attain a more abstract understanding of numbers. The gradual development is suggested by Shneur Zalman in describing how the nourishment of milk allows the child to develop teeth with which to chew solid food.

The Israelites do not go directly from Egypt to the revelation of God's Presence on Mount Sinai. They journey for forty-nine days. They wonder how they will sustain themselves. They need to understand and make sense of the new realities of life in different circumstances. They require time to interact with the world to achieve this understanding.

The process of cognitive development occurs not only in childhood. As we struggle with new life situations, we recapitulate the developmental process. Encountering a changed environment, we find ourselves disoriented and confused, lost in the desert. We do not know how to nourish ourselves. We do not quite know where we are going or how to get there. We may long to return to our old environment, to a world that is familiar. We find mentors and guides for ourselves. We learn through a process of trial and error, step-by-step. In time, we may experience moments of revelation, intuitive leaps in which our goals and methods for achieving those goals become clear.

Connection with God as Archetypal Mother

The experience of this time of year is also characterized as a time of connection with the Archetypal Mother. In relationship to the mother, the infant's understanding develops out of the biological connection in the womb, a foundation that is strengthened and developed when the mother nurses and provides daily care. In the same way as a mother fills the infant with her milk, the feminine aspect of God known as the *Shechina* fills and nourishes all life. This experience of God as the Divine Mother is known as *Memaleh Kol Almin,* the immanence of God as "filling all worlds." The image of God as Archetypal Mother is consistent with the sense of ourselves and the Israelites as infants. During the forty-nine days of counting, we learn from our interaction with our environment. We experience God's Presence mediated by the experience of our world.

Learning to Speak

Shneur Zalman also associates this time of year with the process of learning to speak, a task that not only makes sense with respect to the archetypal experience of childhood but also is consistent with the image of God speaking from the top of Mount Sinai. To speak, we begin with the breath. The breath is invisible and unitary. We experience the breath when it is translated into sound. The same breath can produce many different sounds. The infant learns to differentiate the breath into the five vowel sounds. In developing the capacity to speak, the first step is the differentiation of sounds in this way.

This process can be applied to connection with Spirit. God, by definition, is unitary, infinite, and unknowable. How do we come into relationship with this Presence? The breath of life that emerges from the mouth of God differentiates into the various spiritual energies, the *Sefirot* that are associated with the seven weeks of counting. Breath cannot be seen or heard; however, differentiated into vowels, it can be perceived. God's Essence is beyond our perception, but the spiritual energies are manifest and revealed. In the same way, we begin to differentiate the confusing, chaotic world around us into separate categories and objects.

A PSYCHOLOGICAL PERSPECTIVE:
LEFT-BRAIN LEARNING

If you like puzzles, you should find life very enjoyable.
© Ashleigh Brilliant

The barley offering, made each day for forty-nine days, corresponds to spiritual realization based on systematic observation and logical analysis of experience. For example, in making the decision to buy a house, a person might consider the issues systematically and analytically. Each house is evaluated according to specific criteria such as cost, location, layout, landscape, condition, neighborhood, and so forth. Similarly, in psychotherapeutic process, we may make discoveries about ourselves through detailed self-observation of patterns of behavior, thinking, feeling, and interacting. We may analyze these patterns, consider the sources of the habits in early life experience, and gain extensive insight about the reasons for these patterns. We may further assess the value of these habitual responses and conclude that some, perhaps helpful to us at one time, are no longer helpful in current life situations.

This learning can be understood in terms of psychological theories concerning differing functions of the two hemispheres of the human brain. For most of us, the left hemisphere is associated with the right side of the body, right ear, and right eye; the right hemisphere is associated with the left side of the body, left ear, and left eye. The two hemispheres process information in different ways. The left hemisphere operates step-by-step, linearly, temporally, logically, and analytically, reducing data into parts. It utilizes language and mathematics. The right hemisphere operates holistically. It processes visual and spatial perception, nonverbally and intuitively. It synthesizes information simultaneously from many different sources, recognizing patterns and faces. It is timeless and diffuse in its orientation. The step-by-step, linear, and analytic learning of the forty-nine days can be associated with left-hemisphere mental process.

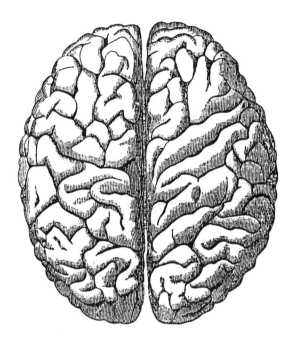

The confusion, exploration, trial and error, step-by-step learning associated with this time of year is illustrated by the following example. Saul entered therapy a few days before he was to move out of his house into his own apartment; he was leaving his wife and family, taking the first step on the road to a divorce. He had not wanted a divorce; after more than a year of counseling, his wife decided she did not want to continue the marriage. Saul was confused and disoriented. He did not know where to begin.

Saul did not need an empathic but passive counselor who would just listen. This was not a time for analysis of the reasons for the marriage ending or for exploration of early childhood experiences that impacted on the present. Saul was in the desert, dependent and lost like a young child. Saul was in crisis; he needed guidance and structure to help him cope with immediate issues of transition. I took the lead, suggesting we begin by focusing on immediate survival issues, coping with the transition. He agreed. We made specific plans concerning the physical environment of his new apartment. We discussed how he would spend time on weekends and evenings. We clarified how he might talk with his children about the changes. We established guidelines for dealing with his wife, defining issues that might better be avoided, issues about which he needed to be assertive, and strategies to protect the children from being placed in the middle of their battle. We identified several friends whom he could ask for support and companionship when he was overwhelmed and lonely. I offered to be available by telephone for emergencies. He left the session with specific, practical plans for getting through the next week, day by day.

For Saul, who was struggling with the transition of a divorce, our work initially focused on creating structure rather than exploring reasons. In the preliminary stages, I sometimes asked him to act on faith as I guided him, suspending judgment even though he might not understand the reasons. For example, Saul did not think it was important to fix up his new apartment. I asked him to invest some time and energy in decorating and find out whether that eased his transition. As he experimented, we both learned more about what he needed.

PERSONAL APPLICATION OF PRINCIPLES

The days from Pesach to Shavuot, Sefirat Ha'Omer, serve as a bridge from the experience of redemption to the experience of revelation. We are pulled from slavery by miracles, by powers outside of ourselves. Changes in our lives—both positive and negative—pull us out of our habits, out of our constrictions. It may be a change in work life, relationships, health, a new stage in the life cycle. Then we begin to make sense, to try to understand what this means and how to deal with it.

During the days of counting, we use the archetypal images of the *Sefirot* as guides. Our job is *Tikkun*—repair—of the attributes. One of the qualities of an archetype is that it is ambiguous, can be defined in many different ways. Through meditation, contemplation, and analysis, we clarify the ways in which we might interpret each of the *Sefirot* negatively in ways that are not helpful and positively in ways that help us with our struggles.

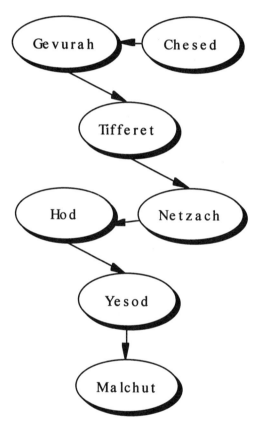

Each week is devoted to one of the seven *Sefirot*. For example, during the first week, the *Sefira* of *Chesed* is the focus. One might meditate on a variety of topics: What are my experiences of unconditional love? What are my definitions and beliefs about love? How have my life experiences affected my understanding and beliefs? What can I learn from experiences of others about love? What can I learn about unconditional love from the texts and commentaries of the tradition? What can I learn from story, myth, or

psychological theory? Is there any way in which my understanding
is incomplete or faulty? What new perspectives might I adopt concerning the nature of unconditional love? How do changes in
understanding affect my approaches to current life situations and
issues? One might ask similar questions appropriate to the focus
for each week.

Not only does each week have a unique focus; each day within the
week also has a particular significance. Each of the *Sefirot* contains
aspects of the others. For example, the first week is associated with
the *Sefira* of *Chesed*. The days of that week are linked to the various
Sefirot subsumed in *Chesed*: *Chesed* in *Chesed*, *Gevurah* in *Chesed*,
Tiferet in *Chesed*, *Netzach* in *Chesed*, *Hod* in *Chesed*, *Yesod* in
Chesed, and *Malchut* in *Chesed*.

Following is a brief definition of each of the *Sefirot*. Exact definitions are not made of the *Sefirot* or of the particular manifestation
on each day. The purposeful ambiguity leaves to each person an
opportunity for making individual discoveries through contemplation and meditation.

> *Chesed*—Loving-kindness: *Chesed* is also known by the name
> *Ahavah*—love. It is associated with Abraham, the patriarch
> who was known for his hospitality and care for others. It
> refers to the experience of unconditional love and accep-
> tance. It is the ability to see the positive in everything, to
> appreciate and accept all aspects of life.

> *Gevurah*—Strength: *Gevurah* is also known as *Yirah*—awe or
> fear. *Gevurah* is associated with Isaac. It refers to strength
> that comes from containment, the power to contain and
> hold the energy of love. It is the power of inhibition, the
> power of discrimination and judgment that allows one to
> make choices. It refers to our ability to know when not to
> express or act. In the kabbalistic story of creation, God's first
> attempt to create the world ended in the breaking of the ves-
> sels of the *Sefirot*. They were unable to contain the energy of
> spiritual manifestation.

Tiferet—Beauty: *Tiferet* is also known as *Rachamim*—merciful-ness. It is also a symbol of peace because it is represents the perfect balancing of the left and right sides, integrating love and containment, *Chesed* and *Gevurah*. *Tiferet* is associated with Jacob.

Netzach—Victory: *Netzach* begins the second triad of the *Sefirot,* associated with the translation of feeling into energy. *Netzach* is linked to Moses, the archetypal leader who guid-ed the Israelites through the desert. It refers to the quality of power, desires, and plans which translate feeling into form. The quality of loving-kindness becomes more specific, man-ifesting as a particular image of when, how, and to whom that feeling might be expressed.

Hod—Glory: *Hod* refers to the quality of presence and being, the light in a person's face. *Hod* is associated with Aaron, the high priest, and brother of Moses. It parallels the *Sefira* of *Gevurah* insofar as it is more receptive than active. In con-trast to the plans and images for expressing feeling, *Hod* refers to the experience of feeling.

Yesod—Foundation: *Yesod* represents the integration of *Netzach* and *Hod,* the balance between power and presence. Joseph, the son of Jacob, is linked to this *Sefira.* It is associ-ated with sexual energy, the expression of the life force in the body.

Malchut—Kingdom: *Malchut* represents manifestation, the translation of energy into action, doing in the material world, behavior. *Malchut* serves as the intermediary between the spiritual domain and the material world. For this reason, *Malchut* is associated with the *Shechina,* the feminine aspect of God's Presence that flows into creation. King David is associated with this *Sefira* as the one who brought fruition to the Israelites dream for a land.

These definitions provide only one possible basis for meditation. For some, the intricacy of the kabbalastic system offers a rich and wonderful resource. For others, it may be confusing. What is required of us during the forty-nine days of counting is that we do our own work, step-by-step in the form that best serves us. It is exactly the nature of the task that we make our own definitions. It may equally serve you to construct your own forty-nine steps.

JOURNEY THROUGH THE DESERT

- In what respects do you experience your life as a journey through the desert?

- For what do you cry out? What are your needs?

- Who sustains you and responds?

- What are the rules which you need to follow?

- What is the personal "Egypt" to which you sometimes want to return when times are difficult? What stops you from regressing?

- What do you learn each day concerning your situation? What are the new understandings?

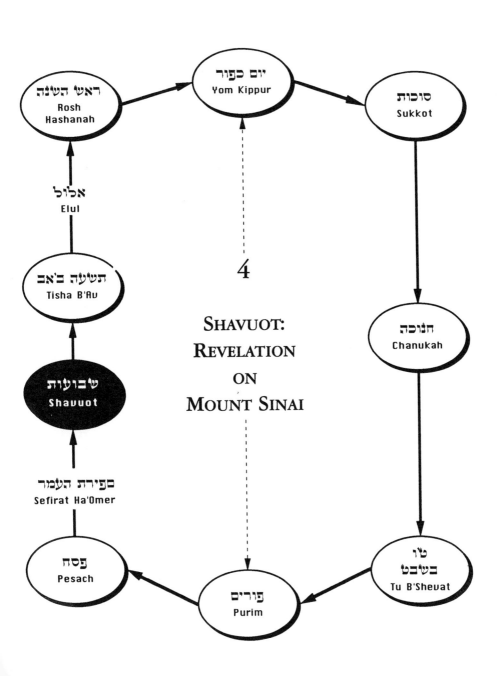

ראש השנה
Rosh
Hashanah

יום כפור
Yom Kippur

סוכות
Sukkot

אלול
Elul

תשעה ב'אב
Tisha B'Av

שבועות
Shavuot

ספירת העמר
Sefirat Ha'Omer

פסח
Pesach

4

SHAVUOT:
REVELATION
ON
MOUNT SINAI

חנוכה
Chanukah

ט'ו
בשבט
Tu B'Shevat

פורים
Purim

Shavuot, celebrated on the sixth (and outside of Israel on the seventh) day of the month of Sivan, marks the occasion when the Israelites received the Torah. Freed from slavery in Egypt, the Israelites wandered in the desert for forty-nine days. On the fiftieth day, they experienced God's Presence:

> There was thunder and lightning in the morning with a heavy cloud on the mountain and an extremely loud blast of a ram's horn. The people in the camp trembled. Moses led the people out of the camp toward the Divine Presence. They stood transfixed at the foot of the mountain. Mount Sinai was all in smoke because of the Presence that had come down on it. God was in the fire, and its smoke went up like the smoke of a lime kiln. The entire mountain trembled violently. There was the sound of a ram's horn, increasing in volume to a great degree. Moses spoke, and God replied with a Voice.
>
> [Exodus 19:16–18]

ASPECTS OF REVELATION

The encounter with God at Mount Sinai serves as an archetypal symbol of the discoveries we make as we struggle to make sense of the changes in our lives and to clarify how to cope with these changes most effectively. The step-by-step learning of the forty-nine days establishes a foundation for personal revelation, a qualitative change in our consciousness that allows us to understand our situation in a new way.

Revelation as a Personal Experience

At the time of revelation, God is described with reference to the redemption from Egypt: "I am YHVH, your God, who brought you out of Egypt, from the place of slavery" (Exodus 20:1).

Shneur Zalman notes that God does not refer to the more powerful identity as the creator of the heavens and the earth who manifested the material world out of nothingness. The reference to Egypt, the place of constriction, is deliberate: we come to know God through our experience, from our time in Egypt, not through the more indirect association with creation.

The Transcendent Experience of Revelation

At Mount Sinai, God says, "I am the Lord," using the first-person pronoun to indicate a direct face-to-face experience of God. In everyday life, we do not usually perceive God's Presence directly. Our understanding is constricted and limited by what we have learned through the course of our lives. Although we have left Egypt, we still make sense of our situation with the minds of slaves. Even the discoveries of the forty-nine days are limited by the constrictions of human perception and understanding. On Shavuot, we transcend those limits, making a direct connection with God.

These limits in our understanding are embedded in the structure of the human body. The brain's capacity to see is mediated, constricted, and distorted by the material limits of the eye. The brain's capacity to hear is shaped by the capacity of the ear to register sound. The eye is not able to perceive the entire visual spectrum of light. The ear does not register the entire range of sound. Our bodies limit our capacity to see and hear. According to Shneur Zalman, when God reminds us that we have been taken out of Egypt, the reference is not only to the historic event. The body is our personal Egypt that enslaves our understanding, constricting and limiting our ability to know. At the time of the exodus, the constriction from which the Israelites were freed was physical. At Mount Sinai, they were freed from the constrictions of limited knowledge and understanding. For each of us, this limited understanding is transcended at the moment of revelation as we experience the oneness of life.

Nullification: Surrendering Old, Constricted Knowledge

Sometimes I think I understand everything, then I regain consciousness.

© Ashleigh Brilliant

According to the tradition, the souls of the Israelites left their bodies as they heard each of the Ten Commandments. Shneur Zalman understands this image as a reference to a nullification of "self," an experience of God beyond anything we can understand or know cognitively. The Israelites fully and directly experienced God's Essence and Presence at Mount Sinai. In this respect, as we hear the Word of God, our old understanding dies, creating a possibility for new learning.

A Transformation of Consciousness

This change in consciousness is symbolically noted in the description of how the Israelites "heard" the lightning and "saw" the thunder at Sinai, as it says in the Torah: "All the people saw the sounds" (Exodus 20:13). They now can see and understand what was previously unknown, hidden, and heard only from the distance. They distance themselves from that which previously was understood, seen, and thought to be close. In this same way, as we gain experience of our new situation, we may "see" it in a new way that allows us to cope more effectively. I realize that my old understanding is inaccurate: the habitual strategy for responding does not really apply to my new circumstance. Perhaps denying and ignoring pain helped me at one time in my life, but that approach does not serve me at this time; or, fighting my pain may have helped me previously, but ignoring it may serve me more now.

The structure of the ritual helps us access this quality of consciousness. We disconnect from ordinary consciousness through the prohibitions regarding work and ordinary activity. On Pesach and Sukkot, the ritual involves physical tasks: the removal of *chametz* and eating of *matza* on Pesach and the building of the *sukkah* and prayers with the four species of vegetation on Sukkot. In contrast, on Shavuot, no special ceremonial objects are used in the ritual. There is a custom of eating dairy foods because the Torah nourishes us like milk. The rituals of Shavuot focus on learning: we spend the night in study of the Torah. Depriving ourselves of sleep facilitates connection to the dreamlike state of trance in which we have more access to images and nonlinear associations. In this consciousness, we not only read the story of revelation but experience ourselves as standing at Sinai, open to revelation and ready to commit ourselves to the vision we receive.

Understanding as a Basis for Action

The revelation at Mount Sinai was not only a mystical, intellectual, and inner experience. God's Presence manifests in concrete and practical form, in the Ten Commandments engraved in stone, and in the Torah with the 613 *mitzvot,* action imperatives that guide and inform every aspect of life. According to Shneur Zalman, at the time of revelation on Mount Sinai, the light of God's Essence, the *Ayn Sof,* the Infinite, is manifest through the Torah. In the same way, the personal revelation we experience is not limited to a cognitive discovery that remains within us. It translates into new rules and guidelines for ourselves in how to approach our situation more constructively. Understanding informs action.

Making Commitment

I love information; what I don't like is having to do something with it.

© Ashleigh Brilliant

When the Israelites are invited to receive the Torah, they respond enthusiastically with the words "We will do and we will hear." They promise to act even before they completely understand, committing themselves to live by the *mitzvot.*

The experience at Mount Sinai is described using the image of a wedding in which God is the groom standing under the marriage canopy—the *chuppah*—with the Israelites as the bride. God and Israel make an eternal commitment to one another. God gives the Torah, and the Israelites pledge to adhere to its precepts. A wedding represents the beginning of a relationship. Although vows are made, the young couple must still struggle to translate those vows into reality, overcoming differences and difficulties. In the same way, the commitment made at Sinai also represents a beginning of relationship. There are many difficulties to overcome: shortly after Moses ascends Mount Sinai, the Israelites make the golden calf, losing trust and violating their commitment.

This beginning is also symbolized by the offering of the first ripe fruits that begins at this time: "The day of first fruits is when you bring a new grain offering to God as part of your Shavuot festival. It shall be a sacred holiday to you when you may not do any mundane work" (Numbers 28:26).

For this reason, Shavuot is also known as *Yom HaBikurim,* the day of the first fruits. We not only harvest the agricultural produce; we also begin to nourish ourselves with the fruits of our learning.

This same quality of commitment is reflected in the story of Ruth, which is read during the Shavuot service. Ruth, the ancestor of King David, is respected because of her commitment and devotion in caring for her mother-in-law, Naomi. Ruth, whose husband had died, returns with Naomi to the land of Israel rather than stay in the land of her birth, Midian.

The images of Shavuot allow us to receive a personal revelation that transforms our understanding, help us clarify a vision of our future, and motivate us to make a commitment to manifest that vision. We define rules for ourselves and commit ourselves to allow those rules to guide how we act.

SHAVUOT IN RELATIONSHIP TO SEFIRAT HA'OMER

The themes associated with Revelation at Mount Sinai are echoed in other aspects of the ritual, symbols, and stories associated with Shavuot. Shavuot also marks the end of the forty-nine days of the counting of the *omer*. On this day, the offering of barley is replaced by a bread offering, marking the beginning of the wheat harvest. The step-by-step learning from the forty-nine days of counting provides a basis for revelation, an intuitive leap in which we are able to transcend what we know from logic. In contrast to the left-brain, logical, experiential learning of Sefirat Ha'Omer, on Shavuot, our learning is based on synergistic discoveries associated with the right hemisphere of the cerebral cortex. Shneur Zalman describes the moment of revelation as an experience of the archetypal Father that builds on the connection to the archetypal Mother during the forty-nine days. He also links Shavuot with the twenty-two letters of the alphabet, complementing the association of the forty-nine days with the vowels.

	Sefirat Ha'Omer	Shavuot
Historic antecedent	Fifty-day journey	Revelation at Mount Sinai
Mythic experience	Wandering and learning	Receiving and committing
Ritual	Sefirat Ha'Omer— counting of days	*Tikkun*—All-night study
Agricultural cycle	Barley harvest	Wheat harvest
Sanctuary service	Barley offering	Bread offering
God as parent	Archetypal Mother	Archetypal Father
Speech	Breath differentiated into five vowels	Twenty-two letters of alphabet
Learning	Analytic study	Intuitive discovery
Psychology	Left-brain analysis	Right-brain intuition

Shavuot: Completing the Fifty Days of the Counting of the Omer

In the Torah, we are commanded to count fifty days. In practice, we only count forty-nine days. The fiftieth day of Shavuot is not explicitly counted. Shneur Zalman explains this discrepancy as an indication that the experience of the fiftieth day is qualitatively different than that of the other forty-nine, paralleling the difference between analytic, experiential learning and intuitive, synergistic knowing.

Counting the *omer* marks the journey in which we work to discover and understand the particular archetypal energy associated with each day. We count the days until we get to the fiftieth. The counting of the forty-nine days of the *omer* is necessary to access this experience of revelation that is achieved at the giving of the Torah on Shavuot (*Likutei Torah,* 20:B).

On the fiftieth day, an integration occurs that incorporates and transcends the previous learning. We surrender what we think we know to a higher understanding. We link the spiritual Essence to the material level of existence. At this time, all the parts are integrated, subsumed into a larger oneness. An integration occurs in which the whole is more than the sum of its parts. There is no need to count the fiftieth day, because it represents the integrative principle. There is no need to count the fiftieth day because that discovery comes from beyond what we know.

Offering of Barley and Offering of Wheat

On Shavuot, the bread offering replaced the barley sacrifice from the days of the *omer.* The wheat offering serves as a further symbol of transcendent, integrative learning. According to Shneur Zalman, the Tree of Knowledge in the Garden of Eden was actually wheat, indicating that wheat refers to a particular kind of knowledge. Wheat, the food of humans, nourishes the higher soul. The bread offering of Shavuot signals the manifestation of the quality of "wheat," integrative and intuitive learning in contrast to the barley offering of the *omer,* which nourishes the "animal" soul associated with the *Sefirot.*

Connection with the Archetypal Father

This quality of learning is also symbolically described as a connection with God as Father in contrast to the image of the Divine Mother associated with the counting of the *omer*. The mother's role in nourishing the child with her milk is direct and clear. The father's role is more difficult to comprehend, associated traditionally with the role as economic provider. The mother offers the infant milk, and the father puts the bread on the table. An infant does not immediately understand the father's role, the connection to its father, or the basis for feelings of love. According to Shneur Zalman, an infant learns to cry for its father once it tastes wheat. The child is too young to understand logically, but wheat gives the infant a knowledge that transcends what can be understood through the logical cognitive processes. The infant feels the connection and expresses it. The infant longs for the father, has trouble separating from the father, and cries when the father leaves. An infant cries out for its father even though he or she cannot explain the connection. In the words of Shneur Zalman, the pain is so great that the child "nearly gives up its soul to the tears." This knowledge is more powerful than the logical process. It is this aspect of God we experience at Shavuot.

In the experience of God as Divine Mother as we count the *omer,* the nourishment, like the manna in the desert, is directly received and perceived. At Mount Sinai, we make connection with God as Divine Father, receiving a nourishment that is complex and less obvious. In the language of Jewish mysticism, the connection with the archetypal Father is the experience of God as transcendent—*Sovev Kol Almin,* who "surrounds all worlds"—in contrast to the connection with the archetypal Mother, the experience of God as immanent—*Memaleh Kol Almin,* who "fills all the worlds."

Connection with the Twenty-Two Letters

Shneur Zalman associates the bread offering with the twenty-two letters of the Hebrew alphabet using the mystical process known as *gematria* for making connections through numerology. The Hebrew

word for *wheat*, חטה , adds up to twenty-two, the
same as the number of letters in the Hebrew alphabet.
Once we have the basic sounds of the vowels associated
with the time of the counting of the *omer,* we can combine them with letters to produce words, sentences, and
conversations, the traffic of relationship. The letters represent the transcendent experience of Shavuot and the
giving of the Torah.

ח	= 8
ט	= 9
ה	= 5

	22

A PSYCHOLOGICAL PERSPECTIVE:
RIGHT-BRAIN LEARNING

The nature of spiritual experience at the time of Shavuot is associated with the right hemisphere of the cerebral cortex, the part of
the brain that uses intuitive, synergistic, and associational learning.
For example, in making the decision to buy a house, a person might
use the right hemisphere, walking around the house, getting an
intuitive "feel" for it and its desirability in contrast to the left hemisphere, systematic, analytic consideration of specific criteria.
Similarly, in psychotherapeutic process, we might experience a sudden moment of spontaneous realization. It might occur at a time
when we are busy and occupied with something else or appear in a
dream. We are graced with revelation, a vision, an image, or a new
thought rather than pursuing a logical analysis of current patterns in
terms of present realities.

Learning requires both parts of the brain, both left and right
hemispheres. For example, in learning to drive a car, there is a step-
by-step learning as one struggles to coordinate the different movements involved in the process: using the steering wheel, the acceler-
ator, the brake, the clutch, keeping eyes on the road. Each separate
aspect of the skill is practiced. Eventually one achieves a point of
coordination in which one simply drives. The particular individual
aspects are subsumed into a larger integration.

In scientific investigation, this same dichotomy exists. One begins
with investigation of particular aspects of a phenomenon, gradually

increasing understanding. Eventually, these discrete, often contradictory pieces of understanding are subsumed under a more comprehensive, systematic theory. For example, astronomers first attempted
to explain the movements of the stars and planets by conceptualizing
a model of the universe in which all heavenly bodies rotated around
the earth. As more and more data were collected, the model became
more and more cumbersome: the various planets appeared to move
in orbits that were increasingly complex. Finally, astronomers like
Galileo came up with a new model in which the planets, including
the Earth, rotated around the sun. With this model, the movements
could be described more simply. Initially, Galileo's model was rejected as heretical; eventually, his view prevailed. All of the discoveries of
the past were vital to the new model that incorporated and transcended the previous view. Similarly, Einstein devised a model that
incorporated and transcended Newtonian physics. In our time, theo-
reticians like Steven Hawking struggle to integrate two contradictory models for explaining the nature of light—as a wave and as a par-
ticle—into a more comprehensive model.

Psychotherapy involves both processes, integrating systematic, analytic, and logical exploration of issues with synergistic, nonlinear, intuitive discoveries that integrate and subsume the pieces. For example,
in learning to create more satisfying relationships, one might consider
the various skills needed: active listening; making direct statements of
one's own perceptions, feelings, and needs; responding to others'
needs; resolving conflicts through negotiation; and so forth. One's
competence increases as each of the component skills is mastered.
Eventually, a breakthrough occurs: all the pieces become integrated,
without focusing on each as an individual skill. The prior learning dissolves into a new synergy, a whole greater than the parts, a more intuitive, nonlinear integration. The step-by-step, left-hemisphere learning from the time of the counting of the *omer* provides a foundation
that is integrated and transcended by the intuitive synergistic learning
of Shavuot.

This process is incorporated in Assagioli's (1976) two-stage model
of psychotherapy. In the first stage, one engages in an analysis of the

"lower self," identifying and describing the various "sub-personalities." In the second stage of therapy, the parts of the self are reintegrated, subsumed under a new organizing principle—the "higher Self." Rossi (1993), in his articulation of Erickson's approach, focuses on use of right-brain trance state in which we open ourselves to revelation: a message from the unconscious in the form of a voice, an image, a feeling, or an association that transforms our understanding.

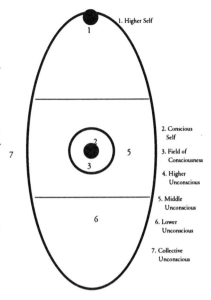

1. Higher Self

2. Conscious Self

3. Field of Consciousness

4. Higher Unconscious

5. Middle Unconscious

6. Lower Unconscious

7. Collective Unconscious

The experience of revelation is illustrated by the following example. Alan came to therapy as a result of a chronic back problem that interfered with every aspect of his life: work, recreation, and intimate relationships were all disturbed by debilitating and persistent pain. Medically, it had been determined that there were no organic, structural or skeletal abnormalities. The pain seemed to be the result of chronic tension. Alan began to discuss the various situations that caused frustration. He was overloaded by responsibilities at work as a lawyer. He was hesitant to let his girlfriend know the extent of his problem, fearing she would end the relationship. He zoned out while working at his computer, which exacerbated his physical tension. As we explored each situation, a pattern began to emerge. He tended to be unaware of what he needed; when he was aware, he held himself back and did not speak up assertively. In his family growing up, he was one of eight children. His youngest brother was stricken with leukemia. The family focused on helping the child. His parents were rigid and authoritarian. He learned to be quiet and acquiescent to get along in the family.

After several months, he arrived at a session animated and excited, a departure from his usually depressed mood. He had failed to speak up when given another assignment at his job and worked evenings and weekends to finish the project. His girlfriend was angry because he had canceled a date and he was overwhelmed by pain. That night he dreamed about his brother, flooded with images of him sick in bed with both parents by his side while Alan played alone with some blocks. All of a sudden, he realized that he kept hoping that someone would see his pain and give him some attention. Unfortunately, as an adult, no one noticed, not his girlfriend and not his supervisor at work. He realized that he needed to speak up if he was going to be able to heal himself.

A PSYCHOLOGICAL PERSPECTIVE ON MAKING COMMITMENT

Until one is committed, there is hesitancy, the chance to draw back, always ineffectiveness. Concerning all acts of initiative and creation, there is one elementary truth, the ignorance of which kills countless ideas and splendid plans: that the moment that one definitely commits oneself, then providence moves too. All sorts of things occur to help one that would never have otherwise occurred. A whole stream of events issues from the decision, raising in one's favor all manner of unforeseen incidents and meetings and material assistance, which no man could have dreamed would have come his way. Whatever you can do or dream you can, begin it. Boldness has genius, power, and magic in it. Begin now.

Goethe

Insight is meaningless if it does not translate into change in what we do and how we respond. For example, in working with addictions, twelve-step programs such as Alcoholics Anonymous stress the need for making a commitment to change. There is also a recognition that commitment does not instantly translate into behavior. For this reason, the recovering addict is enjoined to take "one day at a time." Sometimes, one is not able to sustain the commitment, falls back into old addictive behavior, and must begin once more in the struggle for recovery.

In the same way, for each of us, as we develop our understanding of new situations and how to cope with them, we arrive at a point where we are able to make a commitment to change. Although this is an important step, we are only beginning: much effort is needed to translate that commitment into reality.

This process is illustrated by the work with Lila. Lila was involved in an abusive relationship with a man who lied to her about involvement with other women and then accused her of being paranoid when she challenged him. Initially, she did not question the relationship, believing that she was overly suspicious. Over a period of months, she began to realize that her lover was unreliable and dishonest. She then made a commitment to end the relationship. In the same way as Shavuot represents the beginning of a commitment, this decision also represented the beginning of a process. She then had to work to translate the commitment into reality. She was unable to break off the relationship immediately: she needed to develop other social support so she could have the help of others when she was tempted to reestablish contact.

In this same way, as each of us experiences a moment of revelation, we then need to make a commitment to that vision, so that the thought and idea can be translated into reality. We spend the rest of the cycle of the year in that process.

REVELATION AT MOUNT SINAI

- What is your personal revelation? What are the intuitive realizations that occur?

- What is the commitment you need to make as a result of the new understanding of your situation and how to cope with it?

- What is needed to translate that commitment into reality?

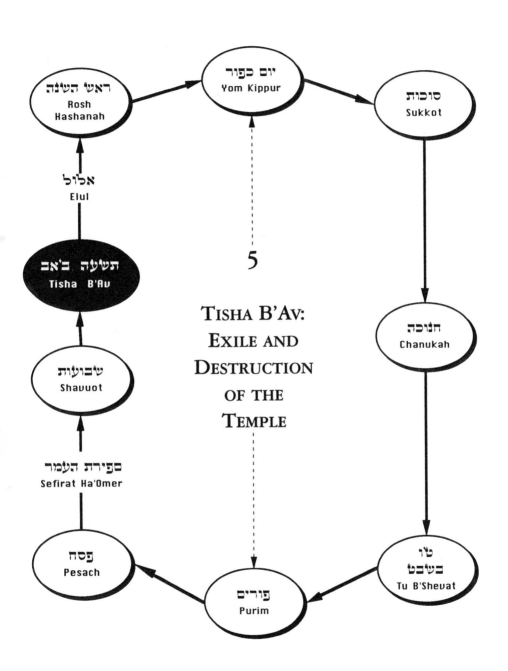

ראש השנה
Rosh Hashanah

יום כפור
Yom Kippur

סוכות
Sukkot

אלול
Elul

תשעה ב'אב
Tisha B'Av

5

TISHA B'AV:
EXILE AND
DESTRUCTION
OF THE
TEMPLE

חנוכה
Chanukah

שבועות
Shavuot

ספירת העמר
Sefirat Ha'Omer

פסח
Pesach

פורים
Purim

ט"ו בשבט
Tu B'Shevat

sitting by the rivers of babylon
escaping, for the moment,
the heat of an unrelenting summer desert sun
in the shade of a tree
rooted in a land not my own
not to rest,
but, at least, thank god, to catch my breath
and remember my lost home
in the land of zion

the land of promise
too far away
the road ahead leads only further away still

not just my promise broken,
but a promise shattered
stretching back in time,
back from generation to generation
to the days when we stood at sinai,
back further to the days of abraham and sara
who traveled this road
full of hope and trust towards Jerusalem

we knew, god told us,
exile, slavery, and pain
will steal us from our home,
our holy land;

we knew that the inevitable exile
also leads to redemption far beyond.

little good that promise
when we sit enslaved,
oppressed in egypt
trying to save our children
from their fate in the river
far from us their hope, when,
the children of jacob have no food
to nourish us in the land of promise
far from us their hope
when we find ourselves on trains of death
carrying us and our families
inexorably to camps of death

i remember the land of promise
after six days war of miracles.
full of hope
i explored the streets of the old city of Jerusalem,
united in peace again.
jogging the walls of that old city
hitchhiking through jericho, nablus, jenin
enjoying summer heat and hospitality
in the tradition of our common ancestors
abraham and sara.

only now to return
more than twenty years later,
no more to visit east Jerusalem or west bank
a land of stones
new roads built to keep us separate and away.
feeling terror not hope
when darkness of night and a wrong turn
take us off the road of the jews
to a road of blue license plates
dead ending in an unknown arab village
from which we turn,
hurrying back,
fearing for our lives,
no longer a safe and hospitable place
now we fear our cousins
may greet us with rocks
instead of expresso and arak.

i remember the promise
long delayed in coming
seeing my child's first smile,
but now I sit, weary, sleep-deprived,
working too hard,
to feed, clothe, and shelter
by suburban standards
enslaved by
lists
errands,
unrelenting pressures
too much to do
never enough time,
everything done inadequately
little sense of satisfaction
we curse the promises
which doom us to a life of misery
a lifetime of dreams which
we cannot put aside
nor fulfill,
dooming us to failure, pain, and misery
as we face the limits of
mortality
time
space,
resources
energy.

resting for a moment
by the waters of Babylon
in the shadow of a tree
rooted in a land far from my home,
not to rest,
but at least, thank god, to catch my breath
and let flow the tears
as I remember
the land of promise,
longed for,
achieved,
then all too quickly lost again.

there is relief in the tears,
a short reprieve,
before we once again
pickup our load and
pray for strength and help
to find our way
back again to
Jerusalem.

The summer heat is punctuated by a three-week period of mourning. It begins on the seventeenth day of the month of Tammuz , a fast day commemorating the breaching of the walls of the first Sanctuary by Nebuchadnezzar in 586 B.C.E. and of the second Sanctuary by Titus in 70 C.E. According to tradition, this was the same day that Moses came down from Mount Sinai and smashed the tablets when he found the Israelites worshipping the golden calf.

The three weeks of mourning culminates in the fast of the ninth day of Av, the day in which both the first and second Sanctuaries were destroyed. This loss deprived the Israelites of their center for communal life and ritual observances, the dwelling place of God on earth. The ninth of Av also marks the time when the Israelites rebelled against God and wanted to return to Egypt after hearing the reports from the spies sent by Moses to scout out the land of Canaan.

The historic events mirror a process that parallels our experience. In the same way as the Israelites lose faith only a short time after

receiving the Torah, we also fail in the effort to manifest our intuitive discoveries in daily life. The archetypal stories validate the difficulty of translating insight and commitment into consistent behavior. We fail despite our good intentions and our vows; we do not heed the warnings, and we ignore the reminders. In the end, the worst occurs, we suffer the consequences, and we are left with our grief and powerlessness. The commemoration of these events creates the time and space to mourn the tragedies of our own lives.

We do not only fail God; God also fails us. Misfortunes sometimes occur in spite of our best efforts. Not all adversity is the result of our limited capabilities. The innocent children who were tortured when invaders destroyed the Sanctuary did nothing to deserve that fate. During this time, we grieve the losses that unfairly bring suffering to our lives.

In a time of grief, there is permission to experience and express sadness, fear, rage, vulnerability, powerlessness, and other feelings. We struggle with hopelessness, self-blame, and guilt. We do not attempt to deny, minimize, or avoid facing the realities of our situation. We do not attempt to reflect on our situation, figure out how to cope, or overcome the problems. We do not even attempt to console ourselves or find hope. Similar to the days of *shiva* after someone has died, we sit with the pain rather than try to avoid it or fix it. Later on, during the Days of Awe, in the next part of the yearly cycle, we focus on self-improvement and discovering new ways to cope. However, before one can begin to engage in that process, time is needed simply to grieve.

THE PROCESS OF GRIEF IN RITUAL, STORY, AND SYMBOLS: FACING REALITIES AND VOICING FEELINGS

How can I possibly have come so far, and yet still have so far to go?

© Ashleigh Brilliant

Grief begins with acknowledgment of the realities. Fearing that the pain may be too overwhelming, we may not acknowledge our losses even to ourselves, or we may distance ourselves from our feelings. In the agricultural cycle of the Holy Land, the climate at this time of year fits the mood. The summer is a time of no rain, hot sun, and desert heat that is relentless and oppressive. The ground is parched and scorched and cannot sustain life; all vegetation withers away, and nothing can grow.

Ritual Enactment

The customs associated with this time of year parallel many of the practices associated with the period of mourning after the loss of a close relative. The seventeenth of Tammuz is a fast day: one refrains from eating and drinking from sunrise to sunset. Special penitential prayers are included in the regular daily services. The three weeks that follow are marked by restrictions on celebrations and joyousness: no weddings are held. We traditionally refrain from public entertainment such as movies and swimming; we do not cut our hair. Beginning on the first day of Av, there are additional restrictions: we do not eat meat as a further sign of mourning.

The ninth of Av is also a fast day. In addition to abstaining from eating and drinking, we also do not engage in sexual intercourse, nor do we wear leather shoes; we also refrain from washing and from using oils and perfumes. The ninth of Av is the one day in the Jewish year when study of the Torah is also prohibited because study is viewed as a joyful activity. One is allowed to study only those tractates of the Talmud that describe the destruction of the Sanctuary.

On the eve of the ninth of Av, we read the book of Lamentations, the prophet Jeremiah's grief-filled description of the destruction of the Sanctuary and exile. The text is read with a special mournful melody to the light of candles. In the custom of mourners, we sit on the floor rather than in chairs. The curtain is removed from the ark which holds the Torah as a further sign of our anguish. Following the reading of the book of Lamentations, we recite *kinot,* expressions of sorrow written through the generations to mark Jewish suffering and misfortune. During the morning prayers, as a sign of sadness, one does not put on the tallit and *tefillin* because these ritual garments are considered to be adornments inappropriate to the experience of loss. Additional *kinot* are recited as well.

During the three weeks, as we tell the stories of our tragedies, our connection is not solely intellectual and abstract but visceral and emotional. We see ourselves and connect to our own grief as we tell the stories of the golden calf and the breaking of the tablets, of the spies' report and the Israelites rebellion, of the destruction of the Sanctuary and the exile of the Jews, and of tragedies through the generations. These stories invite us to recall and tell the stories of death, failure, and loss that we experience and may not otherwise allow ourselves to acknowledge.

The Golden Calf

The Israelites had direct experience of God, first in Egypt, then by the sea, and finally standing at Mt. Sinai. They made a commitment by saying, "We will do, and we will listen." According to the *midrash,* the lowliest among the people experienced more than any prophet or mystic of succeeding generations.

Nonetheless, that enlightenment was fragile and incomplete. According to tradition, the Israelites were overwhelmed by the intensity of revelation. They were unable to receive the entire Torah directly. In the Torah text, the Israelites received only the Ten Commandments directly from God. According to tradition, their experience of revelation was limited to hearing the first letter of the first of the Ten Commandments, the letter *aleph,* a vowel with no sound. Their faith was insufficient to sustain their initial commitment. As soon as Moses disappeared, they became insecure. Moses ascended to the top of Mount Sinai for forty days while the Israelites waited below. Despite the moment of ecstatic experience, they became distrustful:

> And when the people saw that Moses delayed in coming down from the mountain, they gathered themselves together around Aaron and said to him, "Rise up and make for us a god who will go before us, because we do not know what has become of this man Moses who has taken us up out of the land of Israel. . . .
> And all the people broke off their golden rings which were in their ears, and brought them to Aaron. And he received it from their hands and fashioned it into a molten calf; and, they pro-

claimed, "This is your god, O Israel, which brought you up out
of the land of Egypt."

[Exodus 32:1–4]

The failure of the Israelites has consequences. When Moses
returned, he was angered by the people's lack of faith; he smashed
the tablets. The people were stricken with a plague. Our experience
is mirrored in the story of the Israelites. We understand, we commit
ourselves, but we are unable to sustain that commitment on our
own. The story validates the tentativeness of our own commitments
and the consequences that occur when we fail in our trust.

The Spies

As the Israelites approached the land of Israel, Moses sent twelve
spies, a representative from each tribe, to journey to Canaan and
report back to the people. When they returned, they confirmed that
the land was a beautiful, fertile place, a land of "milk and honey."
However, the spies, except for Joshua and Caleb, also frightened the
Israelites, predicting that they would be unable to conquer the land
of Canaan:

> *And they spread an evil report of the land which they had spied*
> *out unto the children of Israel, saying: The land through which*
> *we have passed to spy it out, is a land that eats its inhabitants,*
> *and all the people that we saw in it are men of great stature.*
> *And we saw there the Nephilim, the sons of Anak, who come*
> *of the Nephilim; and we were in our own sight as grasshoppers,*
> *and so we were in their sight. . . .*
>
> *And all the congregation lifted up their voices, and cried, the*
> *people wept that night. And all the children of Israel mur-*
> *mured against Moses and against Aaron; and the whole con-*
> *gregation said to them: Would that we had died in the land of*
> *Egypt! Or would we had died in this wilderness! And why does*
> *the Lord bring us unto this land, to fall by the sword? Our*
> *wives and our little ones will be a prey; were it not better for*
> *us to return to Egypt?*
>
> [Numbers 13:27–14:3]

The Israelites lost faith. They forgot the miracles of the plagues in Egypt, the moment at Sinai, and the sustenance in the desert. Caleb and Joshua attempted to convince them to trust in God, but they were unsuccessful.

The story of the spies speaks to the human experience in which a loss of faith leads to passivity or withdrawal. "I could never change my job." "There's nothing I can do about my bad back." We do not believe something is possible; consequently, we make no effort to achieve the goal. God's decree expresses this principle:

> You said that your children will be taken captive, but they will be the ones I will bring there, so that they will know the land that you rejected. You, however, will fall as corpses in the desert. . . . The punishment shall parallel the number of days you spent exploring the land. There were forty days, and there shall be one year for each day, a total of forty years.
>
> [Numbers 14:31–34]

The Israelites realized their mistake, but it was too late. God did not relent. This story parallels the moments in our own lives when realization comes too late. In contrast to the story of the golden calf, the consequences are not always reversible. Sometimes our opportunities are lost.

Destruction of the Sanctuary

While they were still in the desert, God warned the people that living in the land of Israel is conditional: they will be able to live in the land only when they follow in the path of righteousness:

> If you act corruptly and make a graven image in the shape of any thing, and do what is evil in the sight of the Lord your God, so as to provoke God's anger, I call heaven and earth to witness against you today, that you will soon utterly perish from off the land which you are going over the Jordan to possess; you will not prolong your days upon it, but will be utterly destroyed. And the Lord will scatter you among the peoples; and you will be left few in number among the nations, where the Lord will lead you away. And there you will serve man-

*made gods of wood and stone, that neither see nor hear, nor
eat, nor smell.*

[Deuteronomy 4:25-28]

According to the rabbis, the second Sanctuary was destroyed
because the Jews were hateful toward one another. When the
Israelites fail to keep their commitments to live according to the
Torah, the prophet warns them that they face consequences. We read
his words on the three Sabbaths before the ninth of Av:

*The celebration of your new moons and your holy days, my
soul despises. They are a burden to me and they make me
weary. When you raise your hands up, I will hide my eyes from
you. When you speak prayers, I will not hear them; your hands
are filled with blood. Wash yourselves, make yourselves clean;
put away your evil ways from before my eyes, cease to do evil.
Learn to do well, seek justice, relieve the oppressed, judge the
fatherless, plead for the widow.*

[Isaiah 1:14–17]

The warnings are ignored. The seventeenth of Tammuz marks the
beginning of the siege of Jerusalem before the destruction of both
the first and second Sanctuaries. On the first day of Av, the attack-
ers break through the walls of the city. On the ninth day of the
month, they overcome the last Israelite resistance and occupy the
Sanctuary. The Sanctuary is destroyed. This moment is described in
the *Selichot,* the penitential prayers recited on the fast day:

*The enemies destroyed our Sanctuary, and the divine Presence
fled from the corner of the Palace, and we were betrayed into
the hands of the wicked to be consumed,*

*We were scattered from city to city, and our old and young
were taken captive; our city was destroyed, and set on fire.*

Kalir, a poet from the seventh century, writes this description of
the horrors experienced by the Jews at the time of the destruction of
the Sanctuary:

*When women could devour their own offspring, the children of
     their tender care*
*When compassionate women could boil their own children
     that were so carefully nurtured*
*When the tresses of their heads could be cut off, and tied as
     adornments upon the enemy's fleet horses*
*When the tongue of the infant could cleave to his palate
     through parching thirst*
*When one woman could moan to another: "Come let us boil
     our shrieking children"*
*When the flesh of fathers were prepared as food for their chil-
     dren in caves and ditches*[1]

The Sanctuary is not yet rebuilt. Although we once again live in
Israel and Jerusalem, this story is still unfolding. There is not yet
peace. We struggle with conflict, hatred, war, death, and suffering.
It is up to us to bring a positive resolution. In contrast to the stories
of the golden calf and the spies, the story of the exile from the land
of Israel allows us to identify with those tragedies in our own lives
that have not yet been resolved. As we speak the details of the
tragedy that happened to us long ago, we also recall and speak the
details of the tragedies and losses in our own lives.

We do not only remember the events. We also connect with the
feelings. In the liturgy of the ninth of Av, we find a variety of emotions expressed as the prophet Jeremiah responds to the tragedy of
the destruction of the Sanctuary:

Sadness: My eyes are spent with tears, my spirits are troubled; My
     heart is poured out in grief over the destruction of the
     daughter of my people, while infants and babies faint in the
     streets of the city. (2:11)

Despair: Indeed, he has made my teeth grind on gravel, and made
     me cower in ashes. And my soul is far removed from peace,
     I have forgotten what happiness is. So I said: "Gone is my
     strength, and my expectation from the Lord." (3:16–18)

Loneliness: For these things I weep, my eyes shed tears,; For the
     one who might comfort me is far away; My children are des-
     olate, for the enemy has prevailed. (1:16)

Regret: The Lord is righteous, for I have rebelled against his word; Listen, I pray, all you peoples and behold my pain; My maidens and youths have gone into captivity. (1:18)

Guilt: Who has commanded and it came to pass, unless the Lord ordained it? Is it not by command of the Most High, that good and evil come? Why should a living man complain when punished for his sins. Let us search and examine our ways, and return to the Lord. Let us lift up our heart and hands to God in heaven. We have transgressed and rebelled. (3:37–42)

Blaming: Our fathers have sinned and are no more, and we have borne their iniquities. (5:7)

Rage: Behold, O Lord! See whom you have afflicted! Whether it be women devouring their own offspring, those whom they tenderly held, or, the priest and prophet slain in the Sanctuary of the Lord. (2:20)

Vengefulness: Pay them back, O Lord, according to the work of their hands. Give them a weakness of heart, may your curse be upon them. Pursue them in anger, and destroy them from under the heavens, O Lord. (3:64–66)

Pleading: Restore us to you, O Lord, that we may be restored! Renew our days as of old. (5:23)

Hope: The kindnesses of the Lord never cease! God's mercies never fail! They are new every morning; great is your faithfulness. "The Lord is my portion," says my soul. "Therefore will I hope in God." (3:22–24)

According to tradition, it is said that the *Shechina,* the feminine aspect of God's Presence, descends into exile with the Jews, accompanying us wherever we go. God is present as witness—listening, empathizing, and acknowledging the truth of the pain. In the working through of grief, we need the presence of another who can allow for the expression of grief in whatever form it takes.

The feelings that Jeremiah expresses offer a mirror for us to know our feelings as well. This connection is enhanced insofar as the images embedded in the readings and prayers repeatedly use metaphors from the human experience: the loss of the Sanctuary is compared to the experience of a woman who is widowed at a young age, to a mother whose child dies an untimely death, and to similar images. Our shattered dreams are also our children, some of which never grow to maturity, victims of an untimely death. As we allow ourselves to experience our losses fully, we begin a rocky journey through feelings of guilt, regret, sadness, fear, rage, vulnerability, powerlessness, despair, resignation, and depression, each in its own measure. There is no formula for what to feel, how to express it, or how much time is needed. We need the Presence of the *Shechina* who listens, empathizes with, and acknowledges our experience.

This quality of presence during this time of grief is different than what we experience at other times in the cycle of life. At Pesach, God

intervenes to free the Israelites and prevent their destruction in slavery. God is compared to a nurturing parent who provides the infant with protection, safety, and nurturance. During the three weeks, we do not experience God as a redeemer, but God does sit with us in our suffering and acknowledge the depth of our hurt. At Shavuot, God offers us revelation, new insight, and understanding. During the three weeks, the task is not to make sense of our experience. On the ninth of Av, we are not even allowed to study. During the Days of Awe, the next stop in the cycle through the year, we are encouraged to engage in self-reflection and make changes in how we respond. During the three weeks, we do not focus on self-improvement. We need time to sit with the loss, without trying to fix it, understand it, or take responsibility for our part in creating it.

According to Shneur Zalman (*Likutei Torah,* 96B), God sees our pain and responds; our tears cause God's Presence to flow down to us. Even when the gates of prayer are locked, the gates of tears are never closed. Having time to sit with grief is intrinsically healing. Experiencing and expressing the feelings reduces the tension and allows us to continue living.

THE PSYCHOLOGICAL PERSPECTIVE: A CLINICAL EXAMPLE OF THE GRIEVING PROCESS

Rabbi Meizlish of Cracow was a well-to-do merchant as well as a scholar. When his students learned that the rabbi's fortune was lost in one day as a result of a shipwreck, they wanted to break the news gently. One of his favorite students came to him with a question about a passage in the Talmud: "It says that we are to thank God for the evil that befalls us as well as for the good. How can this be done?" The rabbi explained the matter in terms of its hidden meaning, clarifying how every crisis is an opportunity for learning, how we do not always understand the ultimate result of what seems to be a tragedy in the moment. The student then replied, "And if my rabbi were to learn that all his ships had been wrecked, would he dance for joy?" The rabbi said, "Yes, of course!" "Well, then," responded the student, "you can dance—all of your ships are lost!" The rabbi fainted. When he came to, he admitted, "Now, I confess I no longer understand this passage in the Talmud."

This process of grief is illustrated in the experience of Bruce who initiated therapy when he began to experience periodic episodes of pain in his chest. Bruce grew increasingly concerned that he was developing heart disease, but his physician conducted a thorough evaluation and assured him that no medical condition appeared to be causing his symptoms. He suggested that the pain might be caused by stress and advised Bruce to seek counseling.

When Bruce explained his situation to me, I asked him if he was aware of any tensions. He talked about some dissatisfaction with work but did not regard the problems as very significant. He also mentioned to me that his father had died when he was 11 years old; however, he was not aware of any obvious connection between this trauma and the current problem. Bruce showed no emotion in talking about the death of his father. Had he come to terms with events from long ago? Or was he somehow cut off from his feelings?

I asked him to tell me more of the details surrounding his father's death. In bits and pieces the story emerged. His father had been stricken with cancer. The disease progressed quickly; he died sixth months after contracting the disease. Bruce's mother remarried shortly after the death of his father; they moved to a new town; he was adopted by his new father and took on his last name. His biological father was never mentioned. There were no pictures of his father in the new house. He did not even know the date of his father's death. He had few memories of his childhood and no memories of the events around the time his father died. I felt sad and angry as I heard his story. I shared my feelings with Bruce. He told me he experienced no feelings as he talked about his childhood.

I asked Bruce about his lack of feeling. Bruce acknowledged that something seemed missing. His new father had been uncomfortable with the notion of being a stepparent. To ease the awkwardness, his mother tried to remove all traces of her first husband from the house. In the process, Bruce had been denied time for normal grief. Bruce's wife sometimes complained about his lack of emotion. Was there a connection? And how could he make himself feel? I suggested that he might begin by doing some research, trying to learn more about the events of his childhood.

Bruce began asking questions of his family, using their memories to fill in the blanks in his own recollections. An aunt, with whom he had not communicated in years, told him the date of his father's death. She also provided him with the date of his father's birthday. Bruce came to therapy, excited with the new information. His father died at the age of 38. Bruce was approaching his 38th birthday. Perhaps his anxiety about death was somehow connected. Could he unconsciously have known his father's age at death?

Over time, fragments of his own memories emerged—an image of his father in a wheelchair, a teacher asking him why he looked so glum. And with the memories came feelings, first in a trickle, then in a flood. One afternoon, while mowing his lawn, he suddenly recalled the first time he mowed the lawn after his father was taken ill. As he told me of his memory, his eyes became puffy and he began to cry. Then he was sobbing. I sat next to him and held his hand. I did not attempt to analyze him or intellectualize in any way. He cried for what seemed like an eternity, though it was only fifteen minutes by the clock. After he regained his composure, he was still teary, but he felt relieved and satisfied to have found his tears.

Through months of therapy, he slowly and steadily took time to grieve. More and more memories emerged, sometimes evoked by commonplace events of daily life, sometimes by dreams. He brought these memories to our sessions, took time to tell me the stories and feel the feelings. His original symptoms occurred less and less frequently. Bruce had indeed been suffering from heartache. As the tears flowed, the tension dissolved.

GRIEF AS A HEALING RESPONSE TO POWERLESSNESS

We need time to express grief when we experience a loss. Grief is normal and necessary. When we do not have the opportunity to grieve, we can, like Bruce, literally make ourselves sick. This healing quality that emerges from the expression of grief is described by Clark Moustakas (1961), a psychologist who has written extensively on the subject of loneliness. Moustakas describes the experience of being with his daughter while she was hospitalized as a child:

> I noticed a slight tensing, her arms pulled away from her body, the fingers twisted and extended. Her entire body grew rigid. She went into a series of jerky, stretching movements—contortions—convulsions—grotesque and terrifying. Immediately I realized she was having a brain seizure. Her entire being was in a state of extreme agitation. She began biting her tongue. I slipped a pencil in her mouth, shouted for the nurse, and urged

that the surgeon be called immediately. The nurse looked in briefly and left. I stroked Kerry's hair and whispered her name, but each time I touched her she moved away with violent, gross movements. I had to hold her body because she twisted and turned so violently there was danger she would fall off the bed. In those moments I experienced indescribable loneliness and fear and shock. In some measure my body writhed with Kerry's. I paced, and stretched, and turned as I witnessed the seizure. The most intolerable feeling was the realization that she was beyond my reach, beyond my voice and touch. She was in pitiful plight—entirely by herself. She was without anyone or anything. I tried to commune with her. I whispered her name softly, gently, over and over again. "Kerry, Kerry. Kerry, my darling. It's Daddy. I'm here right beside you. I won't leave. Kerry, I'm here. Kerry. Kerry. Kerry." She opened her eyes. A horrible sound issued from her throat—then several more utterances of anguish and pain and fear.

At last the surgeon arrived, took one look, and shouted to the nurse, "Brain edema. I'll have to give her a shot of glucose." The word "Shot" struck the center of her terror. She tried to form words to speak, but no sound came; she shook violently in an effort to scream out an alarm. Then came an instinctual cry, emitted from deep within her being, a cry of raving terror followed by excruciating moans. . . . The doctor asked me to leave but I refused; I knew I had to stay whatever happened. Kerry's eyes were wide and fitful. . . . I held her arms as the surgeon inserted the needle again. She looked at me with utter contempt and hatred. Her eyes were full of pain and accusation. I whispered, "I know how much it hurts." I could feel her pain and terror in my own nerves and bones and tissues and blood, but at the same time I knew in that moment no matter how fervently I lived through it with her, how much I wanted to share it with her, I knew, she was alone, beyond my reach. I wanted so much for her to feel my presence, but she could not. She was beyond my call, beyond the call of anyone. It was her situation in a world entirely and solely her own. There was nothing further I could do. Each time she screamed her voice ripped through me, penetrating deeply into my inner being. . . .

> *Starting with these experiences before and during the hospital-*
> *ization, I began to discover the meaning of loneliness. I began*
> *to see that loneliness is neither good nor bad, but a point of*
> *intense and timeless awareness of the Self, a beginning which*
> *initiates totally new sensitivities and awareness, and which*
> *results in bringing a person deeply in touch with his own exis-*
> *tence and in touch with others in a fundamental sense. I began*
> *to see that in the deepest experiences the human being can*
> *know—the birth of a baby, the prolonged illness or death of a*
> *loved relative, the loss of a job, the creation of a poem, a paint-*
> *ing, a symphony, the grief of a fire, a flood, an accident—each*
> *in its own way touches upon the roots of loneliness. In each of*
> *these experiences, in the end, we must go alone.*
>
> *In such experiences, inevitably one is cut off from human com-*
> *panionship. But experiencing a solitary state gives the individ-*
> *ual the opportunity to draw upon untouched capacities and*
> *resources and to realize himself in an entirely unique manner.*
> *It can be a new experience. It may be an experience of exquis-*
> *ite pain, deep fear and terror, an utterly terrible experience, yet*
> *it brings into awareness new dimensions of self, new beauty,*
> *new power for human compassion, and a reverence for the pre-*
> *cious nature of each breathing moment.*[2]

As a child learns to ride a bike, there is a time for words of advice and caution, for coaching the child on how to ride. But when the child takes a fall and comes crying with bloody knees, a wise parent knows that the time for advice and admonition can come only after the child is comforted. A wise parent offers open arms, hugs, reassurance, and tenderness. Once the child is comforted, the wound is cleaned, and the bandage applied, once the child regains composure, then one can figure out what to do. One can assess whether the bike is defective, consider whether the child needs more instruction, or discuss why it might not be a good idea to try to ride over that curb.

Death is woven into the fabric of life. No one can avoid loss. Not only do we experience death of those who we love, we must also face our own mortality. The cycle of our lives are further punctuated by endings: taking leave of relationships, jobs, residence, and the developmental changes in childhood and adult life. The three weeks offer us time and space to recall the tragedies, the losses, the frustrations, and the failures. The three weeks offer us time to experience and express the feelings associated with that grief.

For many Jews, the fast of Tisha B'Av seems inappropriate because the state of Israel has been reestablished. How can we grieve the destruction of Jerusalem when we can stand once again at the western wall? However, we have not rebuilt the Sanctuary, a dwelling place for God on earth. Although the state of Israel has been reestablished, the exile and its impact continues to affect us as a community, a religion, and members of an extended family. Our land is filled with strife and tension. In our own lives, the world is not yet whole. The Messianic era has not yet come. There is much to grieve and much that is still in disrepair.

FROM GRIEF TO CONSOLATION

Although it is vital that we give time, space, and energy to express our grief, it is also important that we not remain stuck in our grief. We also need to maintain hope, optimism, and commitment to our future. The shift from grief to consolation is illustrated in the experience of Yael who initiated therapy after trying unsuccessfully for three years to conceive a child. For eighteen months, she had tried *in vitro* fertilization. Each month was an emotional roller coaster as she endured the pain of invasive medical procedures to harvest her eggs, fertilize them in a test tube, and then reimplant them. This was followed by a time of anxious waiting, and then grief when the egg failed to implant. Yael was highly motivated, intelligent, and persistent. She was determined to keep working. However, she knew she needed more support as she worked through the grief that she experienced each month. Her husband was loving and supportive, but he coped by focusing on practical concerns and distanced himself when she expressed sadness. She felt that she had become a burden to her friends as well.

As we worked together, we discovered what Yael needed as she coped with each stage of her monthly cycle: space and time to grieve. She did not need any problem solving or advice. She simply needed time to talk about her sadness, fear, frustration, and despair. She needed to know that I cared. After several months, she came for a session just before a trip to the clinic. The doctors once again were going to implant a fertilized egg. She talked about how frustrated she felt. She expressed some anger at one of the doctors who had failed to return a phone call and talked about how uncomfortable the procedure felt.

Yael looked at me, sat silent for a moment, and then asked, "Do you think this is ever going to work? Will I be able to have a baby?"

I was flustered for a moment. I did not quite know what to say. I am not a psychic. I cannot predict the future. I did not want to hold out false hope. I also did not want to discourage her. I was all too aware of how mental attitude can profoundly affect the body. How could I respond? In my heart, I felt hopeful about her situation, though I did not have any objective basis for that hope. "I don't have a crystal ball," I said, "and I can't speak as a medical doctor. But I can tell you that I feel optimistic. I don't know why, but I feel very hopeful that you will have your baby."

"Well, I don't feel hopeful," she replied. "I'm sick of this, and I've gone through it too many times."

I did not want to try to convince her to feel hope. I wanted to respect her grief; nonetheless, I could see, in her eyes, that my hope was somehow important. "Let's make a deal," I suggested. "I wouldn't expect you to feel hopeful after what you've been through, but I feel a lot of hope. So, how about if I hold onto the hope for you for a while?"

She smiled, and the tension went out of her face. She persisted; five months later, she conceived and gave birth to twins.

The balance between expressing grief and orienting ourselves with hope toward the future is embedded in the Jewish tradition. In the ritual associated with death, we take time to grieve and sit with our despair, but that time is also contained. After a death, there are prescribed times for mourning. We observe seven days of mourning, *shiva,* to take time to grieve the loss of a close relative. During that time, the mourner sits on a low stool, wears clothing that has been torn, and does not wear leather shoes. On the morning of the seventh day, the mourner goes through a transition. Although the mourner continues to grieve for an entire year, after seven days, one returns to the activities of daily life. I recall the sensitivity and gentleness with which a friend's family approached this moment. After the morning service on the seventh day, the rabbi invited the mourners to sit on regular chairs and put on their shoes. He poured everyone a *schnapps* so they could wish each other *le'chayim,* praying for life and health. Then he escorted us all outside, taking a short first walk around the block, beginning the return to life in the outside.

Tisha B'Av reminds us to allot time for comfort as well as for grief. In the same way that a mourner ends the week of mourning by returning to daily life, toward the end of the day of Tisha B'Av, we turn our attention outward. In the afternoon service, we put on the *tallit* and *tefillin,* adornments that we could not use in the morning. Our grief is softened as we listen to words of hope from the prophets, reminding us that healing will come from forces outside ourselves. We can hear the words even if we can not yet quite believe them or digest them. We allow God to hold the hope:

> *For as the rain and the snow come down from heaven, and return not thither but water the earth, making it bring forth and sprout, giving seed to the sower and bread to the eater, so shall my word be that goes forth from my mouth. . . . For you shall go out with joy, and be led forth in peace; the mountains and the hills shall break forth into singing before you, and all the trees of the field shall clap their hands. Instead of thorn shall come up the cypress; instead of the brier shall come up the myrtle; and it shall be to the Lord for a memorial, for an everlasting sign which shall not be cut off.*
>
> [Isaiah 55:10–13]

After the fast ends, it is customary to say the blessing for the new moon, a ritual that alludes to the Messianic era. According to tradition, the Messiah will be born on the ninth of Av, and the day of mourning eventually will be transformed into a day of celebration.

This theme of consolation and trust is expressed in the readings from the prophets for the next seven weeks on the Sabbath. The theme of consolation is also expressed in the stories of the golden calf, the spies, and the destruction of the Sanctuary. Misfortunes are never disastrous; the covenant between God and the Israelites is a pledge that adversity will always be overcome:

> But when you will seek there the Lord your God, if you will search with all your heart and with all your soul, you shall find God. When you are in distress, and all these things happen to you; then in the end of your days you will return to the Lord your God and hearken to God's voice. For the Lord your God is a merciful God, God will not fail you nor destroy you; and will not forget the covenant made with your ancestors which God swore to them.
>
> [Deuteronomy 4:27–29]

We experience the power of this pledge throughout history. After the breaking of the tablets, the Israelites are regretful. Moses intercedes with God on their behalf and once again ascends the mountain to receive the tablets: "God said to Moses, 'Carve out two tablets for yourself, just like the first ones. I will write on those tablets the same words that were on the first tablets that you broke' " (Exodus 33:1). This story affirms the possibility of being able to have a second chance, even after a failure that seemed devastating.

Similarly, in the story of the spies, despite the Israelites' lack of faith, they are not utterly destroyed. They suffer consequences. They are unable to enter the land of promise; nonetheless, the dream is not lost. Their children are able to complete the journey. In this same way, even when we suffer consequences, we can learn from our mistakes and continue in our journey.

Although we once again live in the land of Israel, the Sanctuary is yet to be rebuilt. In this uncompleted journey, we can find inspiration to sustain hope in our own lives for wounds that have not yet healed or crises that have not yet resolved: we can draw inspiration from our ancestors through the generations who sustained their hope for two thousand years of exile.

DIFFERENTIATING CONSTRUCTIVE GUILT FROM SELF-ABUSIVE GUILT

One of the worst of my many faults is that I'm too critical of myself.

© Ashleigh Brilliant

In responding to grief, one often experiences guilt, holding oneself accountable for the tragedy in some way. Sometimes the sense of guilt is a constructive, courageous, and honest effort to take responsibility for ways in which we have contributed to the negative outcome. This kind of guilt allows us to change our responses in the future. There are other times when the sense of guilt is self-abusive, a destructive distortion of reality. This self-abusive guilt may protect us from experiencing feelings that are overwhelming, or self-criticism can help us contain rage that may be unsafe to communicate to those who have hurt us. We do not initially realize that we are being self-abusive; we perceive ourselves as simply telling the truth. In this situation, we need help to identify the self-abusive quality, understand the fears that prevent us from feeling the underlying emotions, and build enough safety to abandon the primitive protection.

Constructive Guilt

It may appear paradoxical for the enlightenment of revelation at Shavuot to be followed so quickly by the catastrophe and misfortune associated with the three weeks. However, upon deeper examination, the sequence accurately reflects the reality of human experience. In the process of growth and development, an initial moment of intuitive discovery does not translate immediately into a new reality. Sometimes, the new understanding may only serve to heighten awareness of the discrepancy between the possibility and the all too painful reality of current life.

The stories of the three weeks speak to the difficulty of translating our commitments into action. The intuitions and insights, the peak experiences, and the moments of clarity help us know our path. We fully intend to act on the basis of those understandings.

However, we fail in our efforts. Events overwhelm us. We forget our promises, reacting in the moment. Our insights are lost or overpowered by our primitive habits. The tablets are broken; we do not enter the promised land; the Sanctuary is destroyed, and we are exiled. This crisis carries a seed of opportunity because the shock can motivate us to change.

Constructive guilt is exemplified by Lucille's experience. Lucille's partner was a very likable man. He loved her. He had a wonderful sense of humor. They had fun together. However, he was horribly irresponsible with regard to money. He was successful in his work and had a stable job, but he was unable to control his spending. He gambled compulsively. He ran up large balances on his credit cards. He often threw out bills or let them pile up on his desk. He had failed to file taxes for the last three years. In a crisis, he turned to gambling hoping that he would have a lucky streak. As a result, his life was in constant turmoil with creditors pursuing him. When he turned to Lucille for help, she was unable to say no. She had given him thousands of dollars to bail him out of various difficulties.

Lucille wanted to set limits. She knew that she only reinforced his irresponsibility when she rescued him; however, she lost her determination when her refusal to provide needed funds could result in his being jailed. She was not deceived by his promises that this would be the last time, that he had learned his lesson, that he would cut up his credit cards and learn to manage his finances; nonetheless, he was very convincing, and she wanted to believe him. In the end, each time, she capitulated. Lucille's own financial health was threatened as a result. She was unable to save and found herself scrimping even on necessities.

My efforts to help Lucille learn to set limits were singularly unsuccessful. I tried everything I could imagine to help. We analyzed the patterns in the relationship. I carefully outlined the ways in which her attempts to rescue Frank only reinforced his irresponsibility. We examined her finances and computed exactly how much money she had given him. We discussed what the loss of that money meant for her own life. We brainstormed alternative ways for her to set limits when he came to her for money. She made agreements with me to stop giving in to him. In spite of our intentions, nothing worked.

Finally, Lucille was forced to face up to the realities of Frank's problem. Against her own best judgment, she lent Frank her bank card. Over a period of a month, unbeknownst to her, he withdrew the maximum each day in order to pay off a debt. She bounced several checks, including her mortgage payment. She received a threatening letter from the bank. She had no reserve and was unable to pay her obligations.

Like Lucille, we may have cognitive awareness of our situation and how we need to respond; nonetheless, the cognitive awareness is, in itself, not strong enough to prevail. For example, in working with addictions, there is a recognition that change may result only when a person "hits bottom." Unfortunately, it sometimes takes a disaster, or a near-disaster, for a person to come to terms with changes. The alcoholic cannot be "rescued" by warnings or admonitions. Sometimes, change occurs only when the alcoholic is arrested for drunkenness, loses a job, destroys a marriage, or begins to suffer health problems. Trying to protect the person from experiencing the consequences of one's actions only reinforces the dysfunctional behavior. In these situations, the only road to change is to allow the worst to occur and hope that the person will finally acknowledge the reality of the situation. At this moment, the response changes. Sitting with the pain, the grief, and the tears may be the beginning of real change.

Freud also believed that cognitive insight was not enough, in itself, to facilitate change. He believed that insights required a working through in which the person gradually integrates that understanding with time and effort. Ernest Rossi's (1993) model of state-dependent learning is also helpful in understanding this process. In one part of the brain, we may gain insight and make commitment to a new way of being. Nonetheless, when stress occurs, it activates a different part of one's brain, deactivating the part that has the more evolved understanding. We fall back to a more primitive pattern of response and act on that basis.

Jewish Images of Self-Abusive Guilt

The Rabbi refused to ask God for forgiveness for his sins. "Why should I ask God for forgiveness? I did not ask to be born into this world he created. I did not create this world filled with darkness, suffering, and misery. I struggle my best to address that pain, to ameliorate the suffering, and bring light in the darkness. No, I will not ask God for forgiveness for my failures. It is God who should ask me for forgiveness. And, I will forgive God this year, give God another chance, and agree to work again in hopes that God will do better next year.

Although it is important to be willing to reflect on our own behaviors and to take responsibility for ways in which we have contributed to difficulties, we must be equally vigilant to identify and confront external forces that also contribute to difficulties. We are tempted, at times, to try to avoid facing tragedy that makes no sense, to hold back from confronting God for the pain of human suffering, seeking solace instead in self-accusation. The stories of our ancestors mirror our own, making us aware of the tendency to avoid the grief with inappropriate self-blame, validating the need to confront authority, and modeling responsiveness by those in authority to challenge.

The Golden Calf

In the incident of the golden calf, after Moses breaks the tablets, God threatens to destroy the people:

God then said to Moses, "I have observed the people, and they are a stubborn group. Do not try to stop Me when I unleash my wrath against them to destroy them. I will then make you into a great nation."

[Exodus 31:9]

Moses does not passively accept God's decree, nor is he intimidated by God. He resists being seduced by a promise that offers him personal benefits. Instead, Moses challenges God:

Moses began to plead before God his Lord. He said, "O God why unleash your wrath against Your people, whom you

brought out of Egypt with great power and a show of force?
Why should Egypt then be able to say that You took them out
with evil intentions, to kill them in the hill country and wipe
them out from the face of the earth. Withdraw Your display of
anger, and refrain from doing evil to Your people."

[Exodus 31:10]

God responds. The threat is withdrawn, and Moses receives a new set of tablets. In this respect, the Torah validates the legitimacy of challenging authority, even when that authority is God. We can apply this teaching to our own lives, validating the legitimacy of our own challenges.

The Spies

In the story of the spies, a similar process occurs. When the Israelites lose faith and rebel, God once again threatens them, and Moses challenges God:

God said to Moses, "How long shall this nation continue to
provoke Me? How long will they not believe in Me, despite all
the miracles that I have done among them? I will kill them
with a plague and annihilate them. Then I will make you into
a greater, more powerful nation than they."

[Numbers 14:11–12]

Moses replied to God, . . . "Now, O God , is the time for You to
exercise even more restraint." You once declared, 'God is slow to
anger, great in love, and forgiving of sin and rebellion.'. . . With
Your great love, forgive the sin of this nation, just as You have
forgiven them from the time they left Egypt until now."

[Numbers 14:15–19]

God once again responds to the challenge and withdraws his threat. The legitimacy of Moses' challenge is again effective. We are provided with another validation for our own right to challenge authority that is overly rigid and punitive.

Destruction of the Sanctuary

In response to the destruction of the Sanctuary, the liturgy also includes similar challenges to God. In one of the *kinot* recited on the ninth of Av, Kalir describes a conversation in which the prophet Jeremiah goes to the burial sites of the ancestors and asks them to confront God. Each of them speaks:

> *Then all of them burst forth into lamentations over the loss of the children; they whispered in a voice of supplication before the one who dwells in heaven saying: "O what has become of the promise you made when you said 'I will remember for their sake the covenant with their ancestors?' "*. . .

> *Then Abraham, the father of the great multitudes cried for their sake, and implored the Presence of God on High: "In vain was I tested with ten trials for their sake, for behold, I now look on at their disaster! What has become of your promise when you said 'Fear not O Abram?' "*. . .

> *Next did Isaac cry out* . . . *"O what has become of the promise you made when you said, 'And I will establish my covenant with Isaac?' "*. . .

> *Jacob who was reared in the academy poured forth tears like the serpent's fountain, "My little ones, whom I nurtured and O how in a faint, alas, they are cut off from me by the butcher's knife, and how payment was demanded from me by shedding copious blood of many thousands"* . . .

> *The faithful shepherd Moses wallowing in ashes and dust, opened his lips and said: "The sheep that were tended in my bosom, alas! They are sheared before their time! O what of the promise: 'That Israel is not widowed?' "*

> *Leah, beating her breast, sobbed bitterly; her sister, Rachel, wept for her children, and Zilpah was bruising her face, while Bilhah wailed with both hands uplifted in grief.*
>
> [*Kinot* for Tisha B'Av[3]]

God initially tries to answer back to each of these challenges. However, as additional confrontations are made, God no longer continues to rationalize the destruction: "Return to your resting places, O perfect ones," the Divine Presence interjected; "I will surely fulfill your requests!" Again, the liturgy validates the justice and necessity for challenge of authority, providing us with a model that we can apply to parallel situations in our own lives, as well as an example for those in authority of how to respond.

A Clinical Example of Working through Self-Destructive Guilt

Shmuel commissioned a tailor to make him a suit. The suit was promised for delivery at the end of the week. The man appeared at the appointed time for his suit but was told, "It's not ready yet. Come back tomorrow." Shmuel was angry because he was leaving the next day on a trip that would take him away from home for a year. However, there was nothing to be done about it.

A year later, he returns to his home and goes to the tailor for his suit. "Come back in three days," the tailor responds. "It's almost ready." Shmuel is upset, but he knows the tailor is quite highly regarded. He returns in three days. He is delighted with the suit. It fits perfectly. Shmuel says to the tailor, "I have to admit this is a beautiful suit. I have never had a suit such as this. But I don't understand why it had to take so long. After all, God created heaven and earth in six days!" The tailor responded, "Look at this suit! See how perfect it is, how every seam is straight, how well it fits! Now look at the world!"

The work with Sally provides an example of the working through of self-destructive guilt. When Sally was stricken with cancer, she became very depressed. A veteran of years of therapy, she was certain that she had caused her own cancer, the result of being unable to work through and resolve the rage of her childhood. The disease itself was proof that she had failed and was guilty of the worst of sins. If only she could work harder, she was positive that the cancer would go into remission. And, as long as the cancer remained in her body, she took it as proof of her own guilt.

Sally's guilt offered her some sense of empowerment. If the cancer were caused by something she did, she could cure herself if she could only identify her failing and change. Her guilt allowed her to have some sense of power. In so doing, Sally avoided facing her powerlessness. In some situations, her habit of reflecting on her own actions was constructive; she was willing and able to admit mistakes and learn. However, in this situation, instead of helping herself, she became self-punitive, lacking compassion, tenderness, and patience for herself. As Sally realized her misguided self-reflection, she allowed herself to experience her grief more fully, to feel rage at her disease and fear at her powerlessness. She experienced this grief as relief.

Sally had grown up in a fundamentalist religious community. Although she had rebelled against its rigidity and intolerance, she had replicated some of its poisonous teaching, dressed up in a sophisticated new-age language that unfortunately paralleled the fire-and-brimstone threats of childhood. Sally remembered one situation in particular. A bully had attacked her on the playground. She came home to her mother in tears; she was angry and hurt. Her mother was not sympathetic: she reminded Sally that the best response to violence was to "turn the other cheek." She discounted Sally's claims that the attack had been unprovoked and unwarranted. Surely Sally had done something to provoke the attack. She sent Sally to her room to pray for forgiveness and think about what she had done wrong.

As she told this story, Sally became angry. She realized that she never felt angry with anyone after that day; she always assumed that if something went wrong, it was her fault. I asked Sally to imagine her mother sitting in the room. Now she could express her anger. Sally spoke to her with a strength in her voice that I had never heard before. "You didn't listen to me. You taught me to turn the other cheek when I needed to learn to fight back. Do you know the result of your poison? I have allowed myself to be hurt again and again when I should have fought back. You were vicious with me because you were scared of anger. I deserved better than that!"

As Sally developed the capacity to feel and express anger, she discovered that there were several situations in her life where she became overly self-critical when she was, in truth, justifiably angry with someone else. One of the technicians at the hospital where she had chemotherapy was consistently rude. One day she confronted him. He failed to respond. She complained to a supervisor and arranged to have someone else work with her.

A Psychological Perspective on Working Through of Self-Destructive Guilt

Alice Miller (1986, 1990), a Swiss psychoanalyst, has written extensively on the tendency to avoid grief and anger by focusing on self-destructive guilt. According to Miller, a traumatized and abused child does not want to view an adult who is supposed to provide love and nurturance as the cause of pain. The child desperately seeks to find a way to avoid that truth. Believing oneself to be the cause provides some relief. If the abuse can be perceived as just punishment for some failure, faith can be maintained.

When the survivor stops the denial, grief is experienced as the impact and effects of the trauma become conscious. The result is not only re-experiencing the feelings that may have been denied or repressed in the past but also feeling the effects of the learned patterns on the rest of one's life. Out of this realization, the victim begins to acknowledge what was done and to feel appropriate rage with the perpetrator of violence.

Miller hypothesizes that Freud's theory of oedipal conflict was an example of inappropriate, self-abusive guilt. She suggests that Freud himself was in denial and unable to assimilate the truth. Unable to acknowledge the validity of patients' reports of incest, he mistakenly concluded that the feelings were the results of internal fantasies and feelings rather than the residues of violence.

When our pain and powerlessness are denied or distorted, when we cut ourselves off from the truth of our feelings about these adversities, we place ourselves in danger of failing to recognize and address difficulties in the present and future. A person who was beaten as a child and fails to acknowledge the violence and its effects may unconsciously do the same to his or her child. In facing the challenge of acknowledging that violence and its effects, one can recognize it in the future and exercise more choice. For the cycle of violence to stop, we must not only end the denial of that violence and its effects, we must also begin to appreciate how that violence has been transmitted generation to generation.

The stories of Tisha B'Av are not only archetypal events that allow us to make sense of our lives; they are also the stories of our family history. Tisha B'Av offers us a chance to revisit the traumas of our forebears and reflect on ways in which we carry the scars of their suffering in our lives. Roberto Assagioli (1945) wrote a paper about the Jewish community shortly after World War II. He describes how the various subgroups in the culture have been affected by the Holocaust. Each subgroup has coped in a different way; each looks to a different solution as a way to overcome the tragedy and protect themselves for the future. Some return to religious practice; some commit themselves to political idealism; some emphasize tribal self-protection; some focus on personal well-being; some take a universalistic perspective. Each perceives the others as misguided and a threat. As a result, the community dissolves into conflict rather than respond to one another as part of a common group. The senseless hate that still haunts our community has its roots in the past. When that pain is acknowledged, we can begin to free ourselves from the effects in the present day.

Differentiating Constructive Guilt from Destructive Guilt

William Glasser (1965) compares the use of punishment with the experience of natural, logical consequences of one's actions. A punishment is an arbitrary infliction of pain, designed to control behavior through fear and hurt, exemplified by a parent who spanks a child for failing to clean up a mess. In contrast, allowing a child to experience the consequences of one's actions is not punitive but rather enables the child to learn something about the world, about cause and effect. In the same way as a child learns about gravity by dropping objects and seeing how they fall, a child also may learn when a parent allows the child to experience natural consequences. For example, a parent may choose to ignore the mess. Struggling to find things, the child may eventually decide to keep the room more orderly. The parent may also set up logical consequences to help the child learn. For example, the parent may temporarily remove toys that are not put away. The parent helps the child realize that toys may be lost or broken if they are not returned to their proper place.

We can read the stories of Tisha B'Av with two contradictory perspectives: we can view our ancestors as learning from the experience of the consequences of their mistakes, or we can view them as struggling to challenge the punitive harshness of a God who is acting unjustly. The same stories that can exemplify constructive guilt can also exemplify dysfunctional guilt. How are we to know the difference? The ambiguity of the stories and the possibility for such divergent interpretations parallels the ambiguity we experience in making sense of the events of our own lives.

For example, Alice Miller (1991) reads Jeremiah's laments as the prophet's unsuccessful attempt to find comfort in the thought that the tragedies he has experienced are a just and necessary punishment for his sins:

> The kindness of the Lord will never cease; God's mercies will never fail. They are new every morning; great is your faithfulness. "The Lord is my portion," says my soul, "Therefore, I will find hope in you." The Lord is good to those who wait, to the soul who seeks you. It is good that one should wait quietly for the salvation of the Lord. It is good for a man to bear the yoke of youth. . . . Who can command and have it come to pass if not the Lord? Is it not by the command of the Most High that good and evil come? Why should a living man complain for the punishment of his sins?
>
> [Lamentations 3:22–27, 37–39]

However, Miller fails to note that the prophet's self-blame is not the only feeling expressed. He also repeatedly expresses the simple truth of his pain:

Slaves rule over us, and there is no one to deliver us from their
hands. With peril to our lives, we find bread because of the
sword of the desert. Our skin is parched as if by a furnace,
because of the heat of our hunger. They have outraged women
in Zion and virgins in the cities of Judah. . . . For Mount Zion
lies desolate, and foxes prowl over it. But, you, O Lord remain
forever, your Throne endures through the generations. Why
have you forgotten us forever, forsaken us for so many days?

[Lamentations 5:7]

We walk a delicate balance between the images of responsibility
and the images of compassion. On the one hand, we have the image
of a just God who caused the destruction of the Sanctuary and the
exile because the Jews failed in their mission, forsaking the principles
of the Torah. The Israelites were deprived of the opportunity to enter
the land of Israel because they did not trust they could achieve their
goal. It is important to realize that our failures have consequences. If
we lack trust, we will not be able to achieve our goals. The Sanctuary
is destroyed because the Jews were guilty of the sin of senseless hate
of their neighbors. When we fail to treat one another as brothers and
sisters, our community cannot withstand outside threats. God not
only punishes but also offers compassion, going with the Jews into
exile, feeling their pain, and reassuring them that they will return
once again, strengthened, and even more successful.

On the other hand, we have the image of a punishing, autocratic
God, a God who has lost control, who threatens and inflicts violence.
This God, we must challenge, repeatedly if necessary, until the violence is recognized and stopped. We must identify and challenge
what appears to be the word of God but insidiously perpetrates violence. In this respect, we must also challenge distortions that have
become embedded in our tradition, parading under the garb of
authority.

Recognizing that we may need to keep both perspectives in mind
allows us to ask the right questions, so we may balance acknowledgment of our own guilt with challenges to forces of external
oppression. The answer varies: sometimes it is most constructive to
focus inward, sometimes to focus outward; often, the truth includes

a mixture of both. For example, the concept that we create our own reality has helped many to empower themselves in response to chronic and catastrophic illness. We can change our patterns of diet, exercise, and time management to reduce stress, which improves our well-being and maximizes the effectiveness of our immune systems. We can also use that concept in a way that is self-abusive, blaming ourselves unduly and ineffectively for problems that are only partially the result of our own actions.

Like a good parent who knows when to be firm and allow the child to experience and learn from consequences and who knows when to nurture and soothe the wounds, the seemingly contradictory images of a firm and a compassionate God must be accessed with proper timing and balance. The mixture of images from this time of year encourages us to clarify the nature of that balance.

THE HEALING PROCESS OF GRIEF

- What are the deaths, failures, and losses in your life? the dreams that have not been realized? the children who have not been born?

- What are your feelings in relationship to those losses? Have you allowed yourself to be aware of sadness, fear, grief, relief, rage, despair, loneliness, regret, guilt, blaming, vengefulness?

- What provides comfort to you when you feel each of those feelings?

- In what ways is your guilt constructive and helpful in taking responsibility for the consequences of your actions? In what ways is your guilt destructive, anger turned against the self which should be directed towards those who ought to be confronted?

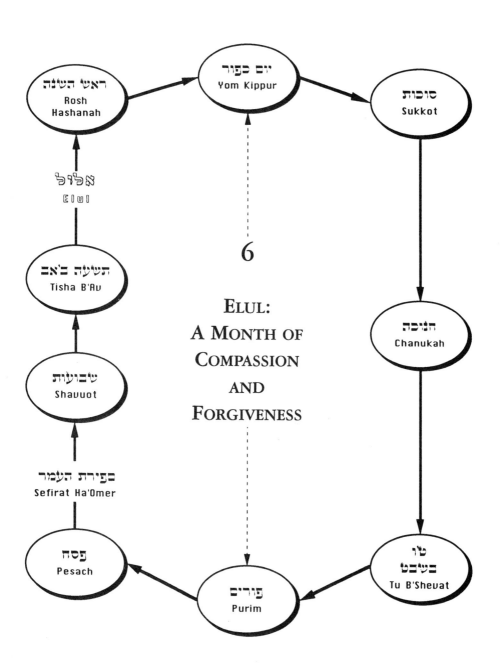

6

ELUL:
A MONTH OF
COMPASSION
AND
FORGIVENESS

During the month of Elul, we heighten awareness of what we do, think, and feel. We become conscious of how we fail to manifest our spiritual Essence in coping with the difficulties of life. We approach this work of self-reflection with an attitude of compassion and understanding, realizing that our intentions are positive, that these habits may have been constructive solutions at some time in our lives, and that we continue them because we do not fully realize what we do or the impact of our choices. As we become more conscious, we take responsibility for hurts we have caused others by acknowledging what we have done and seeking forgiveness. We also open ourselves to others who approach us and seek our forgiveness.

The month of Elul, coming just after the end of the month of Av, marks the beginning of the fall holy days. After the month of Elul comes the new year—Rosh HaShanah, the day of judgment. This is followed by the *Aseret Y'mai Teshuvah,* the ten days of "returning." This period is climaxed by the fast day of Yom Kippur, the day of At-One-Ment.

On Pesach, we are saved by miracles and a God who reaches out to us from above; at this time of year, *we* initiate the efforts. During Shavuot, the focus is on cognitive transformation, new insights and ideas, and a conscious commitment; now, we focus on the emotional aspect, the subconscious and unconscious, more primitive and fundamental habits that operate independently of our conscious cognitive processes. We are asked to make an accounting of our soul,

Cheshbon Hanefesh. For this reason, these Holy-Days are known as *Yamim Nora'im,* the Days of Awe.

SELF-REFLECTION AND COMPASSION

Late one night, in the city of Chelm, known to be populated by fools, Shmuel happened upon his friend Avrum. Avrum was down on his hands and knees, underneath the street light, searching for something. Shmuel inquired as to what Avrum was doing. "I've lost my keys," he replied. "Perhaps you'll help me search." Shmuel joined him. After half an hour, they had still had no success. "Avrum, where exactly did you lose the keys? Maybe we can concentrate our efforts." Avrum replied, "I lost them in that alley over there." Shmuel was dumbfounded, "So, why are we looking here?" Avrum looked over at his friend, "Why are we looking here? Because the light is better here, that's why!"

The self-reflection that occurs during the month of Elul is a continuation of the work that began at Pesach. Until this time of year, we have been unconscious of our ineffective responses. The revelation at the time of Shavuot has not completely integrated into our consciousness. Now, we compassionately and gently reflect on the failures that we grieved at Tisha B'Av. We begin not by trying to change but by working to gain awareness of the previously unconscious coping strategies, the old Ego structure. During the Holy-Days of Rosh HaShanah and Yom Kippur, we surrender that Ego

Pesach through Tisha B'Av	Unconscious dysfunctional responses	Identification with old Ego structure
Elul through Yom Kippur	Conscious dysfunctional responses	Disidentification with old Ego structure
Sukkot through Chanukah	Conscious effective responses	Manifestation of new Ego structure
Purim	Unconscious effective responses	Identification with new Ego structure

and return to the Essence of our being, the Self, so we can reinvent ourselves. We search for new, more constructive ways of responding, a new consciously developed competence. By the end of the year, at Purim, that new way of responding will be fully integrated, solidified as a new Ego that can operate unconsciously (*Likutei Torah*, 32A–34B).

Acknowledging how we have made mistakes is a difficult task. We need to be understanding, gentle, and compassionate with ourselves. On the ninth of Av, we are overwhelmed by despair as we realize the extent to which the insights and commitments of Shavuot have not consistently manifested. During the month of Elul, we consider the same issues and themes with a different attitude. We are less devastated, freed from the punitive, dysfunctional, self-abusive criticism of ourselves.

Shneur Zalman underscores this theme as he contrasts Elul with the Holy-Day of Yom Kippur. Both times are identified with the thirteen qualities of mercy. Since the month of Elul is associated with this powerful aspect of God's Presence, one might imagine that these days would be commemorated with observances similar to those of Yom Kippur, but, such is not the case. The days of the month of Elul are not differentiated from daily life activity; they are not filled with prayer and special rituals. Except for the blowing of the *shofar* and the addition of one psalm, there are no special observances; they are ordinary working days.

Shneur Zalman explains this inconsistency by suggesting that the uniqueness of Elul lies in God meeting us where we are, in the course of daily life within our usual structure for organizing time. Even there, we have access to God's compassion, without needing to create a special, separate, consecrated time and space.

This same theme is expressed in the Torah itself when God tells the Children of Israel: "And you shall search for me from <u>there</u>, and I will come to you." Shneur Zalman interprets the use of the word <u>there</u> as a reference not to our geographic location but to our emotional and spiritual "place." We can only find something we have lost if we search in the place where we lost it. In the same way, if we are to reconnect with our spiritual Essence, we begin from the place in which that connection was lost, the source of our existential dilemma.

Shneur Zalman extends this notion to apply not only to searching from the places of darkness within our lives but also to undeveloped potentials. He uses a geographic metaphor to suggest this theme. He contrasts the desert with an inhabited settlement. The undeveloped potentials within ourselves are like a desert that has been undeveloped. The land is fertile but requires effort to make it produce. The desert symbolizes the undeveloped aspects of our lives, those ways in which we live automatically and unconsciously, those aspects that are disconnected from an awareness of their spiritual Essence. During this time of year, we examine the deserts of our lives, begin to cultivate them and make them fertile. As we do so, we discover the spiritual Essence within them.

The month of Elul is associated with God manifesting through the attribute of mercifulness and compassion. We call on God's thirteen attributes of mercy, repeating the words spoken by Moses at the time when the Israelites made the golden calf:

> Lord! Lord! You are merciful and gracious, patient, bountiful in kindness and truth; You show mercy for thousands of generations, forgive mistakes, deliberate misdeeds, and unconscious wrongdoing, and cleanse us, forgiving our misdeeds, unconscious wrongdoing, and deliberate misdeeds.

The connection between the month of Elul and the quality of compassion is also suggested by a phrase from *Shir HaShirirm,* the Song of Songs, written by King Solomon. The first letters of the month Elul, *Aleph-Lamed-Vav-Lamed,* are the first letters for the phrase *"Ani Ledodi Vedodi Li."* On the surface, these are the words of a love song: "I am to my beloved; and my beloved is to me." The Kabbalists interpret it as a statement of love between God as the bridegroom and Israel as bride; we can experience this love during the month of Elul.

SELF-REFLECTION AND THERAPEUTIC PROCESS

But he can make no progress with himself unless he becomes
very much better acquainted with his own nature.

Carl Jung

The task of self-reflection that occupies us during the month of
Elul parallels the stage of psychotherapy in which we heighten
awareness of unconscious patterns by focusing on here-and-now
awareness. The work with Lily exemplifies this process. Lily, a par-
ticipant in a therapy group, had been struggling unsuccessfully to
control periodic episodes of binge eating. She realized that binge eating was dangerous to her health, and she carefully developed plans
to exercise more restraint. However, her carefully developed plans
seemed to evaporate; her revelations and understanding had been
insufficient to empower her to make changes.

When I asked Lily if anything particular triggered her binges, she
replied that she usually binged on potato chips and sour cream dip. I
asked her if she would be willing to bring chips and dip into the next
therapy group. She showed up for the session with the a bag of chips
and a container of dip. We set up the food in bowls. We began with
where Lily was. As she smelled the chips and dip and looked at the
food, the visual and olfactory stimulus of the food served as a trigger
to the feelings of craving. Lily was able to describe visceral, physical
responses associated with this craving. She could feel herself wanting
literally to reach out. She could sense salivation in her mouth and an
empty feeling in her stomach. I asked her to continue to sit with the
sensations without eating and to notice whether these sensations were
familiar. She acknowledged that this was the same feeling she experienced when she binged. I asked to let her consciousness float back in
time, recalling moments when she had felt like this before, and then
to notice whether she recalled the first time she had this feeling.

After a few moments of concentration, a smile came to Lily's face.
"Where are you?" I queried. Lily described a scene from her childhood.
She was 12 years old, it was her birthday, and she celebrated the occasion with a sleep-over party of girlfriends. They stayed up through the
night telling stories and sharing secrets while eating immense quanti-

ties of chips with sour cream dip. She recalled the warmth, the trust, and the intimacy as she connected deeply to her friends.

Lily had recently separated from her husband. She was living alone for the first time in five years. As Lily continued to reflect, she realized she tended to binge when she was home alone at night. Lily had tried to control her bingeing by substituting foods that were more healthy; however, now she understood that she had tried the wrong approach. She was not hungry for food; she craved attention and support from people. She could not fulfill that need with popcorn and carrot sticks. The chips and dip provided a link with friends who cared. Starting from where she was allowed Lily to gather valuable information: she could focus her efforts more effectively on finding social connections when she was lonely instead of bingeing.

The focus on the present moment allowed Lily to discover the source of her difficulty and learn how to make a shift. This empha-

Gestalt Cycle
of Awareness & Need Satisfaction

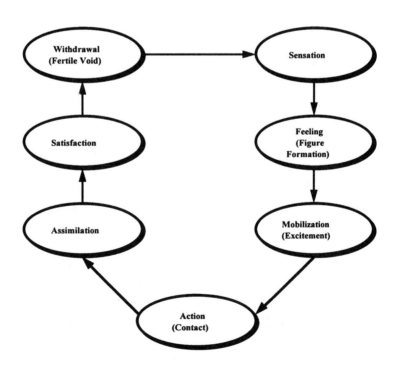

sis on here-and-now awareness is a central element in Gestalt therapy, developed by Fritz Perls. Perls based his approach on the belief that our conscious awareness is guided by the process of need satisfaction. For example, as our need for food develops, we become aware of sensations that we identify as hunger, and we mobilize into activity to eat. After we have satisfied the need, we no longer sense hunger, and a new need can come into consciousness. When we focus our awareness on the here-and-now present experience, sensations associated with unsatisfied needs come into consciousness. Those needs may have to do with the immediate moment, or they may be unmet needs from long ago that are still present. In this way, we can discover which issues are most important.

The focus on here-and-now experience is also important in hypnosis. From the perspective of state-dependent memory learning and behavior, the insights attained during the time of Shavuot are locked into a particular consciousness, the state associated with the celebration of the Holy-Day. On Tisha B'Av, we discover that insight is not available to our ordinary daily consciousness. We need to access the particular state in which we experience difficulty so that the learning is integrated with the state of consciousness activated at the time of stress. In the words of the Torah, we have to "search" from where we are. Elul offers us an opportunity to sit with how we are and to observe ourselves compassionately. As we search from where we are, we learn more about the habitual modes of response, enabling us to make changes.

This exploration is not limited to discovering negative patterns; we may also fertilize the desert, connect with previously unrealized potentials as well. For example, a student in a class I taught on meditation and psychotherapy experimented with eating consciously while meditating. He finished the meditation with a heightened consciousness. As he meditated, he thought about the complex biological processes involved in the growing of the food; he thought about all the people who had worked to grow the food, transport it, and prepare it. He thought about the process going on within himself as the food digested. As he did, he experienced an expansion of

consciousness and a sense of heightened spiritual connection. He fertilized a desert within himself.

COMPASSION AND THERAPEUTIC PROCESS

*I have to live with myself, so I have to tolerate many things I
dislike about me.*

© Ashleigh Brilliant

A Clinical Example of Compassion

Working to increase here-and-now awareness is not enough: we
must also include compassion. This quality of honest, compassionate, accepting, nonjudgmental awareness is exemplified by the work
with Alex. The teachers both hated Alex and felt sorry for him. He
was a disaster to have in the classroom. Although he was quite intelligent and did well on all the standardized tests, he never did his
homework; he passed on to the next grade only because no one
wanted to endure his presence for another year. He was not overly
belligerent, but he infuriated other children: he stole things from
classmates, then feigned ignorance when confronted. Everyone knew
the reasons for his difficulty. His parents were divorced. It had been
an ugly separation. His father had taken up with the wife's best
friend. The affair had been discovered. Eventually, the couple
divorced, and the father married his ex-wife's friend, moving into her
house in the same town. Alex's mother started drinking heavily. His
older brother flunked out of school and began using drugs. Alex was
extremely resistant to anyone who tried to talk directly with him
about his problems. The school contracted with me to try to help.

I realized I could not establish trust with Alex by sitting down
with him in my office and asking him to talk about his life. He did
not even want therapy. I went to Alex's class, introduced myself as a
counselor appointed by the school to help him, and asked if he
would like to meet with me. He replied, "Can I go with you and get
out of math?" I said that I would be able to take him at that time.

He smiled and agreed to meet. I returned to his class at the agreed-
on time and took Alex out of class.

"What are we going to do?" he asked.

"Anything you want, as long as it doesn't break any school rules,"
I replied. His eyes twinkled. Adjoining the school with a nature preserve, complete with a swamp and bird sanctuary. Alex wanted to
spend his time roaming through the swamp.

Although I had provided consultation to the school for several
years, I never had much opportunity to wander through the nature
preserve. Alex was quite provocative. He walked ahead of me and
disappeared into the woods. I began to be nervous that he had run
away, called out for him, and heard no reply. Just as my patience
wore out, he reappeared like an elf, smiling. He knew exactly what
he was doing. I complimented him on his ability to make me nervous and on his exquisite sense of timing in stopping the provocative
behavior just before I became exasperated enough to set a limit. I did
not try to pursue the discussion. For months, each week when I
asked Alex what he wanted to do, he led me off to the swamp. Each
week, we repeated this encounter with endless variations.

As winter came, we moved indoors. We met in a small room that
was used by the teachers for conferences. I continued to give Alex
the control over how we spent time together. He continued to be
provocative. He told me stories of his "tricks," how he had flashed a
wad of dollar bills around school, making the kids jealous and the
teachers nervous. He described an elaborate, and ingenious booby
trap, a "paint bomb." It was designed to protect his locker from his
teacher, whom he suspected of surreptitiously searching for items
that had been stolen from the classroom. I again complimented Alex
on his talent, especially since I was not certain if the story of the
paint bomb was true or if it had been fabricated and deliberately told
to me to keep the teacher away from his locker.

I spent many hours listening to Alex's descriptions of his tricks.
Alex had talent as an artist and enjoyed drawing. I suggested he
make a book of tricks. He loved the idea with the caveat that he
would make all the drawings; since he hated writing, my job was to

write all the text as he dictated. I agreed. His drawings were beautifully executed and filled with detail. Some of his schemes were fanciful, others quite realistic. I sometimes felt uncertain about whether to intervene more actively; I did not want to be passive if there was a threat of physical danger to him or others. I told Alex I was not going to tell anybody else anything he told me unless there was a physical danger to him or others. Alex consistently proved himself to be the master trickster. He seemed instinctually to know my limits, never quite pushing me to the point where I had to intervene more actively.

As winter gave way to spring, we returned to our walks in the nature preserve. One day while we were walking, Alex said, "I thought I was tricky, but you are trickier than me. I know what you've been doing. You are smarter than those other counselors. You are just trying to get me to like you and trust you; you're doing whatever I want so that I'll think you are my friend." I was struck again by Alex's perceptiveness. I knew it was going to be impossible to con him, and I realized that this might be an opportunity to begin to address issues directly. "You're right, Alex. I am also tricky. I knew you have had lots of reasons to distrust adults. Most of the time adults haven't listened to what you want or need. You've been smart enough to be sneaky, and I was smart enough to know better than to try to tell you what to do or what to talk about. You're right. I was hoping you'd start to trust me and talk about all the things that are going on in your life. I was tricky because a kid who is 11 years old deserves to have some adult in his life to whom he could tell the truth."

Alex did not respond directly to my statement, nor did I pursue the conversation. However, he began to reveal more and more information to me. He showed me how he set fires in the swamp, explaining how he liked to watch them burn in ever-expanding circles, demonstrating how he carefully selected locations in which the fires would burn out safely. He took me to his house, showed me his secret hideout, a closet under the stairs on the first floor. Sitting in that closet, he could monitor conversations throughout the house, listening to his mother on the phone in the kitchen or his brother in his upstairs bedroom with his girlfriend. He told me about his mother's drinking, his brother's drugs, and his father's lectures. I continued to listen without offering advice or attempting to intervene.

Eventually, Alex gave me permission to talk with his parents and even agreed to participate in some family counseling. My success was limited, much of the stress in the family remained: the mother continued to drink, Alex's brother committed suicide, and Alex never completed high school. However, Alex stayed away from drugs; and his father took a more active role, learning to listen instead of lecture. Alex developed enough trust with his father to be able to turn to him during times of crisis.

A Psychological Perspective on Compassion

This quality of unconditional, nonevaluative, positive attention that Alex needed to build trust is an important principle in the psychotherapeutic process. Irving Yalom (1985), a psychologist and expert in group therapy, conducted a research study in which he studied the outcomes of a variety of different psychotherapeutic methods. He concluded that the effectiveness of group therapy did not depend on the type of therapy, whether it was process oriented, Gestalt therapy, psychodynamic therapy, or any other method. The effectiveness of the therapy was most consistently associated with therapists who were viewed as empathic and caring by their clients:

> *The ideological school told us little about the actual behavior: the effectiveness of a group was, in large part, a function of its leader's behavior. The higher the caring, the higher the positive outcome. [pp 501–502]*

Carl Rogers (1972) based his approach on a similar principle, suggesting that the cornerstone of psychotherapy was unconditional positive regard and acceptance. From his perspective, the process of self-reflection and change required only that the therapist provide an environment of empathy and acceptance. According to his ideas, when the clinician accepts and validates the client, the person feels safe enough to be honest and open, to acknowledge difficulties and problems:

> *I find that the more acceptance and liking I feel toward this individual, the more I will be creating a relationship which he can use. By acceptance I mean a warm regard for him as a person of unconditional self-worth—of value no matter what his condition, his behavior, or his feelings. [p. 5]*

This same concept is also central to the ideas of Eric Berne (1985), the originator of Transactional Analysis. Berne originated the concept of strokes, a basic unit of social recognition. He identified four types of strokes. *Unconditional positive strokes* refer to empathic, supportive, acceptance of all responses: "I love you regardless of what you do." *Conditional positive strokes* are responses that reinforce particular behaviors: "I love you when you do what I want." *Unconditional negative strokes* are global negative responses: "Regardless of what you do, I don't love you." *Conditional negative strokes* refer to negative evaluations of particular behaviors: "I don't love you when you do things that displease me."

Unconditional Positive Strokes	Conditional Positive Strokes
Unconditional Negative Strokes	Conditional Negative Strokes

Each of us requires a foundation of unconditional positive regard to develop the capacity to face difficulties without losing self-confidence. Conditional negative and conditional positive responses sometimes help us make important discoveries that support continued learning and growth. Unconditional negative responses are never helpful; they only serve to depress and anger someone.

PERSONAL APPLICATION: COMPASSIONATE SELF-REFLECTION

Shneur Zalman describes the nature of our relationship with God during this time of year through analogy to the ruler of a country. The monarch who sits on the throne is inaccessible. Only with difficulty can we gain access: time is highly scheduled, and advisers form a shield to impede direct contact. However, when the monarch travels through the countryside, she or he is accessible, friendly, and welcoming, open to petitioners who approach. This phenomenon is not restricted to the aristocracy of Shneur Zalman's time. We can observe the same dynamic in our politicians, shielded from direct contact with the public during normal times but who reach out to their constituents while campaigning, meeting them in shopping malls, factories, schools, or even jogging. During the month of Elul, God responds to each of us with this same quality of compassionate attention as a monarch traveling through the countryside. God is approachable and open to our requests. God is with us where we are, in the darkness and the difficulty. The Source of Life compassionately welcomes us, helping us gain awareness of aspects of ourselves that have previously been unconscious. We are still loved, perhaps especially loved, as we honestly face parts of ourselves that have been clouded with shame or vulnerability.

HEALING WOUNDS IN OUR RELATIONSHIPS: MAKING AMENDS AND FORGIVENESS

Sometimes it takes courage to be kind.

© Ashleigh Brilliant

Whereas Tisha B'Av stands as a symbol of failure, the month of Elul stands as a symbol of having another chance. Although failure is inevitable, we can also count on the possibility for renewing ourselves and beginning again. Even though the Israelites lost faith and worshipped the golden calf, they acknowledge their mistake and God forgives them. Although the first tablets are destroyed as a result of the incident with the golden calf, the Israelites get a second chance. On the first day of Elul, Moses ascends the mountain, returning on Yom Kippur, the fortieth day, with a new set of tablets:

> *God said to Moses, "Carve out two tablets for yourself, just like the first ones. I will write on those tablets the same words that were on the first tablets that you broke."*
>
> [Exodus 34:1]

Working at the spiritual level alone is insufficient. According to tradition, ritual alone does not suffice to create forgiveness and transformation: we must also work to resolve issues between us for the ritual to be able to be effective. As we approach this difficult task of repairing our relationships, we may be tempted to reduce our efforts to a formulaic conversation devoid of meaning and feeling. If we are to achieve true forgiveness, we must work to acknowledge our misdeeds, make amends, and give space for expression and working through of feelings. Then, we can wholeheartedly forgive and be forgiven.

A Clinical Example of Making Amends

This complex process is illustrated by the Bill, who began therapy to overcome marital problems. Bill's wife, Lisa, was furious. She was ready to divorce him, but their troubled economic situation made it impossible to maintain two households and provide the basics for their children. Lisa had carried much of the responsibility for the family during the past two years while Bill was supposedly incapacitated by back pain. Recently, Bill had confessed that his back pain was much less severe than he had claimed; he had pretended to be incapacitated to avoid carrying his share of the family responsibilities. It had not been a conscious lie: Bill had even pretended to himself that he was truly incapacitated. However, after his father died, Bill had returned to visit his parents' home for the first time in many years. Looking through a scrapbook, he saw a picture of himself in a cast. Suddenly, he remembered that he had deliberately injured himself as a child. This insight stimulated him to reflect on his life. He realized how he had deceived his wife, and he resolved to reveal this secret as the first step in confronting this problem.

Bill wanted her forgiveness, but Lisa was unforgiving. She was furious that he had taken advantage of her, forcing her to give up so much while he pretended to be in pain. She did not want to "work" on the problem. It did not matter to her that it was unintentional. As she spoke, she became more and more agitated and angry. She saw no reason to talk about the issue. She did not want to do any counseling. She stood up and walked out of the therapy session.

Bill and I sat in silence for several minutes, stunned by the power of her words and the suddenness of her departure. I did not know what to do. On the one hand, I could understand Bill's wish for forgiveness. After all, he had the courage to confess his secret when he might easily have continued the charade or simply pretended to get better. I could also understand Lisa's rage as I thought about what she had endured as a result of his deceit. I asked Bill what he wanted. He said he wanted to save the marriage and was prepared to do whatever it might take.

We devised a plan. He would try to re-establish trust by making a radical transformation in his behavior. He would find a stable job and commit himself to providing the financial support he had previously left to his wife's responsibility. He would also make a clear commitment to the physical care of his children, which he had also avoided by claiming to have a "bad back."

When he returned the next week, Bill reported that he had taken a job. He had also taken on responsibility for the bulk of the household chores, sat with his 8-year-old son every night to help with his homework, and taken care of the late-night feedings for his infant daughter. His wife was not mollified. She did not want to sleep in the same bed. She asked him to move out of their bedroom as well. He agreed to do so. Bill realized that his wife was not going to soften after a week. She continued to feel furious.

Over the course of the next year, Bill continued to honor his commitments. He worked hard in therapy to understand the roots of his difficulty. Throughout childhood, his mother had complained of a variety of mysterious illnesses that were never diagnosed but left her quite incapacitated. We discussed, over and over again, the incident in which he deliberately injured himself. He realized that he had no other way to get attention in his family; his mother's powerful complaints continually focused the attention away from him and onto her. Bill spent months enraged with his mother's irresponsibility. He also began to identify his father's role in the dynamic: his father had been extremely passive, never intervening to stop his mother's inappropriate, neglectful, and abusive self-centeredness.

Bill also focused on current situations in his life, examining his actions so as to identify the often unconscious tendency to "play sick" and avoid responsibility. He realized that some of his avoidance stemmed from a difficulty in his work identity. He was an artist, a sculptor who worked in metal. Unable to support himself and his family from his art, he had worked half-heartedly as a welder. He had been at an impasse, neither committing himself to his art nor coming to terms with economic realities. Considering the issues consciously, he reaffirmed the need to provide for the economic security of his family, especially in light of the strain in his marriage. At the same time, he realized he needed to make a commitment to his art. He also scheduled time each week for sculpting.

Lisa was cordial but distant. She acknowledged that the change in his behaviors had been helpful, but she continued to feel enraged. It was hard for Bill to continue in his efforts while his wife remained so angry. I both admired and questioned Bill's persistence. Was the damage to the relationship too great to repair? Was he hanging on to a relationship that was dead? I could not pretend to have the answer to those questions; only Bill could make that judgment.

Finally, after thirteen months, Lisa asked to participate in a therapy session. She said she now was ready to work on the relationship. Over the course of the year, she had come to trust that Bill's commitment was solid. He had been dependable and given her space, not pressured her to respond. Lisa said she still felt enraged but wanted to rekindle her love. We decided to take some time for her to express her anger; she described the suffering she had experienced during the two years she had been the caretaker while he pretended to be incapacitated. Lisa spent several sessions, describing, in detail, the minor and major inconveniences, the effects of tending to him, taking care of their children, and working full-time. Often, they were both in tears as she talked.

Bill shared with Lisa his insights about his family, telling her what it had been like for him growing up, describing the isolation he felt. He discussed his frustration at not being able to spend time sculpting and his efforts to make some commitment to his art. He talked about his struggle during the year, his determination and fear. Lisa and Bill came to a full reconciliation. She did forgive him; she asked his forgiveness for taking so long to respond to his dramatic transformation.

A Psychological Perspective on Making Amends during Elul

The process that Bill completed parallels one of the steps emphasized in self-help programs like Alcoholics Anonymous. In these programs, a key element of recovery includes the attainment of forgiveness. One of the crucial steps is to make an inventory of injuries we have caused others. A person then takes concrete steps to make amends to the extent possible. This may include not only acknowledging to others that a wrong was committed but also taking active steps to ameliorate or undo what one has inflicted on others as well.

In this same, way, the month of Elul is a time for us to reflect on our relationships, to identify what we need to do to forgive others and to be forgiven ourselves. What is required can vary. Sometimes it is enough when we simply acknowledge that we have caused hurt and that we feel regret. Sometimes, we need to do something additional to make amends for what has happened to build trust that it will not reoccur in the future. We work to find out what others need from us, and we work to be clear about what it is that we need from others who have hurt us.

BALANCING DOING AND NON-DOING: COMPASSIONATE SELF-REFLECTION AND ACTIVE EFFORT TO ACHIEVE FORGIVENESS

A couple came to the Rabbi to resolve a dispute. The husband told his story. The Rabbi listened, stroked his beard, sighed, and replied, "I think you are right in this situation." Then it was the wife's turn. She told her story. The Rabbi listened, stroked his beard, sighed, and replied, "I think you are right in this situa-

tion." The Rabbi's assistant, standing off to the side, interrupt-
ed. "Rabbi, how can this be? First, you tell the husband that he
is right. Then, you tell the wife that she is right. How can they
both be right?" The Rabbi listened, stroked his beard, sighed,
and replied, "I think you have a good point. You are also right!"

The tradition, as we have come to expect, provides us with contradictory themes. On the one hand, we are given space to reflect:
relieved from changing anything so we may heighten our awareness.
On the other hand, we are asked to engage in action: to work hard
to achieve forgiveness in relationships. Behaviorists start by encouraging us to act, hypothesizing that the changes in what we do will
result in changes in how we feel and think. Dynamically oriented
therapists might suggest we begin by focusing more on self-reflection, believing that internal changes will eventually translate into
changes in how we act.

By including both a reflective and an active component in the
process, the cycle of the Holy-Days helps us value both approaches,
encouraging us to struggle with the balance and not allowing us to
find refuge in simplistic answers. Sometimes, it is important to start
with action so as to create an environment that is peaceful enough
to engage in an internal process. Sometimes, it is vital to start internally because we are unable to make changes until we work with our
internal process. In providing us with both perspectives, we are
forced to struggle to find the most effective combination of the two
for ourselves. Losing that balance, we may either become too focused
internally while continuing to cause injury in relationships, or we
may focus too much on externals without attending to internal patterns and habits.

PRACTICAL APPLICATION AT ELUL

The Internal Process of Compassionate Self-Reflection

- Begin with an attitude of compassion, understanding ways that any dysfunctional habits are the result of our best efforts to cope with stresses, trauma, incomplete understanding, and powerlessness.

- Identify situations in which we have been unable to manifest our cognitive insight and commitment into new patterns of response.

- Cultivate the quality of compassionate self-observation in which you heighten awareness of your dysfunctional responses—physical sensations, feelings, beliefs and attitudes, habits of behavior, and responses in relationships.

Repairing Interpersonal Relationships

- List relationships that are troubled.

- Consider your role in those conflicted relationships. What is it that you have contributed to the difficulties? What are the consequences of those responses for others? What is it that others need from you to forgive you?

- Consider the role of others in conflicted relationships. What is it that they have contributed to the difficulties? What are the consequences of those responses for you? What is it you need to forgive others?

- Make a commitment to take action based on your conclusions!

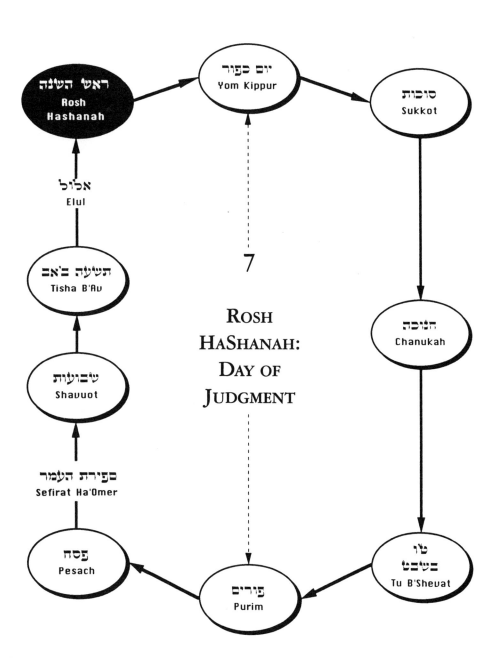

ראש השנה
Rosh Hashanah

יום כפור
Yom Kippur

סוכות
Sukkot

אלול
Elul

תשעה ב'אב
Tisha B'Av

7

**ROSH
HASHANAH:
DAY OF
JUDGMENT**

שבועות
Shavuot

חנוכה
Chanukah

ספירת העמר
Sefirat Ha'Omer

פסח
Pesach

ט"ו
בשבט
Tu B'Shevat

פורים
Purim

Rosh HaShanah is celebrated for two days, the first two days of the month of Tishrei. In the Torah, Rosh HaShanah is referred to as *Yom Teru'ah*—the day of the sounding of the *shofar*. It is also known as *Yom HaZikaron*—the day of remembrance, and as *Yom HaDin*—the Day of Judgment. Rosh HaShanah is traditionally regarded as the birthday of the world, the anniversary of creation and the time of its renewal.

The unconditional acceptance of Elul shifts to confrontation on Rosh HaShanah. God is seated on the throne of judgment. We are asked to be accountable, to take responsibility for our actions and clarify the ways in which we are the authors of our own destinies. We face a God who offers confrontation and critical feedback. In response to that challenge, we work to make changes. This process, known as *Teshuvah*, includes two aspects: (1) *Eetkafya*, the active effort to change our external behaviors, and (2) *Eethafcha*, the inner work to dissolve dysfunctional impulses and connect with our true underlying needs and wants.

ACCOUNTABILITY—DAY OF JUDGMENT

Before you can start going the right way, it's often necessary to stop going the wrong way.

© Ashleigh Brilliant

185

One of the central themes associated with Rosh HaShanah is the
image of this day as a Day of
Judgment. The melodies used for
the prayers and readings from
scripture are written in a minor
key, conveying the atmosphere of
solemnity through the music, an
atmosphere reinforced by the
sounding of the *shofar*. God is rep-
resented as a monarch sitting on a
throne, reviewing the life of each person and determining who shall
live and who shall die in the coming year:

> *It is true that you are the judge and decider, knower, and wit-*
> *ness, inscribing and sealing, counting and numbering; you*
> *remember all the forgotten things; you open the book of*
> *remembrances and read from it, and the signature of each per-*
> *son is contained in it.*
>
> *The great* shofar *is sounded; a gentle whisper is heard; the*
> *angels tremble with fear and declare: "The day of judgment is*
> *here, all the hosts of the heavens have their appointed times to*
> *be judged." They are not blameless in your eyes in judgment.*
> *And all creation pass before you like the hosts of the heavens.*
> *Like a shepherd who tends his flock, making his sheep pass*
> *under his rod, so do you make all living souls pass before you*
> *to be counted and numbered, fixing the lifetime of each cre-*
> *ation and writing its destiny.*
>
> *On Rosh HaShanah their destiny is inscribed, and on Yom*
> *Kippur it is sealed: how many shall pass on, and how many*
> *shall be brought into existence; who shall live, and who shall*
> *die; who shall come to a timely end, and who die before their*
> *time; who by fire, and who by water; who by sword, and who*
> *by beast; who by earthquake, and who by plague; who by*
> *strangling and who by stoning; who shall be at ease, and who*
> *shall wander; who shall be at peace and who shall be torn*
> *apart; who shall have comfort, and who shall be disturbed; who*

shall become poor, and who shall become rich; who shall be
lowered, and who shall be raised.

[Rosh HaShanah Liturgy]

This image can incorrectly be reduced to a simplistic, childlike image in which we represent God as a rigid, perfectionistic, stern, and punitive father, a cruel God who knows everything we do and punishes us for every misdeed. We feel overwhelmed with shame, guilt, and fear, pleading for mercy and hoping we will succeed in averting the punishment. This image of God is consistent with the perspective of a young child who feels powerless and insecure in relationship to figures of authority. If we stopped trying to make sense of the Infinite in childhood, we may continue to view God in this way as adults.

We need a more mature, appropriate, and adult understanding of God and our relationship with the Infinite. The Source of Life is not a mean, capricious, or punitive God but a God who sees the truth of our lives and who understands the consequences of our choices, behaviorally, emotionally, and mentally. The God of Rosh HaShanah who sits on the throne as monarch and judge is a God of justice. At this time of year, we have the opportunity to hear this truth so that we may reevaluate those choices.

A Clinical Example of Accountability

Give me strength to face my weaknesses.

© Ashleigh Brilliant

The following example from a therapeutic relationship provides a clearer sense of constructive challenge. At the urging of a friend, Joyce reluctantly agreed to go to a party. She expected to feel shy, intimidated, and withdrawn. To her surprise, she met someone, an attractive, successful, and interesting man. They spent several hours talking. However, although Joyce was interested in him, she did not pursue the possibility of getting together again. She was sure he would not be interested in her. He was much too successful. There was no reason to risk disappointment and rejection.

I felt impatient with Joyce's reluctance to follow through. I knew how much she wanted a life partner, how much she wanted to have children. She was 35 years old; a five-year relationship had ended more than a year ago. She had taken time to grieve that loss. If she refused to reach out, she would have little chance of achieving her wish.

I told Joyce I felt as if her mother had suddenly joined us in the session. Joyce was puzzled and taken aback: "What do you mean by that?" she asked.

"Well," I replied, "that's just what I'd expect your mother to say if you told her you met someone. She'd say that if he was successful, he was probably too good for you. Only your mother isn't here. You are doing to yourself the same thing you complain about your mother doing to you."

Joyce got angry with me: "It's easy for you to say. This is how I feel. I can't help it."

I understood why Joyce was reluctant. She had developed low self-esteem as a result of her life experiences. One of the most powerful of these experiences had occurred when she was in college. An excellent student, Joyce received a scholarship to a prestigious Ivy League school. Her family was unsupportive of her ambitions. Her mother, especially, experienced Joyce's desire to leave home as a rejection of the blue-collar community in which the family had lived for several generations. Despite their objections, Joyce persevered and went away to school. She had a terrible year. She was overwhelmed by the academic demands. She was no longer the brightest student and star in every class; sometimes she felt everyone else knew more than she did. Socially, she felt terribly out of place. She stopped doing her homework and missed classes. At the end of the first year, she lost her scholarship and was forced to return home. Her mother was unsympathetic. From her mother's perspective, Joyce had her chance at college. Now she advised her to enroll in the community college in town and get a job as a secretary. Eventually, Joyce would meet someone, get married, and have a family. Joyce never returned to college.

This event had been devastating. Joyce lost faith in herself, in her ability, and in her dreams. She gave up hope in achieving goals. Although she understood that her mother was limited by her own upbringing, Joyce still felt hurt by the lack of support. She was enraged with her mother for failing to recognize that the environment of the university had been overwhelming. Joyce wished that her mother had helped her overcome the difficulties and get back on track or encouraged her to find a different university where she could succeed.

Although it had been important for Joyce to acknowledge her rage with her mother, that same rage had become an obstacle. So long as she focused on her rage, she avoided confronting her own unconscious, habitual tendency to discourage herself and withdraw in the face of frustration.

I did not back down. "I don't believe you are that incompetent. I think you can help it. You have to help it. Your mother said horrible things to you, they caused a lot of pain, and you've been left with deep wounds. Perhaps the most damaging is that you learned to deflate yourself in the same way your mother deflated you. You really want a family. If you don't begin to take steps to meet men, you are going to end up alone and bitter."

Joyce stared at me in silence. Then I noticed her lips curl up slightly in what looked like the beginnings of a smile. "Are you aware that you just started to smile?" I asked. Joyce was taken aback again, ruminated for a few moments, and then acknowledged that she sensed herself smiling. She could not understand why she might smile in response to my challenge. It seemed inappropriate and out of context. All of a sudden, I had an intuition: "I think you've figured out a great way to get even with your mother. You'll show her! She will be really disappointed if you never get married. She'll never have any grandchildren. You'll be miserable. And it will be her fault."

Joyce got angry with me: "I thought you understood, but I can see now that you don't really know what it's like. It's not that simple. I thought you were supportive, but you're blaming me. You're being abusive to me. You're doing the same thing my mother does to me. I don't have to put up with this. I'm getting out of here." Joyce stood up and turned toward the door.

For a moment, I panicked. I did not want Joyce to walk out. Had I approached Joyce too critically? But I did not feel like backing down. "Wait a minute, Joyce. I want you to hear me out before you walk out of here. It's true, I am being critical and your mother was critical. But there is an important difference. I believe in you. I think you are intelligent; I think you are competent; I'm encouraging you to have your dreams. I may not be completely on target; maybe I haven't quite said it in the right way, but I think there's some truth in my words. You can walk out of here right now, and you can take comfort that, once again, you're right. Once again, you confirm that people are abusive, that no one will help, and that you are all alone. But if you win this battle, I think you lose. I want you to stay here and talk this through with me."

Joyce did not move for what seemed like an eternity but was probably less than a minute. Then I saw her shoulders relax, and she sat down. Joyce was an avid tennis player. "I flashed on the image of my tennis coach. He's a cranky and crotchety old man, but for some reason, I never feel like he's abusive. He's always critical, he gets very impatient with me, but he's also very sharp. He sees exactly what's wrong with my form, and he's relentless. He doesn't back off until I get it right. And I do. I get it right, and I walk off the court feeling terrific. Just now, with you, I kind of felt the same way. I think you won't back off until I get it."

At that moment, Joyce made an important shift. She took responsibility for herself. She made herself accountable; she acknowledged her tendency to engage in self-defeating behaviors and also acknowledged her competence; she recognized her ability to become aware of those behaviors and to change them.

A Psychological Perspective on Accountability

I can face anything as long as I don't have to open my eyes.
© Ashleigh Brilliant

We sometimes need to be confronted by others who see a truth that we are unable to recognize. Sometimes we need a push in order to become accountable, to take responsibility and recognize how we sabotage ourselves. Thomas Harris (1973), who elaborated on Berne's theory of Transactional Analysis, describes this unconscious decision as a life script. Based on our experience, we draw conclusions, often unconscious, about ourselves, others, and what we can make of our lives. These beliefs support patterns of response to others and within ourselves that tend to reinforce those beliefs. In Transactional Analysis, these patterns are described as "games" and "rackets." For example, Joyce's low self-esteem caused her to withdraw rather than risk what seemed to be certain rejection or failure. As a consequence, she finds herself alone, further reinforcing her low self-esteem. To overcome the life script, the therapist confronts the client, brings the self-defeating tendencies to awareness, and clarifies the destructive effects of those patterns.

Someone who suffers from the disease of alcoholism may deny the truth of the situation. The person may fail to acknowledge the extent of the drinking or the effects of the alcohol on health, relationships, and daily functioning. The person's family may unknowingly collude in that denial. In such a situation, meeting with the person's spouse, children, friends, colleagues, health providers, and other significant relations can sometimes be effective. Each of the participants confronts the person and describes their experiences of the addiction and its consequences. The participants express their concerns and share their worries about what will happen if the alcoholism continues. They ask the person to end the denial, acknowledge the alcoholism, and agree to receive treatment for that disease. Treatment requires a commitment to end the drinking. This process is facilitated by short-term hospitalization during the physical and emotional withdrawal from the alcohol dependency. Afterward, sobriety is maintained through therapy and self-help programs such as Alcoholics Anonymous.

In this same spirit, on Rosh HaShanah we are asked to push through our denial; make ourselves accountable; become aware of the previously unconscious truths of our thoughts, feelings, and actions; clarify the impact and consequences of those responses; and acknowledge our ability to make choices about our responses. Through the month of Elul, we acknowledge, with compassion, the truths of our lives. On Rosh HaShanah, we find ourselves confronted by God, sitting on the throne of judgment, evaluating our lives, and deciding our fate for the coming year. All aspects of ourselves are judged. Some aspects of ourselves are judged as ineffective or destructive, while others are judged as positive and constructive. In this sense, parts of ourselves are judged for life and others for death.

RESPONDING TO GOD'S CHALLENGE:
THE PROCESS OF *TESHUVAH*

'Tis a gift to be simple, 'tis a gift to be free
'Tis a gift to come down where we ought to be
And when we find ourselves in the place just right
'Twill be in the valley of love and delight

When true simplicity is gained
To bow and to bend we shan't be ashamed
To turn, turn will be our delight
Til by turning, turning we come 'round right.

Although one's fate is decreed on Rosh HaShanah, that fate is not irrevocable: it can be changed through *Teshuvah,* usually translated as "repentance." According to tradition, our names are inscribed on Rosh HaShanah; they are sealed on Yom Kippur. Even before Rosh HaShanah, a special late-night service is added in which prayers—known as *Selichot*—are said to encourage us in this process. Similarly, on the afternoon of the first day of Rosh HaShanah (or the second day if the first day is a Sabbath), we symbolically acknowledge our commitment to change by casting our "sins" into the water in the ritual known as *Tashlich.* This focus on *teshuvah* continues during the intermediate days from Rosh HaShanah until Yom Kippur, known as *Aseret Y'mai Teshuvah*—the ten days of *Teshuvah.*

Although *Teshuvah* is usually translated as repentance, that translation is inaccurate. The literal translation of *Teshuvah* is "answer," suggesting that this process involves a dialogue, a response to God's challenge. The root of the word, *shuvah,* means "turning" or "returning," suggesting a change, a transformation, a turning inward, a return to one's true self. In Kabbalistic imagery, this process involves a reconnection with oneness, a return to connection with God, a surrender of ego and separateness. The liturgy is filled with examples of our forebears who stubbornly persisted in their struggles to realize their goals, who clung to the faith that somehow they could accomplish their particular mission. Hannah persisted in her prayers for a child; Hagar looked to God to save her son; Abraham stayed in dialogue with God even when asked to sacrifice his son.

During this time, we can change our fate through *Teshuvah*— returning to our Essence; *Tefillah*—prayer; and *Tzedakah*—acts of charity. According to Maimonides,[1] a medieval rabbinical authority, *Teshuvah* involves three steps: cognitively, it requires an acknowledgment of one's actions; emotionally, it involves a feeling of regret in realizing the consequences of those actions; and behaviorally, it means a commitment to respond differently. The emotional component of this process occurs in prayer; acts of charity speak to the behavioral aspect.

Shneur Zalman differentiates two facets of *Teshuvah:* an active and a receptive process. The active work involves acknowledging the tendency to behave in opposition to our true Self and true Spirit. We engage in a struggle, an act of will by recognizing the dysfunctional impulse and by encouraging ourselves to respond differently. This struggle is symbolized by the *shofar* in the long blast of the *teki'ah,* which is a call to arms. According to Shneur Zalman, this quality, known as *Eetkafya* and translated as "subduing," is expressed in the experience of ourselves as the "servants of God." It is associated with the kabbalistic concept of *Memaleh Kol Almin,* literally translated as "the One who fills all worlds." We experience God's immanence as we work within the context of everyday life on the material level.

The receptive aspect of *teshuvah* also begins by acknowledging the disconnection with our true Essence. However, instead of engaging in the empowered act of will, we face our powerlessness, our inability to make a change. In facing our powerlessness, we open ourselves to support from outside ourselves. This acknowledgment is symbolized by the *shofar* in the broken sounds of the *teru'ah* and *shevarim,* which mimic the sound of crying. This quality, known as *Eethafcha*—"transformation"—is associated with the experience of ourselves as the "children of God," the kabbalistic experience of God as transcendent—*Sovev Kol Almin.*

Shneur Zalman describes these two facets of Rosh HaShanah in his commentary on the phrase: "This is the day which is the beginning of creation, a remembrance of the first day." Referring to this day as the "beginning of creation" implies that it is actually a day of creation in which God renews and re-creates the world each year. Referring to this day as the remembrance of the first day suggests that it is a commemoration of the first day of creation, a historic event that occurred many years ago. Shneur Zalman suggests that both descriptions are accurate, each referring to a different facet of renewal.

Eetkafya (Subduing)	*Eethafcha* (Transformation)
Servants of God	Children of God
Teki'ah	*Teru'ah & shevarim*
Memaleh Kol Almin ("Filling All Worlds")	*Sovev Kol Almim* ("Surrounding All Worlds")
Immanence	Transcendence
Renewal each year	Creation of the world
Active principle	Receptive principle
Human effort	Crying out & divine help

EETKAFYA: THE ACTIVE PRINCIPLE

The thought manifests as the word,
The word manifests as the deed,
The deed develops into habit,
And the habit hardens into character.
So watch the thought
And its ways with care,
And let it spring from love
Born out of respect for all beings .

Shneur Zalman notes that the Torah does not refer to Tishrei by name when the commandment is made to "Blow the *shofar* on the Month." The Hebrew word for month, *chodesh,* comes from the same root as the word for creation or renewal, *chidush.* Based on this connection, Shneur Zalman suggests that Rosh HaShanah is not merely the anniversary of the historic event of creation, but the time of creation each year. Each year the life force is renewed on Rosh HaShanah. Shneur Zalman draws an analogy between this day in relationship to the rest of the year with the relationship between the head and the body. Although the name of the Holy-Day—Rosh HaShanah—is usually translated as the "New Year," a more accurate translation is the "Head of the Year."

The life energy travels by way of electrical impulses in the nerves from the head to the parts of the body, manifesting uniquely in each body part. Although the manifestation of the life force depends on the condition of the particular limb or organ, nothing can happen without the initial impulse from the brain. In the same manner, the life force on Rosh HaShanah energizes the particular manifestation of life each month and each day of the year:

> *The head of a person is the source of the life force. The life force*
> *radiates from the head to all the parts of the body. The head*
> *contains all the potential energy for the body in its cognitive*
> *functions. The energy is transformed from a potential energy*
> *into actual realization according to the particular specialized*
> *quality of each organ and part, causing the eye to see, the leg*
> *to walk, etc. In the same way, the "head" of the year, Rosh*
> *HaShanah, contains the potential energy of the life force for all*

the days of the year. That energy manifests in each day of the
year according to the particular, unique quality of that day.

[Likutei Torah, 48A]

From this perspective, Rosh HaShanah is literally a re-creation of
the world, a time when God renews creation. This quality of God's
manifestation is *Memaleh Kol Almin,* God's immanence filling all
worlds. The manifestation of the life force does not occur in a vacuum or in isolation. Creation occurs in relationship with humans and
depends upon human activity. When we use the image of God sitting in judgment, it is expressing the idea that God's manifestation
of the life force depends upon the quality of our actions in the material world.

In our efforts to facilitate the manifestation of the life energy for
the coming year, we struggle to overcome our resistance. As we
become aware of dysfunctional responses, we begin *Eetkafya,* the
battle to subdue our habitual, unconscious, rigid patterns.
Awareness alone is not enough because that awareness is fragile and
overwhelmed by the force of habit. It is required that we fight our
"nature," our rigid tendency to respond in the dysfunctional way.

Like a servant who is a stranger and alienated from the master,
who adheres to the orders of the master with the quality of war,
who is reluctant and resistant, but who overcomes these resis-
tances, subduing those tendencies in order to do the will of the
master, . . . [as the servants of God,] we are engaged in a war
in which we have to subdue the resistances; sometimes we are
successful; other times we fail to do so. In this process, we are
judged on our success.

[Likutei Torah, 45B-56A]

Therapeutic Conceptions of the Active Principle

This process is illustrated by Joyce's struggle with her tendency to
withdraw in response to rejection. As a result of her insight, Joyce
decided to take a risk: she would call the man she had met at the party
and find out if he wanted to get together again. The following week
when we met, I could see by the look on her face that something was

wrong. She had been unable to make herself call. She had succeeded in obtaining his phone number from her friend who had given the party; several times she started to dial the number, but she found herself hanging up when he actually answered the phone. Joyce was thrown again into the torment of shame, self-doubt, and hopelessness.

However, something was different. She understood that her impulse to give up was dysfunctional. She gave herself credit for taking the step of getting the phone number and even for dialing the number. She knew she needed to fight the impulse to quit and to push herself to follow through. We agreed that she would make a commitment to follow through during the next week. If she continued to have difficulty, she decided she would make the call from my office at the next session. The next week Joyce came in to the office with a big smile on her face. She had made the call, Larry was happy to hear from her, and they had made plans to get together.

Joyce's success did not result in a complete transformation. She continued to struggle with her impulse to withdraw when she was criticized or rejected. Each time, she struggled against that impulse by using logic and getting support from others to sustain herself in spite of the anxiety. Over time, she found herself more easily able to win that battle: the dysfunctional impulse weakened, and her determination was stronger.

This process is similarly described in Assagioli's (1976) understanding of therapeutic process. Assagioli explains that insight alone is insufficient to produce change. When one has identified a dysfunctional habit, it is necessary to use an act of will to make a change. The insight in itself is insufficient because one has a compulsive, habitual tendency to respond in the old way. Assagioli recommends that one practice acts of will in order to develop that capacity, beginning by making a commitment to perform some arbitrary, even meaningless, task as a way to develop that skill. From this perspective, the act of will needed simply to celebrate the various rituals of the Holy-Day takes on an added dimension; our decision to perform the ritual provides an opportunity to develop self-discipline as we overcome internal and external obstacles that distract us from our commitment.

Eric Berne (1985) identifies a equivalent process in overcoming the tendency to enact a habitual life script. The life script is enacted in games and rackets. *Games* are compulsively repeated sequences of interactions with others that result in the familiar outcome. *Rackets* are the familiar feelings that are reexperienced at these times. Berne notes the importance of gaining insight about these habits. He advocates working to inhibit the impulse to continue reenacting the game so that we are able to experiment with new alternatives.

EETHAFCHA: THE RECEPTIVE PRINCIPLE

Rosh HaShanah is not only a day of creation; it is also a remembrance of the first day. The first day is qualitatively different from the day of re-creation that occurs each year. On the first day of creation, God formed the universe from nothingness; on Rosh HaShanah each year, God only renews and re-creates the universe. The first day of creation occurred before life existed; that manifestation of divine energy occurred without effort and without depending on the merit of human activity. The day of re-creation depends on human activity. For this reason, the remembrance of the first day symbolizes the experience of divine lovingkindness: we receive without needing to act.

We are not only servants of God; we also experience ourselves as the children of God; a child and parent have a natural love and connection that sometimes is clouded or lost for a few moments. We do not have to "fight" our nature to return to connection but simply reestablish the natural connection that is there. The resistances no longer have power, no longer pull us. We are easily able to sustain the connection.

The stages of reconnection, a three-step process, are embedded in the liturgy of the Holy-Day, in the *Musaf* service. During the first part, *Malchuyot,* we describe images of God as the monarch, the ruler of the universe, making connection with Essence of God's Will, the inner quality of spirit that has been corrupted or misunderstood and caused our will to be at odds with the spiritual Will. In the second section, *Zichronot*, we focus on remembering as a way to access an experience of that Essence:

> We only need to make reference to memory when something is far away from us. When we are connected with an experience or it is present for us, there is no need for memory, that word has no meaning. When we talk about remembering something, that means that we are far from it and disconnected from it. And so, on this day, we ask to be reconnected with our memory and thereby to access the experience of God's Essence as it was on that first day.
>
> [*Likutei Torah*, 57B]

In the third section, *Shofarot*, we make the visceral connection. Shneur Zalman contrasts the deliberate, conscious, cognitive, and verbal efforts to make change with a more nonverbal, emotional process. He notes that the head—the brain—receives its life energy from the heart. Although the brain is the source of the life energy for the whole body, the head receives life from the heart: without the blood supply from the heart, the brain cannot do its work. In the same way, the heart is the source of connection with the divine Will.

The heart is associated with deep emotions, especially the experience of vulnerability. On Tisha B'Av, we experience our powerlessness and vulnerability, surrendering to our grief. On Rosh HaShanah, we experience a similar powerlessness. However, we do not find ourselves facing the immediate moment of loss and crisis. We are able to maintain some perspective: we experience regret as we reflect, realizing the extent of our failures to manifest the life force. The experience of powerlessness empowers us, fueling our prayer and becoming a force for transformation:

> As a person meditates in the depth of his heart, experiencing the pain in his soul, realizing the shortcomings and handicaps within and the effects of these flaws, the person cries out to God in this pain. This is known as the Cry of the Heart, in which the heart itself cries out. This pain from the depth of one's heart is so great that it cannot even be expressed in words.
>
> [*Likutei Torah*, 56]

In the same way, the sound of
the Shofar is a simple sound, a
sound without words, a sound
which comes from the depths of
the heart, from its innermost
essence. It is a sound which tran-
scends ordinary wisdom and
knowledge. For this reason, on
Rosh HaShanah, we read a
psalm in which we ask God not
*to listen—'*lekol—*to my voice,*
but to "listen to what is—

bekol—*in my voice," not to the words but to the sound of the*
words and the feelings expressed within them.

[*Likutei Torah,* 54B]

In contrast to Tisha B'Av, the powerlessness and vulnerability and acknowledgment of failure on Rosh HaShanah, are not a time of collapse but rather an important step in transforming ourselves. Shneur Zalman asserts that "anyone who does not shed tears on Rosh HaShanah, lacks an integrated soul" (*Likutei Torah,* 54B). We end our denial and we seek help. The acknowledgment of a difficulty and the need for help in overcoming it represents a more hopeful situation than continued denial of a problem and a rigid clinging to an inflated sense of our own competence and power.

That hopefulness is reinforced by the readings from the Torah on Rosh HaShanah. Abraham and Sarah have been promised by God that their progeny will become a great nation, but they remain childless into old age. We retell the story of the birth of Isaac in fulfillment of that promise. We read the story of God commanding Abraham to sacrifice his son in an apparent threat, once again to that pledge. In the end Isaac's life is not threatened, reaffirming the covenant with God. We listen to the story of Chana praying for a child, arguing with the priest who chastises her when the intensity of her devotion appears to resemble drunkenness. Chana's prayers are answered with the birth of her son, who becomes the prophet Samuel. We are inspired by the prophet Jeremiah's vision of deliverance in which he instills hope that the pain of exile will end in a return to the land of Israel.

Even the foods associated with Rosh HaShanah express our wishes for the new year, offering a light and sweet counterpoint to the themes of judgment and challenge. We dip apples in honey as an expression of our wish for a sweet year. Bread, which on Sabbaths and other holidays is dipped in salt, is also dipped in honey. The breads are baked in special ways as well: in a round rather than oval or rectangular shape to symbolize the crown of the monarch, or in the shape of ladders to remind us of being raised up or lowered. We eat the head of a fish to enact our hope to be the head rather than the tail.

A Clinical Example of the Receptive Principle

This process is illustrated in Gary's work. A year had passed since Gary ended therapy after successfully losing eighty pounds. When he called for an appointment, I could hear the sadness in his voice as he described how he had gained back all the weight he had lost. In our initial work together, Gary had been a model client. He was highly motivated, established clear goals, committed himself to a nutritional plan that allowed him to gradually and steadily lose weight; he stuck with it until he had achieved his goals. What happened? Why had his success turned out to be so fleeting?

As Gary described the events of the past months, I began to understand some of the issues. Gary desperately wanted to find a life partner, to get married and raise a family, but he had not succeeded in developing a long-term relationship. He had always blamed the difficulty on his weight. When he ended therapy the last time, he had been enthusiastic about the possibilities and had actively begun to develop his social life. However, after a short time, he lost momentum. He took a new job in which he was highly successful, but he also began to work evenings, nights, and weekends. He stopped cooking healthy foods and began to rely on junk foods. The weight came back. Caught up in the momentum of his work, he ignored his body.

I asked Gary what he wanted to achieve in therapy this time. Did he want to use the time to take charge of his life again and get back on his diet? Gary responded negatively. I was surprised because Gary was an action-oriented person. In the past, his "to-do list" had never been far from his side. Nonetheless, Gary felt he needed something different. He realized that weight was not the only barrier to finding a long-term relationship. He admitted that when he started to date, he had experienced extreme anxiety and a sense of shame. He did not want to focus on his weight. He felt he somehow needed to be fat to protect himself. He felt shame in admitting that he did not want to lose weight, that he wanted to be accepted as he was, with all the extra pounds.

I respected Gary's courage and his willingness to acknowledge his powerlessness and his vulnerability. I did not need Gary to lose weight for me; he did not have to be a "good" client in order to please me. Gary eyes began to tear. We talked about his childhood, how he had always been a "good" boy, always done what he was supposed to do, and always pleased his parents. After losing all that weight and beginning to date, he found himself entering into relationships with a similar style: he focused on pleasing his partner and forgetting his own needs. He was unable to stand up for himself, set limits, or end relationships that did not serve him. His weight protected him from being overwhelmed, from losing his sense of self. Gary cried as he faced the reality that he was stuck in a life-long pattern that could not easily be changed, a devastating pattern that stood in the way of achieving a basic goal in his life.

Gary's acknowledgment provided the basis for a new course of therapy. He spent two years in a therapy group and committed himself to working through this life-long pattern. In the group, he initially reenacted his pattern: he took care of others, asked little for himself, and never did anything that caused others to become angry. He got frustrated, almost quit the group, but gradually began to speak up for himself, taking the risk to be "selfish." He discovered that, unlike his family, group members actually supported him in these efforts and found him more likable when he showed more spine.

Gary's acknowledgment of his impasse paradoxically provided the foundation to true change. Fritz Perls (1973) expresses a similar idea when he talks about the importance of acknowledging an impasse, a condition of inner conflict in which one feels no possibility for escape or resolution. Transformation occurs by acknowledging the truth of the impasse and by feeling the frustration and the powerlessness. In twelve-step programs such as Alcoholics Anonymous, this principle provides the basis for the first step in overcoming one's addiction. So long as the alcoholic is in denial, no one can help.

God's Response to the Acknowledgment of Powerlessness

On Rosh HaShanah, we acknowledge our powerlessness and inability to change life-long habits in the cry expressed in the broken sound of the *shofar,* in our tears, the vulnerability, and the sound of our voice. As we surrender our old Ego, we are able to receive the life force that is manifested at this time of year. We no longer block the experience with a rigid, inaccurate, and inflated sense of self.

Shneur Zalman describes two factors that create these blocks, symbolized by two places in which the Jews were exiled: in *Mitzrayim,* Egypt, and in *Ashur,* Assyria. *Mitzrayim* is a symbol of suffering and oppression, associated with the word *maitzar,* which is translated as "narrow place." *Ashur* symbolizes materialism, connected to the word *ashir,* which means "wealth." Both suffering and materialism create blocks. Gary's story offers an example of both qualities: he found relief from his anxiety in relationships by succumbing to a food and work addiction. The acknowledgment of the truth of his situation provided a foundation for change.

The effort to change our responses combined with the acknowledgment of our powerlessness and cry for help are powerful. In the spiritual imagery, this acknowledgment causes God to step down from the throne of judgment and move to the throne of mercy. For Shneur Zalman, this concept is expressed in the binding of Isaac, whose story is told on Rosh HaShanah. Abraham and Isaac are not only our ancestors but symbols of archetypal forces. Abraham refers to the force of *Chesed,* Loving-kindness; Isaac refers to the quality of

Gevurah, Strength and Judgment. The binding of Isaac by Abraham symbolizes the submission of the quality of Judgment to the quality of Loving-kindness.

Although we are held accountable, our efforts to change are more effective than we might imagine. In the liturgy of the high Holy-Days, God says to us, "Make an opening for Me the size of a pinhole, and I will open for you a doorway." Despite the overwhelming momentum and force of history that predetermines the consequences, we can shift directions and change what had seemed like an inevitable conclusion. We reconnect with the experience of ourselves as children of God and the experience of God's Presence from the first day of creation, a moment of pure loving-kindness and grace.

MAKING OURSELVES ACCOUNTABLE

- What are the ways in which our coping responses are dysfunctional? in which we create negative consequences for ourselves?

- What are the consequences if we continue to respond based on these dysfunctional habits?

- What do we need to commit ourselves to do to change? What are the specific commitments we must make?

- What are the areas in which we feel powerless to change? How will we pray for guidance and support?

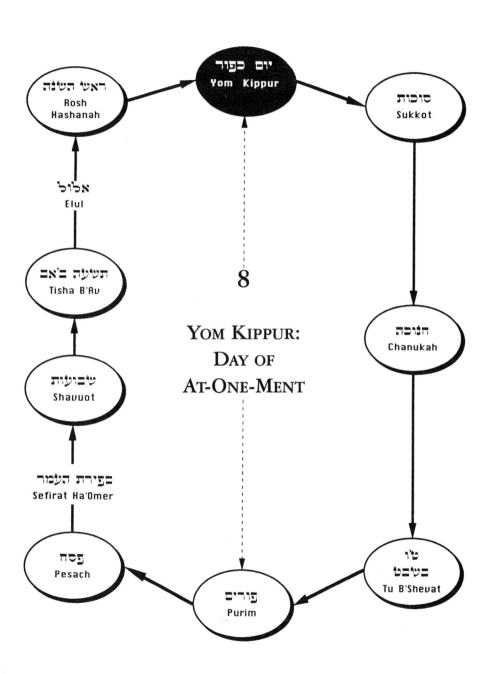

ראש השנה
Rosh
Hashanah

יום כפור
Yom Kippur

סוכות
Sukkot

אלול
Elul

8

חנוכה
Chanukah

תשעה ב'אב
Tisha B'Av

YOM KIPPUR:
DAY OF
AT-ONE-MENT

שבועות
Shavuot

ספירת העמר
Sefirat Ha'Omer

פסח
Pesach

פורים
Purim

ט'ו
בשבט
Tu B'Shevat

On Yom Kippur, the day of At-One-Ment, we experience a completion of the process begun during the month of Elul. Whereas the focus on Rosh HaShanah is with the image of God as judge and an emphasis on the struggle of *Eetkafya*—to acknowledge and interrupt old patterns, the focus on this Holy-Day is with God as the source of mercy and forgiveness, with the process of transforming evil—*Eethafcha*. We separate ourselves from the particular habits and identity which we rigidly and mistakenly regard as our "self," and we reconnect with our Essence. This experience of Spirit and One-ness provides a foundation for a new way of being and a new identity. Through the remainder of the year, we work to integrate that new identity.

TRANSFORMATION OF EVIL INTO GOOD

According to tradition, during the Sanctuary service on Yom Kippur, the High Priest tied a red thread to the horn of the scapegoat and symbolically transferred the misdeeds of the people onto the animal. At the end of the day, a miracle occurred in which the thread was transformed from red as blood to white as snow. In the liturgy, we repeatedly make reference to this image as a symbol of our own transformation. The image suggests that we not only free ourselves from the sins of the past, but that they are mystically transformed into positive forces.

This task is accomplished through a reconnection with our Essence, a moment of at-one-ment. The archetypal expression of this experience is in the climax of the service in the Sanctuary. The High Priest, symbol of the Essence of the people, enters the Holy of Holies, the Essence of all creation. He speaks the YHVH, the name of God which refers to the Essence of Being, a name spoken aloud only at this time of the year.

At the end of the process, that which was negative has dissolved and been replaced by a new form that is more appropriate and constructive. Darkness becomes like light, because it no longer prevents us from seeing. That which was evil is no longer a force but simply a step on the journey of transformation. Instead of being trapped into repeating the past, our history teaches us how we might create a different kind of future for ourselves.

A Clinical Example of the Process of Transformation

Before his death, Rabbi Zusya said, "In the coming world they will not ask me, "Why were you not Moses?" They will ask me, "Why were you not Zusya?"

The image of darkness transmuted into light, of evil transformed into good need not be regarded as an incomprehensible, esoteric, mystical concept. This process is illustrated by the experience of Manny in his struggle with addiction. Every day after work, Manny spent a couple hours in his neighborhood bar where he drank a pitcher of beer. On weekends, he plopped himself in front of the TV and consumed several six packs of beer each day. A few times a year at parties or celebrations, he tended to drink until he passed out. For many years, he had been able to function adequately; he was successful in his work at a computer company and held a high-level position even though he never graduated college. His marriage had ended in divorce, but he felt close to his son and treasured their time together. Manny had never thought that his drinking was a problem until he totaled his car while driving home from his neighborhood bar. Miraculously, he walked away from the accident although his car was demolished. Manny was determined to stop drinking. When he called me, he had not had a drink in two weeks.

When we met together, Manny affirmed his commitment to abstain completely from drinking. I asked him how he felt having stopped drinking. He noted that he did not find it difficult to keep away from alcohol. Usually, when he made up his mind to do something, he was stubborn and persistent in following through on his decision. He reported that he did not notice any feelings, either— not frustration, fear or sadness, relief, joy, or self-satisfaction. In fact, Manny did not feel much at all.

Manny appeared to have his situation under control. Usually, when someone comes for therapy they are experiencing stress and have a goal in mind. I did not understand his purpose in coming for therapy. When I asked him why he had decided to talk with me, he explained that he had initiated therapy at the suggestion of a doctor who warned Manny that it was difficult to stop an addiction without some outside support. He had come for therapy as the result not of an inner need but of someone else's assessment. Manny explained that he had never experienced psychotherapy and had no idea what was involved in the process. He assumed I was the expert and would instruct him.

I could identify some issues that might be valuable to explore. Most importantly, Manny's lack of awareness of his feelings and his needs appeared to be significant. I wondered if Manny's drinking had served as a form of self-medication, a way to calm himself or distance himself from emotions that were too overwhelming.

As we began to discuss his goals for therapy, this issue became more clear. I asked Manny if he had goals for his life, a vision about the future. Other than continuing to abstain from drinking and wanting to spend time with his son, he had no goals, neither personal nor professional. I asked Manny if he had ever had dreams for himself. He could not recall ever having had any dreams; although he had been successful in his work, he had never really been ambitious. He had gone to work in a company at a low-level position; his employer had repeatedly initiated promotions and higher levels of responsibility. In his personal life, his wife had initially pursued him; when they divorced, she also initiated the separation.

I asked Manny to reflect back to his childhood. Had he ever had dreams of what life would be like when he grew up? At this point, Manny informed me that he was a hemophiliac. When he was a child, the prognosis for hemophilia was very poor. He had been told as a child that he probably would not live past the age of 15 or 16. He never had any dreams of growing up, nor was he encouraged to imagine any other possibilities. Manny developed a wonderful capacity to live in the moment, have no expectations, and extract what he could from each day. No wonder he had no dreams. Now he was in his late forties and had already surpassed all expectations. I asked Manny if he still expected to die soon. He replied that, as a result of medical advances, he expected he could live a normal life span, into his seventies or eighties.

On the basis of this discussion, we were able to define some goals. Manny had coped very well with the possibility of a limited life span. However, the same coping skills that helped him survive now interfered with his life. He had no skill or capacity to dream and build realities from his dreams. His drinking had helped keep this deficit out of his awareness. With new awareness, he could begin to work at making a change.

The question remained of how to achieve the goal of having dreams. I suggested that he needed to develop the skill of identifying feelings because feelings are markers that let us know what we want and do not want. Since Manny never had learned about feelings, we needed to start as if it was a new skill, which it was. In the same way as one might start with a child to help name a few simple feelings, I suggested Manny to begin to check in with himself, to ask, "What am I feeling right now?" When Manny found this task too difficult, we devised a multiple-choice question instead: "At this moment, am I feeling sad, mad, glad, or scared?" He discovered he could answer that question. I asked him to keep a journal and record his feelings about those events. After a week of practice, we added another step: working to connect feelings with wants and needs. He experimented with identifying the feeling and noticing if there was anything he wanted or needed.

In time, Manny found himself able to talk about feelings and wants in daily life. There was a colleague at work who made him feel angry. He wanted him to stop talking. He noticed he felt glad when he spent time with his son. He felt sad when he visited his elderly father but could not define what he wanted in that relationship. I suggested he did know something about what he wanted: he wanted to know what he wanted. He smiled and agreed. His expression changed, his eyes softened, and he looked as if he might be on the edge of tears: "That's right," he said, "I want to know what I want in my life." For the first time, Manny identified a want that extended beyond the moment and into the future.

I told Manny I was glad he had discovered a deep feeling and a want. Manny was an engineer. He was not used to questions that had no immediate, practical answer. However, this question had no immediate answer. Nonetheless, his discovery of the want and need represented an important step. I suggested to Manny that he not rush to identify any practical solutions. Instead, I asked if he would be willing to try an experiment for a week, something that I thought would be helpful, although it might seem slightly odd. Always cooperative, Manny agreed. I proposed that every time he looked in a mirror, he say to his image in the mirror, "I want to know what I want." Slightly amused and somewhat skeptical, he agreed to try the exercise.

The exercise helped. Over the next months, Manny began to identify many wants and needs. Despite his success at work, he noticed that he often felt inadequate because he was the only person in his company who had no college degree. Most of his colleagues had advanced degrees. Even though there was no external pressure, he discovered that he wanted to complete his college degree. He had taken courses at various times but had never realized how much it meant to him to finish. He made plans for finishing his course work and made a commitment to completing the degree.

In relationship to his father, Manny realized that he felt sad to see his father living in a house that had deteriorated: it needed paint on the walls, new carpets and linoleum on the floors, and a variety of simple repairs. He decided to spend part of each visit with his father fixing up the house. Manny also noticed some feelings each time he passed by his neighborhood bar, which he no longer visited. He realized that he did not miss his beer, but he did miss the camaraderie and friendship. He was not afraid that he would be tempted to drink, but he was afraid that his friends would make fun of him if he admitted to being an alcoholic. He decided to visit the bar and told his friends that his doctor had discovered that he was allergic to alcohol and had instructed him to stick to seltzer and soft drinks. They accepted his explanation, and Manny found that he enjoyed spending time with his friends at the bar, though not as frequently as before.

At one session, I told Manny how proud I felt about what he had accomplished in a very short time. I felt he had really done a good job. Even as the words came out of my mouth, I knew something was wrong. Manny's face tightened, his eyes narrowed, and he looked away from me. I thought perhaps he found it difficult to receive a compliment. However, I was wrong. He told me he had no problem receiving compliments. He closed his eyes for a moment, checking in with himself to clarify what he was feeling. When he opened his eyes, he looked confused. "I don't understand it, but I feel angry at you."

I didn't understand what was happening either. I asked Manny if he would be willing to sit with his feeling, suggesting that he notice the feelings and body sensations, as well as any images, thoughts, associations, or memories that spontaneously bubbled up into his consciousness. He sat quietly for a few minutes. "I feel like I am about 8 years old. I'm angry." Manny had accessed a memory. He was at the doctor's office. Manny had been a model patient: he never cried, he always did what he was told, and he was consistently cheerful. The doctors and nurses loved him: "You are such a good boy,

Manny. We are so proud of you. We wish all the children were as cooperative as you are." At the time, Manny was proud. He tried hard to live up to his reputation. However, now he felt angry.

I suggested to Manny that it might be helpful to imagine himself at the doctor's office and to say what he had never had a chance to say to the caring but misguided adults.

"Why did you force me to be so good?" he said. "I don't like these transfusions. I don't like the way the hospital smells. I don't like having to be so careful on the playground. I don't like having to be so good. I hate this." Tears rolled down Manny's cheeks. His hands were clenched into tight fists. No wonder Manny was furious when I complimented him on doing a "good" job.

Manny gradually reoriented himself to the here-and-now reality of my office. "I've always been a good boy. I'm sick of being a good boy all the time." He realized he was angry at some of his colleagues at work who consistently failed to do their jobs properly and relied on Manny to fix their mistakes. He was angry with the registrar at his college who made his life miserable with bureaucratic red tape when he tried to obtain credit for courses taken at a different school. He was angry with his ex-wife who repeatedly attacked him in front of their son.

Manny stopped being a "good boy." He stopped covering up for his coworkers. One of them was fired. He carefully documented several incidents in which the registrar had violated school policies and filed a formal complaint. He confronted his wife about her outbursts in front of their son. He decided to take a trip to Las Vegas, even though it seemed decadent and wasteful. Manny had made tremendous progress in learning to recognize and respect his wants.

At our last session together, Manny reflected on his life in the year since his accident. He remembered when he extricated himself from his demolished car and realized he could have been killed. "At the time," he said, "I thought that accident was the worst thing that ever happened to me. It seems strange to say this, but now, I'm almost glad it happened. As a result of the accident, I discovered that I hadn't been fully alive. As a result of that accident, I'm more alive now than I ever was. I feel things. I get angry. I get excited. I have dreams. That accident was a gift."

For Manny, his decision to abstain from drinking allowed him to get to know himself in a new way. He was not a religious man in the traditional sense and would never have thought about praying, but he nonetheless prayed when he decided to experiment with the ritual of saying to himself in the mirror, "I want to know what I want". His exploration of the past led him to discover he had been unable to respect the integrity of his own being. His awareness, regret, and decision to say what he had never said transformed something inside himself, enabling him to speak up in the present as never before. In making these changes, the original trauma that had initially been viewed as negative was itself transformed into a positive experience.

A Psychotherapeutic Perspective on Transformation of Evil

Once you get above the clouds, all the world looks like heaven.
                                            © Ashleigh Brilliant

In psychotherapy, it is important to recognize the archaic, unconscious, rigid, and dysfunctional way of being and responding. Interrupting the previously automatic behavior, we separate ourselves from the old automatic response before attempting to make a shift. As illustrated by Manny's work, we complete that task with a process that parallels that of Yom Kippur in many respects: (1) disidentifying from old patterns of responding, (2) reconnecting with the inexpressible Essence of life, (3) acknowledging our misdoings as a way to separate ourselves from them and clarify new, more constructive responses, and (4) ritually affirming our directions and intention based on the experience of Essence.

> **Jungian Therapy**—In the Jungian perspective, we surrender the Ego and reconnect with the Self as a basis for developing a new, more effective Ego identity. For Jung, this cycle occurred spontaneously as part of the flow of one's life, a reaction to changes in circumstances and context. We become aware of where we are in that cycle through dreams

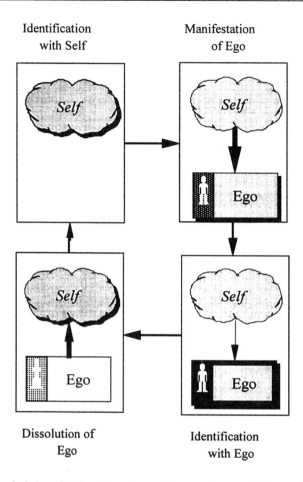

Identification   Manifestation
with Self   of Ego

Dissolution of   Identification
Ego   with Ego

and through identification with myths, symbols and stories. In the Jewish approach, our encounter is structured into the flow of the year at Yom Kippur.

Psychosynthesis—Similarly, in Assagioli's approach of psychosynthesis, after a person successfully identifies all the various subpersonalities—habitual modes of response—the next task is to separate ourselves consciously from those roles, identities, and self-images. We focus not only on interrupting the behaviors but on making an internal change in how we define ourselves. To accomplish this task, a person might make a list of the various roles with which he or she describes him or herself and then actively imagine surrendering those roles until only a core Essence of being remains. Assagioli also stresses the importance, at times, of making an act of will, developing discipline in following through on commitments and overcoming obstacles that stop us.

The Alexander Technique—Another example of this process is in the technique for movement re-education developed by F. M. Alexander. Alexander was a Shakespearean actor who developed a problem with his voice. Observing himself with mirrors, he discovered that his problem was caused by an unconscious movement of his head, his neck pulling back and down, constricting his spine and larynx. When Alexander attempted to change his posture, he discovered that conscious effort to lengthen his neck only exacerbated his tension: his conscious mind did not know how to move differently. Then he experimented with simply noticing the tension, stopping himself when he realized he had unconsciously tried to correct his movement, saying to himself, "Let my neck be free," and continuing to monitor spontaneous changes in kinesthetic awareness. The Alexander technique is based upon the belief that movement habits change by heightening awareness of how we use our bodies. The student of the method uses conscious inhibition to interrupt patterns without trying to change or fix the body. Focused intention is then utilized actively to imagine a shift. Each moment, the student practices interrupting the impulse and substituting the new intention.

TRANSFORMATION AND THE HEALING
OF PAST TRAUMA

You darkness that I come from
I love you more than all the fires
that fence in the world,
for the fire makes
a circle of light for everyone,
and then no one outside learns of you.

But the darkness pulls in everything:
shapes and fires, animals and myself
how easily it gathers them!—
powers and people.

And it is possible a great energy
is moving near me.

I have faith in nights.

Rainer Maria Rilke (translated by Robert Bly)

On Yom Kippur, transformation is symbolized by the thread which turns from red as blood to white as snow. It is difficult to understand how to apply that image to our own lives. Can we actually turn a traumatic hurt from the past into a positive experience? In Manny's work, he understood his trauma in a new way that made the experience more positive, but that falls short of rewriting one's history. In the movie Back to the Future, the hero discovered that events in current life were affected by what had happened before. He traveled backward in time, changed the responses to events, and thereby changed the future. There are times, for each of us, when we wish we could similarly return to the past, armed with the wisdom and knowledge that comes with hindsight and maturity.

Imagine someone who is isolated, withdrawn, and unable to develop satisfying relationships. How wonderful it might be if we could transport that adult back to the first grade classroom, return him to the moment when he mistakenly concluded that he was not likable. At the age of 6, he moves to a new school. He is lost, feels isolated. No one notices his dilemma and pain. He concludes that there is something wrong with himself and that he is not likable. He withdraws, becomes more isolated, and is rejected by his peers.

What if we could rewrite history? We could resolve the problem in many ways. Perhaps a sympathetic teacher, parent, or other child notices his pain, reaches out to him, helping him to develop skills in sports that provide a channel for social interaction and connection. Or perhaps the child finds the courage to speak, asking for help and guidance. As a result of that change, what had previously been a trauma would be transformed into a positive memory, an example of overcoming a problem with inner fortitude and outside support.

It might appear that we are not so lucky, that we are unable to change the past. Are we therefore stuck? Are we imprisoned by the results of events that occurred long ago? Are we limited and forced to live by choices made long ago? Although it is not possible to rewrite history, we can do something that can often help ameliorate and heal the wounds of the past. A variety of psychological techniques allow us to transport ourselves backward in time not only to recall the past but to reexperience our history and transform it. For example, in a trance state, a person can access past experiences very vividly, experiencing the history not simply as a cognitive awareness but as if the past had become present, not simply recalling the memories of childhood but actually reexperiencing them with all the feelings and physiological responses. Although this reexperiencing sometimes occurs spontaneously as it did for Manny, it can also be accessed through the use of hypnosis or psychodrama as well. In hypnosis, active imagination is used to experience vividly and transform the past. In psychodrama, a person reexperiences the events of the past by inviting others to take the role of one of the protagonists and reenact the events.

With either approach, one begins by vividly reexperiencing the events of the past as if they were in the present. In this state of heightened awareness, one can also change history, allowing oneself or others to do something different in the present than happened in the past. In so doing, the traumatic event becomes transformed. In some respects, history is rewritten because one can recall not only the original trauma but also the reenactment in which something different happened.

FROM ESSENCE TO MANIFESTATION:
AFFIRMATIONS, INTENTIONS, AND PRAYERS

If you will it, it is no dream!

Theodor Herzl

Once we succeed in inhibiting a dysfunctional way of being and reconnecting with our Essence, our next step is to translate that understanding back into everyday life. That step is sometimes difficult because we have no experience of anything different. We can begin, as Manny did, with an affirmation of our direction. The ritual repetition of that direction helps orient our being toward creating a new possibility.

The connection between this therapeutic process and prayer is illustrated by the work of Shari, a survivor of childhood violence and abuse. Shari and her siblings were sexually and physically abused through the course of childhood by both parents. Their father was an FBI agent whose specialty was the prosecution of family violence cases. The violence was kept secret because the family was regarded as pillars of the community and model citizens. The truth did not emerge until the daughters, plagued by various physical and emotional symptoms, confronted their past.

For Shari, crises that occurred with her own children motivated her to address her unresolved issues of her childhood. One of these crises involved her eldest daughter, who was married to an alcoholic. Her daughter remained in the relationship in spite of violent incidents that increased in frequency and seriousness. Shari was concerned for her daughter and her 3-year-old granddaughter, whose situation evoked memories of her own childhood.

One day, Shari showed up for her session in extreme distress. Another incident had occurred in which her son-in-law hit the 3-year-old. Shari was powerless because her daughter was unwilling to leave her husband. We discussed the options. There was really nothing Shari could do.

Shari needed to find some positive focus, something she could do when she could not do anything. I suggested we pray together. Shari grew up in a religious family: they went to church every Sunday. However, when I suggested we pray for her daughter and granddaughter, she did not look happy or relieved—she turned white. As sometimes happened, she experienced a flashback to a time when she was 4 years old, recalling how each night, she and her father kneeled beside her bed and said night-time prayers together: "Now I lay me down to sleep, I pray the Lord my soul to keep; and if I die before I wake. . . ." After they finished, her father would climb into bed with her.

The idea of praying together repulsed Shari; sitting alone in a room with a man and praying was too evocative of childhood. We talked about the dilemma. Her abuse had left another scar that contaminated her adult life. It deprived her of the capacity to pray, an activity that offered some sense of hope at times when she was powerless. She wanted to free herself from that contamination. We agreed that we would spend a few minutes each week in prayer. Each week, we took time to compose the words of the prayer—to send light and love to her daughter and granddaughter.

Shari found the experience of praying difficult and healing. Our prayers did not cause any immediate, miraculous transformation in the realities of her daughter and granddaughter. However, it did cause an immediate transformation for Shari. She remained sad, but she was no longer overwhelmed and unable to function in her own life. Her prayers helped her contain her feelings; she continued to do what she could. When her daughter finally made the decision to leave the abusive relationship, she was able to provide support.

THE EXPERIENCE OF AT-ONE-MENT:
THE RECEPTIVE AND THE ACTIVE PROCESS

And if it is true that we acquired our knowledge before our birth, and lost it at the moment of birth, but afterward by the exercise of our senses upon sensible objects, recover the knowledge which we had once before, I suppose that what we call learning will be the recovery of our own knowledge.

Plato

The theme of mystical union on Yom Kippur is expressed in the liturgy through a change in the recitation of the customary manner of declaring the oneness of God. It is customary through the year to recite two verses: *Shema Yisrael YHVH Elohaynu YHVH Echad*—"Listen Israel, *YHVH* Our God is One"—and *Baruch Shem Kevod Malchuto Le'olam Va'ed*—"Blessed Is the Name of God's Kingdom Forever and Ever." The first verse refers to a mystical unification and experience of God's oneness. The second verse refers to the experience of God's Presence in the material world. During the rest of the year, the second verse is recited silently, because we can only partially experience that Presence. However, on Yom Kippur we have direct experience of that Presence, and we can make our declaration in a regular voice.

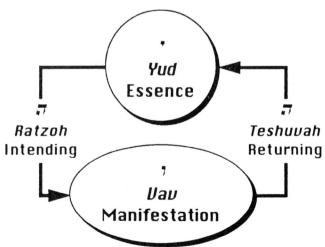

God's unspoken name, *Yud-Heh-Vav-Heh,* encodes the cycle of manifestation, surrender of the material, reconnection with Essence, and manifestation again. The *yud* (ׁ) which is a point, symbolizes Essence before creation: the moment before the breath of creation occurs. The *heh* (ה) is associated with manifestation of spirit into material existence, equivalent to the in-breath of creation. The *vav* (ו), which looks like a *yud* with a long tail extending downward, is a symbol of manifestation, the material world and the ego identity, associated with the moment of holding the breath prior to exhalation. The final *heh* (ה) is linked to the surrender of material existence and of the ego and to the release of exhalation.

This process can be understood through an analogy. In building a house, one begins with an inexpressible sense of the ideal dwelling. We have a concept of a home, a shelter, a sanctuary. That essence is translated into an image that can then be solidified into written plans. The architectural drawings become the basis for building the actual structure.

There is a dynamic tension between the physical edifice and the original concept. Our original idea of a home informs and guides us. Without that foundation, we would not know what to create. At the same time, we cannot live in a concept; we must translate it into a physical reality. Unfortunately, something is always lost in the process. Sometimes, the plans are not executed properly; the carpenters make mistakes, and the building does not reflect our original plan. Sometimes, the plan fails to accomplish what we originally intended: the carpenters did their work well, but the design is flawed. Sometimes, our needs change, making us dissatisfied with a home that previously served us well. The understanding has changed of what is meant by "home."

Consequently, we must return again to the abstract conception. We use what we have learned to redefine the concept of home. Once again, we translate the concept into drawings and then into a new physical reality. Sometimes, we tear down what we built before; sometimes, we abandon one house for a new home. The process is often difficult; change can be costly in terms of money, energy, and stress. Over the years, we may go through this process many times and subsequently adjust our home to accommodate the changes in our lives.

As we return to our concept of how we want our home to be, surrendering for a moment the material manifestation of our design, we reconnect with the essence. We can then examine the material manifestation in terms of that original intention, assess the extent to which it expresses that essence. As we understand what is missing or incorrect, we can redefine how to manifest that vision properly. Similarly, on Yom Kippur, as we separate ourselves from material activity and reconnect to Essence, we are able to understand and acknowledge our failures. In so doing, we understand what we need to do instead.

Similar to Rosh HaShanah, this transformation is accomplished through two types of work, a receptive and an active process. According to Shneur Zalman, the active and receptive principles are suggested by the biblical text. In the Torah, the day of Yom Kippur is referred to in both the masculine and the feminine. In one citation, it is written *Shabbat Shabbaton Hu Lachem*—"A Sabbath of Sabbaths, he shall be for you." In another citation, it is written *Shabbat Shabbaton Hee Lachem*—"A Sabbath of Sabbaths, she shall be for you."

Receptive Principle	Active Principle
Feminine	Masculine
God's Essence	God as Manifest
Yud Heh	*Vav Heh*
Anochi	*Ani*
Hidden	Revealed
Negative commandments	Positive commandments
Deficits injure source of light	Deficits injure capacity to receive light
Yom Kippur	*Teshuvah*

These two principles are also linked by Shneur Zalman to two words God uses when speaking in the first person, the two words for "I": *Ani* and *Anochi.* *Ani* refers to the revealed world and the ways in which God's Presence is manifested on earth. It is associated with the last two letters of God's name—*vav* and *heh,* the letters associated with the material world. It is also connected with the positive commandments because what you do is observable.

Anochi is associated with the hidden world, the world of Essence that is not normally experienced. It is linked to the first two letters of God's name—*yud* and *heh.* It is also connected with the negative commandments, what we are asked to refrain from doing, because what we inhibit cannot be seen.

When we fail to do what we need to do, we create a wound that cuts us off from the light of the Infinite. When we fail to inhibit harmful impulses, we damage the light itself and reduce its power to shine. We reestablish our capacity to receive the light through the process of *teshuvah.* The repair to the source of light is completed through the process of Yom Kippur.

The Receptive Process

Working with the receptive principle, we accomplish the goal through dis-identification with the material world. On the day before Yom Kippur, this separation starts by immersing oneself in a *mikveh,* the ritual bath containing water from rain or a stream. Beginning at sunset and continuing until the next evening, we abstain from eating and drinking, working, engaging in sexual activity, and wearing leather. In this way, we separate ourselves from the identity associated with gender, being a consumer, profession, and our domination in nature. As a reminder of our mortality, at all the services, we wear the garment in which we are buried, a white robe known as a *kittel.* In the same way

as the caterpillar gives up its physical manifestation so as to become a butterfly, we surrender our identity so as to allow for a new possibility.

This theme is expressed in the biblical description of Yom Kippur as *Shabbat Shabbaton*—a Sabbath of Sabbaths. During the six days of creation, God spoke and brought the world into manifestation. On the seventh day, God rested. When God speaks, there is a contraction of the Essence of Spirit that reduces the indescribable, nonverbal Presence to something that can be defined with words. When God rests on the Sabbath, there is a return to the infinite, inexpressible Essence.

In the same way, our words also represent a diminution of our own inexpressible Essence. During the week, we do our work of creating, building a dwelling place for Spirit on earth through everything we do. When we rest on the Sabbath, we reconnect with the Essence of our being. Yom Kippur is also a Sabbath: in not working, we disidentify with our roles as producers; in not eating and drinking , we disidentify with our roles as consumers; in not engaging in sexual activity, we disidentify with our roles as male and female; in not wearing leather, we disidentify with our power over other species and our role as controllers of the universe. In so doing, we return, as well, to the Essence of who we are.

The Active Process

So was I myself a swinger of birches.
And so I dream of going back to be.
It's when I'm weary of considerations,
And life is too much like a pathless wood
Where your face burns and tickles with the cobwebs
Broken across it, and one eye is weeping
From a twig's having lashed across it open.
I'd like to get away from earth awhile
And then come back to it and begin over.
May no fate willfully misunderstand me
and half grant what I wish and snatch me away
Not to return. Earth's the right place for love:

I don't know where it's likely to go better.
I'd like to go by climbing a birch tree,
and climb black branches up a snow-white trunk
Toward heaven, till the tree could bear no more,
But dipped its top and set me down again.
That would be good both going and coming back.
One could do worse than be a swinger of birches.

Robert Frost

Working with the active principle, we use prayer. During the time of the Sanctuary, the High Priest, in the presence of the people, performed rituals and made offerings. He acknowledged his own misdoings, those of his family, and those of the nation, symbolically transferring the sins onto the scapegoat that was sent out into the desert. The burning of the sacrifices on the altar provided a symbolic enactment of the elevation of material existence to the spiritual level; rising as smoke back up to the heavens, the burning flesh of the animal is transformed into its basic elements. The reconnection with Essence was expressed as the High Priest approached the Holy of Holies, the most sacred place in the Sanctuary, the place that was not entered any other time during the year. At this time, the High Priest also said aloud the normally unspoken name of God, the *YHVH.*

Although the Sanctuary no longer exists, the liturgy of Yom Kippur is based on these rituals. On the ninth of Tishrei, before Yom Kippur, the ritual of the scapegoat, known as *Kapparot,* is commemorated with either a live chicken or a contribution to charity. During the day of Yom Kippur, we tell the story of the High Priest in the Sanctuary and prostrate ourselves as our ancestors did when the name of God was spoken aloud.

Since the destruction of the Sanctuary, prayer substitutes for the animal sacrifices because the fire of our prayers raises up the material concerns of daily life to a spiritual level. We use prayer to accomplish the same goals achieved through the sacrifices. We acknowledge and separate ourselves from misdoings, and we connect with the Essence of Life symbolized by the unspoken name of God and the Holy of Holies in the Sanctuary. We also ask for support, guidance, and help to manifest a spiritual dimension in our worldly tasks and concerns.

The activity of prayer allows us to touch the depth of our concerns in the material world and raise them up to the highest level. For this reason, God is compared to a young, supple cypress tree that bends easily: "*Ani kee'brosh ra'anan*"—"I am like a singing cypress tree." Our prayers are raised up like an object placed on the top of a bent tree, carried to the top when the branches are released.

For this reason, most of the day is spent in prayer on Yom Kippur. In addition to the customary services—*Ma'ariv* in the evening, *Shacharit* and *Musaf* in the morning, and *Mincha* in the afternoon—there is also an added service just before to the end of the day—*Ne'ilah*. Each of the services on Yom Kippur includes a confessional—*Vidui*—in which we acknowledge our failings and reach out to the God of mercifulness, the God of the thirteen attributes whom we addressed during the month of Elul.

We begin the holiest day of our year with a disclaimer, in recitation of the prayer—*Kol Needrai*, announcing that all vows, promises, commitments, and pledges made from this year until the next shall be considered null and void. Although one might think it absurd to enter this time of self-reflection by nullifying what we are about to do, this declaration makes sense from the mystical perspective. We begin by acknowledging the limits of words, even prayer, to express the Essence of our being.

We end the day with hope. At the end of the last service, *Ne'ilah,* the time when the gates are closed, we blow the *shofar,* one long blast to mark the completion of the fast. We express our optimism concerning our future as we declare, "*Leshana ha'ba'ah be'Yerushalayim*"—"Next year, may we be in Jerusalem," a wish for the arrival of the messianic era.

PERSONAL PROCESS ON YOM KIPPUR

It is the eve of Yom Kippur. The shul is filled. Suddenly, the silence is broken as the rabbi, a saintly and wise man, jumps to his feet and prays, "Dear Lord, answer our prayers on this day, for we are nothing but dust and ashes." The congregants are moved by his words, return to their prayers with even more intensity. Then, an old man with a long beard, revered for his kindness and compassion, jumps to his feet and prays, "Dear Lord, answer our prayers on this day, for we are nothing; we are dust and ashes." Once again the congregants are inspired. A few more minutes pass. Suddenly, from the back row of the shul, Feivel, the tailor, rises from his seat, throws his arms to the heavens, and prays, "Dear Lord, answer our prayers on this day, for we are nothing; we are dust and ashes." The congregation is quiet. Sitting on the other side of the shul, Moshe, the shoemaker, pokes his friend in the ribs, leans over and whispers, "So, look who thinks he's nothing!"

The theme of Yom Kippur is sometimes misunderstood as inflicting punishment on ourselves, performing penance so that God will have mercy on us. If we punish ourselves, perhaps God will not punish us. However, for the mystics, the process of Yom Kippur carries a different meaning. The focus is on detachment from materialism as our focus rather than penance. From this perspective, dysfunctional behavior is the result of a disconnection from our true Essence, from the Spirit within us that is a spark of Divinity. Immersed in the material world, we lose connection with that Essence, mistaking the means for the end.

It is inevitable that we lose connection with the spiritual Essence as we are immersed in daily life with its pressures and stresses. Yom Kippur provides an opportunity to distance ourselves momentarily, reconnect with that Essence, and allow that experience to inform us as we return to the material world with all its concerns.

In some respects, the notion of reconnecting with our Essence makes no logical sense because we cannot truly be separated from the Source of Life. Although we may talk about ourselves as distant from God, the Source and Sustainer of life is always present as we read in the Psalms: "Your Kingdom is the Kingdom of all worlds." Moreover, God renews creation every day, as reflected in the morning prayers when we say, "You renew the world; everyday is the work of creation." Whatever we do, wherever we are, however we live, at all times, we are connected to the Essence of life.

Despite this immutable bond, the struggle for survival on earth can cause us to become oblivious to that reality. For example, to sustain ourselves, we must address material concerns to provide for ourselves economically. It is easy to lose connection with the Essence of life and make money into our God, viewing economic pursuit as the only reality. Shneur Zalman expresses this understanding when he suggests that all of us are "innocent worshippers of the stars." Our identification with the material world and loss of connection with Essence is an innocent and perhaps unavoidable mistake. The material world, although created by God, functions through intermediaries, astrological forces associated with the stars that control every aspect of life: each blade of grass has its star. As a result, we lose awareness of the real Source of life and "innocently" worship the stars instead of their Creator.

Our relationship with God can be compared to two people standing back to back but not looking at one another. They are physically close but emotionally distant. When they return to focus on one another, they are again face to face. God continues to sustain us and keep us alive, but we lose awareness of the connection. In this respect, we turn our back on God. We do not lose connection, because that is impossible: we lose awareness of our relationship. When we return, like a person turning again to face a friend, we become aware of the connection that has always been there. In the liturgy, God says, "You have turned your backs on me." We, in turn, pray to God, "Return to us, and we shall return to You," to resume face-to-face relationship. As we regain awareness of that connection, we once again experience ourselves in a face-to-face relationship.

In separating ourselves from the material world through fasting and abstinence from material pleasures, we allow ourselves to reconnect with the spiritual Essence. We can then examine how we live from a more objective perspective. What do we do that serves to express the divine Spirit within us? What do we do that inhibits the expression of that Spirit? As we reflect on the sources of our rigid, dysfunctional responses, we discover new possibilities that allow us to transform both the past and the present. From this foundation, we commit ourselves to respond differently in the future.

RETURN TO ESSENCE

- *Disidentifying from Old Patterns* —What commitments do I need to make to abstain from habitual, previously unconscious roles and identities?

- *Reconnecting with Essence* —How can I experience the inexpressible sense of my own spirit?

- *Transforming past traumas* —How can I access and work through events in the past which have shaped my beliefs, feelings, and reactions?

- *Manifesting that essence: intention and prayer* —What affirmations and prayers help me to focus my energy in manifesting my Spirit in daily life?

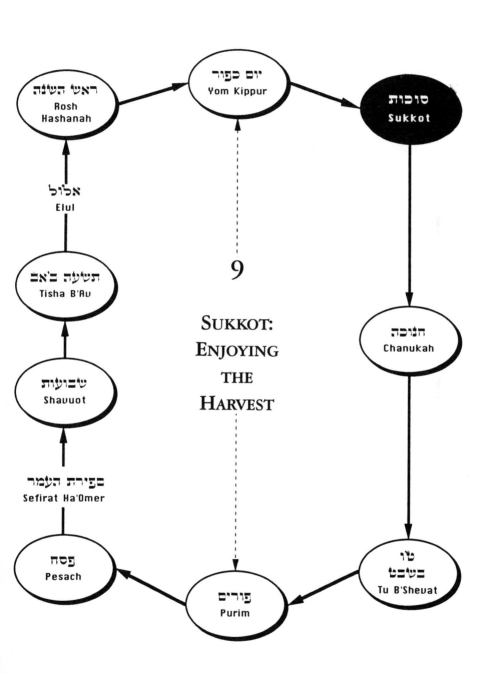

ראש השנה
Rosh
Hashanah

יום כפור
Yom Kippur

סוכות
Sukkot

אלול
Elul

תשעה ב'אב
Tisha B'Av

חנוכה
Chanukah

שבועות
Shavuot

9

SUKKOT:
ENJOYING
THE
HARVEST

ספירת העמר
Sefirat Ha'Omer

פסח
Pesach

פורים
Purim

טו
בשבט
Tu B'Shevat

On the fifteenth day of the seventh month, you shall celebrate
the festival of Sukkot, seven days for God; on the first day shall
be a convocation of holiness, you shall not do any manner of
work; you shall sacrifice a burn offering to God for seven days.
On the eighth day, there shall be a convocation of holiness, and
you shall sacrifice a burn offering to God, it shall be a day of
assembly, you shall not do any manner of work.

[Leviticus 23:34–36]

Sukkot begins on the fifteenth day of Tishrei, five days after Yom Kippur. It is celebrated for eight days. The first day and eighth days are celebrated as full Holy-Days with restrictions on work. Outside of Israel, the first two and last two days are commemorated.

Freed from the constrictions of our personal slavery at Pesach, we wander in the desert until we achieve revelation at Sinai. We experience grief as we realize the difficulty of translating that insight into manifestation, motivating us to enter into the process of self-reflection during the Days of Awe. On Sukkot, we harvest the fruits of our labor, experiencing the pleasure and satisfaction resulting from these changes, allowing our enjoyment to strengthen our efforts. In this spirit, Sukkot is also known as *Z'man Simchateinu*, the time of our joy, and *Chag Ha'Assif*, the Holy-Day of harvest.

Central to the celebration of the Holy-Day is the *sukkah*, the temporary shelter commemorating the tents in which the children of Israel lived when they left Egypt and wandered through the desert:

You shall live in Sukkot *for
seven days; every citizen of Israel
shall dwell in* Sukkot *so that the
generations shall know that God
caused the children of Israel to
live in* Sukkot *when I brought
them out of the land of Egypt.*
[Leviticus 23:42]

The construction of the *sukkah*
is carefully prescribed by tradition,
a three or four-sided structure with
a roof of branches and decorated according to individual tastes. The
sukkah is a temporary shelter but strong enough to withstand the
elements. The covering may not contain metal and, one must be
able to see the stars through the spaces. During the Holy-Day, we
eat, sleep, socialize in the *sukkah*. Insofar as possible, it becomes our
temporary home.

The holiday of Sukkot is also commemorated with a ritual which
utilizes four species of growing things: a palm branch—*lulav,* a cit-
ron—*etrog,* willow branches—*aravot,* and myrtle branches—*dasim,*
as commanded in the Torah:

> *And you shall take on the first day, the fruit of the* hadar *tree,
> branches of palm trees, a bough of the* avot *tree, and willows
> of the brook, and you shall rejoice before the Lord, your God,
> seven days.*
>
> [Leviticus 23:40]

The tradition provides detailed prescriptions concerning the qualities of each of the species. The willow and myrtle branches are
bound together with the *lulav.* After recitation of a special blessing,
the four species are shaken to the six directions—east, south, west,
north, up and down. They are also carried in a procession around the
synagogue, a ritual known as *Hoshanot.*

The seventh day of Sukkot is known as Hoshanah Raba. On this
day, the ritual of *Hoshanot* involves seven circlings of the synagogue
with the four species. At the end of this ritual, willow branches are

beaten against the ground. Hoshanah Raba is viewed as the end of the cycle which began on the first day of Elul.

The last day of Sukkot is followed by the separate festivals of *Shimini Atzeret* and *Simchat Torah* (in the Diaspora, celebrated as two days). We no longer make use of the *sukkah* or of the four species. A special prayer for rain is added as we look forward to the winter growing season in Israel.

Simchat Torah marks the time when we complete the yearly cycle of the reading of the Torah, ending the book of Deuteronomy. It is also the time when we start again to read from the beginning of the book of Genesis and the story of creation. In the evening, the Torah scrolls are taken from the ark and seven circlings, *hakafot,* of the synagogue are made, accompanied by spirited dancing and singing. The same is done on the following morning. To enhance the celebration, Simchat Torah is one of the two times in the Jewish year when drunkenness is encouraged in the tradition. It is also customary to carry the levity into a good-humored parody of the service and the ritual.

During the time of the Sanctuary, the ritual included a flour offering. Libations of wine and of water were also poured on the altar. The water for the libation was drawn from the wells of Shiloah in a joyful ceremony. The Holy-Day was also marked by the sacrifice of seventy oxen, corresponding to the seventy nations of the world, serving as a prayer for peace and well-being for all of humanity.

THE MEANINGS OF SUKKOT

Sukkot carries multiple meanings: a symbol of the transformation as we move out of our homes and into a new structure, a symbol of fragility in its impermanence, and a symbol of protection from the elements. The Holy-Day provides us with a sheltered environment in which we can experience our new way of being in the world. The *sukkah* offers protection from the pressures and stresses of daily life as we embark on this fragile and tentative exploration. Some of the themes which are important on Sukkot are described in the following sections:

Acknowledging Changes

For the Israelites in the desert, the *sukkah* provided a new home after they left slavery in Egypt. The *sukkah* links us to that archetypal experience of change. In this spirit, we begin to build the *sukkah* immediately after the end of Yom Kippur. We move out of the permanent shelter which we habitually regard as home. We move into a new home and establish it as a center for the activities of daily life: eating, sleeping, socializing, and study. The changes in our space are reinforced by changes we make in how we structure our time. After the Days of Awe, we do not return to our regular schedules with normal routines. We set aside a full week for prayer, celebration, and community.

In some respects, the image of the *sukkah* evokes the wandering in the desert associated with the counting of the *omer.* However, there are significant differences. After Pesach, we are thrust into an alien environment; we are confused and dependent. Moments of joy in our freedom are fleeting and unstable. On Sukkot, we experience our competence, autonomy, and power as we build our own shelter. Our joy is built upon a solid foundation as we celebrate our achievements. The image of the *sukkah* as a symbol of change helps us become aware of how we have been transformed as a result of the process of self-reflection which has just been completed. We take ourselves out of the inner "home" of our old personality and move into the new way of being in the world. We take time to be aware of the changes, appreciate them, and deepen our experience of them so they can be integrated fully into our lives.

Joy and Celebration

Sukkot is referred to as *Z'man Simchateinu,* the time of our joy. We not only change, but we also enjoy the change. The rituals emphasize sensual pleasure and enjoyment. They are performed with a focus on joy and celebration. We are encouraged to select a *lulav* and *etrog* which are especially beautiful so as to enhance our pleasure. We continue to cook with honey and eat sweet foods so as to start our year with sweetness. We celebrate in our communities with singing and dancing. With the focus on humor, light-hearted pranks, and drunkenness on Simchat Torah, we make one another laugh; we enjoy one another.

Although we are happy on other Holy-Days, only Sukkot is known as *Z'man Simchateinu,* the time of our joy. According to Shneur Zalman, our joy at other times was limited. The first day of Sukkot is the day when Moses came down the mountain after receiving the second set of tablets. On this day, God once again formed the Sukkot from the clouds of glory surrounding the Divine throne; the clouds of glory had been removed after the sin of the golden calf. Only after betraying their promise and then recommitting themselves do the Israelites really have cause for celebration. At this time, they can begin to build the ark of the covenant, the first dwelling place for God on earth.[1]

The experience of joy and celebration on Sukkot helps us discover and express our own positive feelings. In the process of self-development, it is important not only that we change; we must also experience those changes as positive, pleasurable, and satisfying. As we change our coping responses, we also experience a change in the results. We are better able to resolve the problem that previously overwhelmed or frustrated us. Our self-confidence and self-esteem is enhanced because we feel more power and competence as well as the satisfaction of being able to make changes and take more control of our lives. The pleasure and satisfaction we feel reinforces our commitment to the process and enhances our motivation and our energy. This joy is more mature and dependable than the joy we experience at the time of the liberation from slavery or the giving of the Torah because it is grounded in the reality of human failure and the capacity to learn from our mistakes.

Divine Protection and Support

The Israelites abandoned their security, their homes in the Egypt, for the temporary shelters of the *sukkot* in the desert. According to tradition,[2] the *sukkot* were not built by the Israelites; they were constructed by God. The *sukkot* were not made of ordinary materials.

They were fabricated from the seven clouds of glory surrounding God"s throne, symbols of Divine protection and support.

This theme is also expressed in the ritual of *Ushpizin* in which we invite our ancestors to join us. We are joined by Abraham, Isaac, Jacob, Joseph, Moses, Aaron, and David. Each of the seven patriarchs was a shepherd who knew how to tend and nourish his sheep as they wandered through the fields. Each of the seven also shepherded the Israelites. Now, we invoke their presence to guide us toward our goal, as we read in the Zohar:[3]

> *When the people of Israel leave their homes and enter the* sukkah *for the sake of God's name, they achieve the merit there of welcoming the Divine Presence and all the seven faithful shepherds descend from the garden of Eden and come to the* sukkah *as their guests.*

According to Shneur Zalman, the libation of water in the Sanctuary service is also a symbol of nurturance. He describes this time of year with the image of a young seedling that is first sprouting. In the humility of our self-reflection during the time of the Days of Awe, we make ourselves like the dust of the earth in which a seed is planted. In pouring the water on the altar in the Sanctuary, we water the seed of our new way of being.

The *sukkah* is an unusual symbol of protection. It is a fragile structure, only minimally sheltering us from the elements. However, the Holy-Day offers real protection from the pressures of daily life. We do not return immediately to our regular routines after Yom Kippur. We carve out an island in time in which we nurture the fragile changes we have made.

We do not limit ourselves to the symbols of support and nurturance; the *sukkah* ritual encourages us to the actual experience as we feed one another. We invite guests into our *sukkah* and accept invitations from our neighbors. Difficulty in coping successfully with our stresses is often exacerbated by isolation and alienation. When we regard our problems as too overwhelming or difficult, we tend to expect others to be disinterested or unable to help. As a result of the changes we have made during the Days of Awe, we are more open, honest, and responsive. Others who have similarly worked to change themselves are also more open, honest, and responsive. On this Holy-Day, we strengthen the bonds with others, feeling our ability to give to others and to receive from them.

Extending Outward

In contrast to the inward turning quality of the Days of Awe, on Sukkot, our energies extend out. In the ritual of the four species, we make the blessing and then point the *lulav* to each of the six directions—south, west, north, east, upward, and downward. In the *Hoshanot* and in the *Hakafot,* we circumnabulate the synagogue in a parade. We emphasize prayers for peace and prosperity, for water for our crops, not only for ourselves as a people but for all the peoples of the world. We extend outward towards others as well. We share our meals in the *sukkah,* and we join hands and voices as we celebrate with singing, dancing, and merry-making. The ritual thereby helps us turn our energies outward as well. As we experience changes in ourselves, we begin to translate those changes into our activity in the world. We are energized by our experience and move naturally outward.

THE JOURNEY FROM YOM KIPPUR TO SUKKOT: FROM ESSENCE TO MANIFESTATION

Sukkot serves as a bridge by helping us translate our experience of Essence on Yom Kippur so that we can apply and integrate what we have learned into everyday life activity. Shneur Zalman interprets the rituals in the Sanctuary as touchstones in this process. Through most of the year, sacrifices in the Sanctuary involved fire. According to tradition, when an animal was placed on the altar, a fire descended from heaven in the shape of a lion and consumed the offering. On Sukkot and Shemini Atzeret, there was also a libation of water in which water was poured on the stone of the altar. There were two altars in the Sanctuary: one in the outer court and one in the inner court. The outer court symbolizes the outer aspect of the work of the heart; the inner altar symbolizes the inner work of the heart.

Yom Kippur: Fire and the Silver Altar

The outer work, associated with the element of silver, involves awakening the natural love within each person. This task is accomplished through the fire of prayer which burns our material concerns in the same way that the fire consumes the animal offering. Enmeshed in the material world, we are caught up in the worries over our sustenance, worries which are consumed in the fire of prayer. Quoting from a verse in the *Song of Songs,* Shneur Zalman describes the relationship with God in this process as *Smolo tachat le'roshi* which means, "Your left hand cradles my head." This image suggests that we use our heads, our capacity to understand. We gain perspective as we consider our particular worries and concerns in relationship with the Infinite. In this spirit, we recite the confessional on Yom Kippur.

Sukkot: Water and the Golden Altar

From this foundation, we undertake the inner work of the heart associated with the altar in the inner court, the golden altar. In this process, our relationship with God is portrayed by the end of the verse as *Yemino techabkaini,* which means, "Your right hand hugs me." The image of the hug suggests greater intimacy and closeness than the previous image. Shneur Zalman associates this quality of relationship with the libation of water on Sukkot.

Shneur Zalman explains the emotional changes in the relationship with God symbolized by the fire sacrifice and water libation using the analogy of a parent and child. When the child is separated from the parent, the longing to be close is obvious; the child's heart beats loudly and calls for connection. The child's love is expressed with the heat of a burning fire. However, when the child is close to the parent, the child, feeling the love and connection, becomes calm and relaxed. Love is equally present but hidden within the heart. Water flows down, cooling the heat of the fire, softening, nourishing, and energizing.

In contrast to the upward movement of fire, water naturally falls
downward to the earth. For this
reason, Sukkot is also associated
with the earth. There are two qualities of earth—one implying
humility and the other expansive-
ness. We pray for humility with the
words, "May I be like the dust of
the earth before all of creation"
(*Nafhsi ke-afar lekol tehiyeh*).

Paradoxically, the image of earth is also used to suggest expansive-
ness when God promises Abraham and Sara that their progeny will
be like the "dust of the earth." In this same manner, developing a
sense of humility and an acceptance and appreciation of our vulnerability, we also connect to the source of our power and hope.

Shemini Atzeret: Collecting the Water

On the eighth day, we collect the water we have accessed. It
becomes a well from which we can nourish ourselves as we resume
ordinary life. The connection of the well to *Shemini Atzeret* is suggested by the name of the Holy-Day: *Atzeret* can be translated as
assembly or collection. On this day, we assemble within ourselves the
storehouse of energy which will fuel our efforts through the remainder
of the year, as we bring light into the darkness. Just as we can store
water in a cistern, joy energizes our continued efforts through the year.

We have been able to experience ourselves in a new way while
under the protection of the *sukkah*. On the eighth day, we set aside
the external supports which have helped us to respond in a new way.
We no longer use the *lulav* and *etrog*. We return to our homes and
say farewell to the *sukkah*. In some respects, the props are no longer
necessary—just as a plant which has grown from a seedling no
longer needs special protection from the elements. We are now more
able to support ourselves.

However, we are not completely self-sufficient. The Israelites were
more able to sustain themselves when they reached the land of

Israel. They worked hard to plant and harvest crops rather than rely on the manna for food. However, they still required help from God in the form of rain. On *Shemini Atzeret,* the beginning of the planting season, a special prayer for rain is added to the daily service. In this same spirit, we are able to work hard to nurture our new beginnings, but we still need nourishment to flow down to us from the heavens to help us grow and develop.

Germination of a Seed as a Metaphor for Inner Work

Shneur Zalman also describes the process at this time of year with the image of a planting a seed in the earth. The planting of the seed in the earth is a symbol of humility; when we plant a seed, we cover it with earth. We are like that seed in our process of self-evaluation during the Days of Awe. Even if we perform right actions, the inner intention and understanding is lacking. We are still under the influence of our material concerns. Eventually the seed sprouts and emerges into the light of day from inside the earth. Empowered by the work of self-reflection, the actions take place with a positive feeling. After doing the work of self-reflection on Yom Kippur, we are able to respond whole-heartedly on Sukkot. As we dig into the earth, we find a spring, a well of water that flows up to us from the depths. On *Shemini Atzeret,* we access the "living waters" of salvation which flow the quality of God's lovingkindness, *Chesed.*

Daily Prayer

The process which occurs in the yearly cycle is similar to that which occurs in the ritual cycle of the day. The prayers are said loudly with much fire in *Pesukei Dezimra,* the psalms recited at the beginning of the morning service. We are still far away from connection; we need heat to burn off distractions. However, as we regain our closeness to God, we no longer need to burn with fervor. We have achieved closeness and can speak with a still, small voice: in the silent prayer, we are quieter and cooler. Then we gather the nourishing waters which have washed over us into a deep well within ourselves and draw from this well to cope with daily life.

Yom Kippur	Sukkot	Shemini Atzeret
Fire	Water & earth	Well & earth
Fire offering; lion descends and consumes the sacrifice	Water libation	Collecting of water
Outer altar of silver	Inner altar of gold	
Pesukei Dezimra	*Amida*	After prayer
Consume worries in fire of prayer; awakening love	Requests for what we need	Manifesting God's will
From distance to closeness	Connected	Return to daily activity
"Your left hand cradles my head."	"Your right hand hugs me."	
Warmer	Cooler	
Active	Receptive	
Loud prayer	Still small voice	
Clearing the heart by confession	Flowing outward from the heart	

PSYCHOLOGICAL THEMES ASSOCIATED WITH SUKKOT

Initially, crises in our life motivate us to begin a process of self-reflection. We work to understand our situation and how we cope with it. We identify habitual patterns of response, clarifying ways in which our coping responses help or hinder us in successfully resolv-

Pesach through Tisha B'Av	Unconscious dysfunctional responses	Identification with old Ego structure
Elul through Yom Kippur	Conscious dysfunctional responses	Disidentification with old Ego structure
Sukkot through Chanukah	**Conscious effective responses**	**Manifestation of new Ego structure**
Purim	Unconscious effective responses	Identification with new Ego structure

ing the problems. We make changes in our responses, building on
strengths while stopping and changing dysfunctional responses. As
we do, our efforts eventually make a difference. Having changed
how we respond, the outcome also changes.

At this point in the process, it is very important to acknowledge,
enjoy, and support the changes. When we notice how we have
changed, we are better able to discover ways to have an impact on our
situation. When we notice how our situation changes and how others respond differently to us, we gain confidence and trust. We experience the world around as a nourishing ally rather than perceiving
our environment as a hostile adversary. Our pleasure in the results
reinforces and motivates us to continue and expand our efforts.

A Clinical Example of Psychological Process
Associated with Sukkot

The significance of pleasure is illustrated by the work of the
Stevens family. John and Lily Stevens had begun to argue even
before the session began. Their oldest son, Larry, had unexpectedly
returned home from college to visit his girl friend. At the end of the
weekend, he found himself without a ride back to school.
Succumbing to the pressure, his mother had given him her car.
Then, to make matters worse, Larry failed to return the car to her as
he had promised. John was furious with Lily. Why had she given the
car to Larry when he had failed to plan ahead? Lily was equally
adamant. She did not feel she had been manipulated. She enjoyed
having her son come home and wanted him to feel she could still
"spoil" him; she perceived her actions as motherly nurturance. As
they continued to talk, John and Lily grew increasingly angry with
one another.

My first impulse was to start to work to resolve this conflict.
However, I suddenly found myself smiling. Something was wonder-
fully changed in this family. Although, on the surface, it might
appear that John and Lily were locked into a draining struggle, there
was a significant difference. They were fighting, just as they often
did. They were not listening very well to one another, just as they

often did. John thought Lily was over-indulgent, just as he often did. Lily thought John was too punitive, just as she often did. However, they hadn't even mentioned Alan, their middle son, the focus of our sessions for the last year.

They first initiated treatment as a result of a crisis with Alan, who was struggling with academic and behavior problems at school and who was out of control at home as well. Alan was now doing quite well, a successful student and athlete, enthusiastic about his new school. The concern with Larry was an "ordinary" crisis of a college age child who was a bit self-centered and manipulative. Rather than disengage from one another and operate independently, the Stevens' were now able to discuss the issue themselves. This family was well on the road to healthy functioning.

If this had been the first time I met this couple, I might have focused immediately on the problem. Instead, I shared my observations, pointing out the changes in the family and in the way in which they responded to conflict with one another. We spent the greater part of our session identifying and describing these changes. In the last few minutes, we briefly discussed the issue with Alan and they resolved how to respond to him in the future.

A variety of therapeutic approaches stress the importance of acknowledging changes, enjoying and celebrating progress, allowing and experiencing external support and protection, and extending learning into the context of daily life.

Behavioral Therapy

Noting changes is a central element in behavioral therapy. In working to change behavior, the clinician begins by determining the baseline of the behavior which one is seeking to modify which establishes a basis for measuring changes. For example, if one is seeking to reduce binge eating, the first step is to measure the behavior prior to an intervention. The client records the frequency of binges, details what is eaten, and adds other relevant data such as precipitating factors and consequences. One then carefully observes and measures changes so that the extent of change is clear. Changes are not only measured; they must also be rewarded if they are to be repeated. The most powerful positive reinforcements are intrinsic rewards, direct and natural consequences of the new behaviors.

Behavioral approaches facilitate change by guiding the client through a series of increasingly challenging goals. For example, if a person struggles to overcome the fear of enclosed spaces, one begins by making a list of the situations which evoke that fear, ranking them from most anxiety producing to minimally anxiety producing. The least stressful item is approached first; the person might begin by imagining being in an elevator with a good friend. Then one might go to a building and simply observe the elevator without going inside. Building on a series of successes, one builds momentum, confidence, and competence, able to take on greater and greater challenges.

Feldenkrais Method

Moshe Feldenkrais' technique for reducing chronic tension and gaining more efficiency and flexibility in movement similarly emphasizes the importance of acknowledging changes. According to Feldenkrais, learning occurs when one notices small differences. In helping someone to change patterns of habitual stress, one begins by heightening awareness of existing habits. For example, the practitioner might help a client become aware of chronic tension in the neck using touch, gentle movement, and/or verbal guidance. As the person relaxes chronic tension, current experience can be compared to the initial baseline. Unless we are able to differentiate a more efficient and easier posture from the more stressed posture, it is impossible to be able to choose which pattern to reinforce.

Feldenkrais' approach similarly emphasizes the experience of pleasure as central to the learning process. As one discovers new ways to move, the nervous system registers when a movement feels more pleasurable, easy, and comfortable than another. The natural tendency to prefer pleasure to pain strengthens the person's capacity for learning new possibilities.

Feldenkrais also used a step-by-step approach to learning. In helping someone to relax, one first finds the position of maximum safety and support. For example, a person who has chronic neck pain may find that standing or sitting exacerbates the pain because the spine has to fight gravity. Lying down with just the right support under one's head, knees, and shoulders minimizes the effort needed. In this position, the person may have the least difficulty in relaxing. In this same spirit, if a person experiences most tension in the neck, the practitioner might work initially with another part of the body, helping that part to relax. The initial success creates confidence, optimism, and momentum which can be translated, step-by-step, into new challenges. A foundation is established for working directly with the more tense parts of the body and for working in postures that place more demands on the body such as sitting, standing, or normal daily activity.

Gestalt Therapy

Fritz Perls also emphasized the role of awareness and pleasure as essential to the learning process. Healthy functioning depends upon the capacity for ongoing awareness of here-and-now experience. Our awareness becomes focused on sensations associated with an emerging need. Those sensations crystallize into awareness of a need. That awareness mobilizes us to a state of excitement as we consider how to satisfy that need. After we take action to address the need, taking in and assimilating from the outside world, we experience an internal shift in awareness, a feeling of satisfaction which allows us to know we are satiated and complete. For example, when hunger moves us to eat, we find ourselves feeling full and satisfied as we respond to the body's call. A person who is unable to sense the pleasure and joy of satisfaction lacks an important aspect of experience. Often, a person who overeats is cut-off from feelings of pleasure and satisfaction. The more one is able to listen to the body's messages, the more possibility there is for identifying true needs and also for knowing when those needs have been satisfied.

Gestalt Cycle
of Awareness & Need Satisfaction

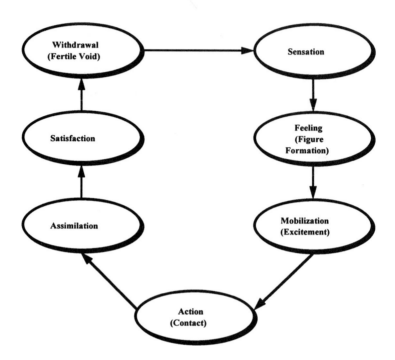

PERSONAL APPLICATION OF PROCESS FOR SUKKOT

On Yom Kippur, we surrender the old way of being and return to an experience of our Essence. On Sukkot, we begin to manifest a new way of being. In the same way that psychotherapy offers a safe place and time in which to experiment with new ways of responding, this Holy-Day offers a protected, nurturing environment in which we can notice and acknowledge changes, express our joy and satisfaction with our progress, receive support and encouragement from outside ourselves, and gradually extend our capacity to respond in new ways and in other contexts which are increasingly challenging.

ENJOYING THE HARVEST

- In what ways have you changed? What do you appreciate about the work you have done?

- What permissions do you need to give yourself to enjoy the harvest of your work?

- What protection do you need to allow these changes to continue to develop? What support do you need from others?

- What are the conflicting polarities in your life that need to be integrated?

- What are the directions in which you need to extend and broaden these changes?

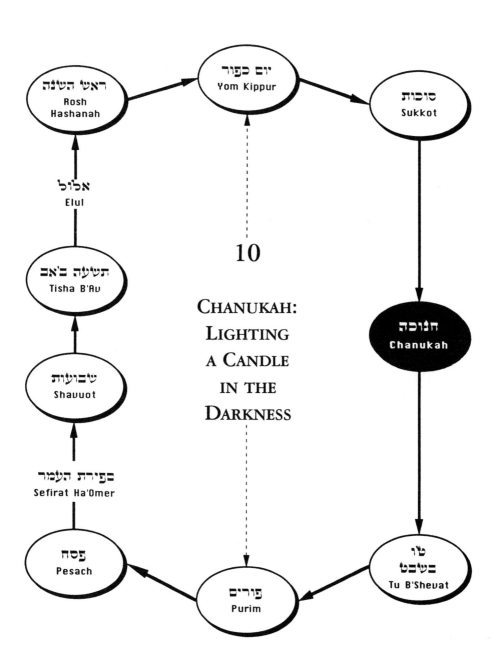

ראש השנה
Rosh
Hashanah

יום כפור
Yom Kippur

סוכות
Sukkot

אלול
Elul

תשעה ב'אב
Tisha B'Av

10

חנוכה
Chanukah

שבועות
Shavuot

CHANUKAH:
LIGHTING
A CANDLE
IN THE
DARKNESS

ספירת העמר
Sefirat Ha'Omer

פסח
Pesach

פורים
Purim

ט"ו
בשבט
Tu B'Shevat

Chanukah is an eight day festival beginning on the twenty-fifth day of the month of Kislev. This festival comes at the time of year when there is more darkness than light. In commemoration of the Jews' victory over their Greek adversaries, we light candles each day. The Holy-Day of Chanukah marks the time for integrating the changes in ourselves that we made during the fall Holy-Days and for applying our learning in the day-to-day struggles of life. We do not change lifelong patterns as a result of one breakthrough or one moment of insight. Again and again, we forget what we have discovered, fall into the same pits, and extricate ourselves. Each time we repeat the process, we deepen and extend our learning. This theme is communicated on Chanukah, through the stories of the battle with the Greeks, and in the symbolism associated with the lighting of the candles.

THE STRUGGLE OF THE MACABEES WITH THE GREEKS AS AN ARCHETYPAL EVENT

Open mine eyes that I may see
Glimpses of truth thou hast for me
Open mine eyes, illumine me, Spirit divine

"Love of my life" I am crying
I am not dying, I am dancing
Dancing along in the madness
There is no sadness, only a song of the soul

What do you do for a living?
Are you forgiving, giving shelter?
Follow your heart, love will find you
Truth will unbind you, sing out a song of the soul

Come to your life like a warrior
Nothing will bore you, you can be happy
Let the light in, it will heal you
And you can feel you, sing out a song of the soul
And we'll sing this song, why don't you sing along?
And we can sing for a long, long time.

Cris Williamson

After the Greek ruler, Antiochus, promulgated laws forbidding the practice of their religion, the Jews, led by Judah Macabee and his brothers, started a revolt that ended in victory over the Greeks. The idols placed in the Sanctuary by the Greek invaders were removed, the altar was reconsecrated, and the Jewish rituals reinstituted:

> *During the period of the Second Sanctuary, the Greek kings issued harsh decrees against Israel: outlawed their religion, forbade them to engage in the study of Torah and the practice of Mitzvot, laid hands upon their money and their daughters, entered the Sanctuary and ravaged it, and defiled all that had been ritually pure. They caused Israel great anguish, till the God of our parents granted them mercy and delivered them from the hands of their enemies. The Hasmonaite Priests prevailed, slew them, and delivered Israel from their hands. They designated a king from among the priests and the Kingdom of Israel was restored for more than 200 years, till the second Destruction.*

[Rambam, *Hilchot Chanukah*, Chap. 3']

As the Macabees cleaned the Sanctuary, they discovered that the Greeks had defiled almost all the oil used to light the candelabrum in the Sanctuary. Only one small container remained; it was sufficient for only a day. Miraculously, the oil lasted for eight days, which was enough time to allow for producing a new supply:

And Israel prevailed against their enemies and vanquished
them, on the twenty-fifth day of the month of Kislev. They
entered the Sanctuary and found only one jar of ritually pure
oil that was sufficient to burn only one day; but they lit the
lights of the menorah *from it for eight days, till they pressed*
olives and extracted pure oil.

[Rambam, *Hilchot Chanukah,* Chap. 3²]

Shneur Zalman derives many meanings from these events to help
define the process of growth at this time of year, including (1) the
spiritual basis of the threat from the Greeks, (2) the importance of
human initiative in battling that threat, (3) the quality of Divine
support, (4) the necessity for step-by-step learning, (5) focusing outward into the world, and (6) the nature of the spiritual victory.

The Spiritual Threat

What makes fantasy different from reality is that reality takes
much longer to produce the same results.

© Ashleigh Brilliant

The crisis of Chanukah differs from the crises of other times in the
Jewish year. At the time of Pesach, the Jews were enslaved. On
Purim, they were threatened with annihilation by Haman. During
the time of the Macabees, the Israelites lived in their own land, but
they were not safe. They were threatened by the Greeks, but the
danger was spiritual, not physical. Their enemies wanted to force the
Jews to abandon the Torah. The Greek oppressors wanted the Jews
to give up their understanding of God and their sense of how to
manifest God's spirit on earth. The Israelites' work to establish a
dwelling place on Earth was not finished simply when they con-
quered the land of Israel and built the Sanctuary. They still needed
to work to manifest their dream.

In the same way, our work is not complete on Yom Kippur when
we experience connection with Spirit. We now have to battle to integrate that new understanding into our daily life. Our work at this
time of year is not primarily with overcoming external forces but
with strengthening our constructive response to those forces.

Although we have experienced a transformation, our old habits are still strong. We experience a battle between the new spirit within us and the old way of being, which mirrors, within ourselves, the battle of the Macabees and the Greeks.

Primacy of Human Initiative

Nobody can do everything, but we can nearly all do more than we think we can.

© Ashleigh Brilliant

In the battle with the Greeks, the Israelites take most of the initiative for the struggle. The Macabees organized the Jews to fight the oppressors. In contrast to the conflict with the Egyptians when God brought plagues and split the sea, no dramatic miracles occur in this war. The Macabees' initiative and responsibility reminds us that we need to take responsibility at this stage of our work to recognize old, dysfunctional responses to problems, interrupt the habitual mode of coping, and respond with our new, more effective way of being.

Divine Intervention

Although more human effort is required, God is also active and present. The Israelites are victorious even though they are fewer in number. In the same way as the tiny candle produces enough light to banish a great darkness, the Macabees' effort produced results beyond what one might have expected from their military prowess. In addition, a dramatic miracle does occur when the oil lasts for an entire week instead of just one day. In this respect, the story of Chanukah is the story of a collaboration between God and the Israelites; as we immerse ourselves in the story, we are reminded that God is with us in our struggles. The old habits, developed and strengthened with years and years of repetition, seem much stronger than our fragile new experiments with change; nonetheless, our efforts to fight the old ways succeed out of proportion to what we might expect.

Step-by-Step Learning

Not everyone who starts can win, but it's even harder to win if you never start.

© Ashleigh Brilliant

When the Macabees regained control of the Sanctuary, they removed the Greek idols. Then, they reconsecrated the altar with a ritual known as *Chanukat Hamizbai'ach*. This event is so important that the name of the Holy-Day, Chanukah, is derived from that reconsecration. This theme is further reinforced in the daily readings from the Torah that describe the offerings of the Israelite princes when the ark of the covenant was consecrated in the desert. Similarly, each day we recite the psalm of David which was associated with the consecration of the Sanctuary.

Shneur Zalman (*Torah Or*, 58A) notes that the word for consecration, the root of the name for Chanukah, is also the etymological source of the word for education, *chinuch*. For Shneur Zalman, this linguistic connection with learning leads to the conclusion that consecration involves a process of "educating" the altar. The altar and the *menorah* provided a material channel for bringing the divine light down to earth. In consecrating the altar, the princes of Israel each brought an identical offering; their gifts helped prepare the Sanctuary to achieve this task of "educating" the altar and those who used it.

In the same spirit, our work at this time of year involves building a dwelling place for spirit, a Sanctuary within ourselves, which manifests God's spirit in our daily life. Just as the princes "educated" the altar by bringing the same offering day after day, we also educate the altar within us, day after day repeatedly practicing the new way of responding.

Outward Focus

The eight days of Chanukah are historically connected to the Holy-Day of Sukkot. The Israelites had been unable to celebrate Sukkot because of the Greek oppression. Judah Macabee established the eight days in Kislev to enable the Jews to celebrate the festival in some way. The reconsecration of the Sanctuary on Chanukah also echoes the consecration of the first Sanctuary during the time of King Solomon that took place during Sukkot. However, Sukkot was ordained by God, transmitted in the Torah, whereas Chanukah was established by the rabbis. On Sukkot, we leave our houses to live in the *sukkah;* on the first and last days, there are restrictions on work. In contrast, on Chanukah we do not stop ordinary activity. On Sukkot, we take time in a sheltered, protected, nourishing environment, removed from daily life stresses, in which we can practice our new responses. On Chanukah we are stronger. We work to integrate that new way in daily life without extra support and safety.

Focus on Spiritual Victory

The political success of the Israelites was limited: 200 years later, the kingdom of Israel was destroyed and the Jews sent into exile, an exile that lasted 2,000 years. In spite of that limited success, we still celebrate eight days, reciting the full version of the traditional prayer of thanksgiving, the *Hallel.* Our focus is on the spiritual victory. We celebrate the miracle of the lights more than the material success of the Macabees. In the same manner, efforts to change our way of being do not always produce immediate results in the world. Our work is difficult, our successes are fleeting, and the struggle is unending. In spite of our limits, we retain a sense of power, competence, and optimism. Even though the results of our efforts are not yet realized, we can celebrate the changes we have made, trusting they will eventually lead to success. Even though we live in darkness, we can light a candle illuminating our way.

THE CANDLE AS A SYMBOL

Those who walk in darkness will see the great light.
Those who yearn for freedom will find a home.
Darkness rules over the lights
and those who stand, still
search for miracles.

Who will light a candle for the future?
Who will sing a song?
Who will find in their heart a new bright light?
In yesterday's torch, the fire will still burn.
Sometimes a great miracle occurs.

The candles are lit on my window sill.
There are some who will know how to solve my dream.
It is the same story, the same play
in those days and at this time.

Don't promise me miracles and wonders.
Even the fog is a sign of the future.
In a stormy season, don't retreat.
On your way you will find hope and light.

Those who walk in darkness will see the great light.

Naomi Shemer

The most important ritual observance on Chanukah involves the lighting of candles, beginning with one on the first day. A candle is added each day until the end of the eight days. The candles are lit in the evening at sunset. Olive oil, the same oil used in the Sanctuary, is the preferred source of light, but other oils or candles can be used as well. We are admonished not to use the light for any mundane purpose; we must have other light available for illumination rather than depend on the Chanukah candles for this purpose. For the same reason, we do not use one of the candles to light another candle; instead, we use a special additional candle, known as the *shamash,* to light all the others.

The candles' importance is not limited to their value as a reminder of the miracle from the time of the Macabees. The use of the candle in the Sanctuary service and our ritual is not arbitrary or simply an aesthetic choice. In the tradition, it is said that "God's candle is the human soul"—"*Ner Hashem, nishmat adam.*" In this respect, as we understand the nature and function of the candle, we can also deepen our understanding of ourselves.

The Candle as Symbol of Experiential Learning: "Seeing" and "Hearing"

No one was closer to the Rebbe than his personal attendant, Shmuel, who was by his side twenty-four hours a day for fifty years. At the Rebbe's death, one of the disciples turned to Shmuel and asked him, "Please, tell me, in these years of such close connection, what was the most significant learning?" Shmuel ruminated for a moment and said, "I learned the most from watching how the Rebbe tied his shoes."

We learn from what we hear, and we learn from what we see. In the liturgy, we recite the words of the *Shema:* "Listen, Israel, the *YHVH* our God, *YHVH* is One!" Shneur Zalman associates listening with the development of cognitive understanding of Spiritual truth. When we see the candles of the *menorah,* we are using a different sensory channel. Seeing is associated with direct experience of that reality; experiencing God's Presence face-to-face is more contactful than hearing the Word of God.

In seeing the candles, we are reminded that our work, at this time, is to "see." We have "heard" the truth, knowing theoretically that a particular response is not helpful. Now we "see" the truth, experiencing it in our lives: the learning is more deeply internalized. For example, a person who always tries to do more and more knows intellectually that rest is needed; however, a different kind of learning occurs when there is a behavioral change. The truth is not only "heard" mentally; it is "seen" and felt. Each step can be digested. The person knows more completely the experience of stopping when tired instead of continuing to work; the person appreciates more fully the results of the new choice in which timely rest allows for more efficient return to work.

Initially, we learn by "listening"; we develop our cognitive understanding of how to manifest Spiritual Essence in our daily life. As a reminder of that way of knowing, we attach the *mezuzah* to the right side of our doorposts: the *mezuzah* contains a parchment with the *Shema* reminding us to "listen" to the word of God. Then we "see" that truth by working to manifest it as an actual experience in the material world. The lit *menorah,* placed to the left side of the entrance, symbolizes the capacity to see and to shine out into the places of darkness. The *mezuzah* raises up our home and helps us make a dwelling place for Spirit. The light of the *menorah* allows that understanding to radiate out into the world. On Chanukah, we integrate the two types of learning symbolized by the *mezuzah* and the *menorah.* That which we have learned through the year by "listening" now can be "seen"; that which we know internally, can now be manifested externally. For this reason, on Chanukah, we do not focus solely on revelation as a cognitive experience as we do on Shavuot when the ritual stresses study of Torah. At this time of year, we perform a concrete and visible act; we light candles to communicate the importance of learning through doing.

The Order of Lighting Candles as a Symbol of Step-by-Step Learning

The rabbis disagreed about the procedure for lighting of the candles. The students of Shamai adhered to the view that we start with eight candles and decrease one each night, ending the Holy-Day with one candle. Their view accurately reflects the historic experience of starting with a full container of oil that is gradually used up. It also expressed the concept of a spiritual enlightenment in which a breakthrough experience fuels our process of change. The house of Hillel had a different opinion, starting with one candle and increasing to eight candles by the end of the Holy-Day. This perspective is based on the notion that we gradually increase the light through continued effort. It is this approach that was accepted as our practice.

As we light the candles each day, we are reminded that the process of transforming life-long patterns of response does not usually occur with one experience of inhibiting a particular, dysfunctional behavior and replacing it with a new response. We often need to re-experience over and over again the same dysfunctional impulse, stop ourselves from acting, and replace it with our new choice. Learning is not only step-by-step and cumulative. It requires a series of successive approximations; at each stage, a new more sophisticated and complete understanding replaces an earlier, more primitive, and incomplete understanding.

The Oil and Wick as a Symbol for Integrating Spiritual and Material Dimensions

The light that shines is the light of love
Lights the darkness from above
It shines on me and it shines on you
Shows what the power of love can do
I'm gonna shine my light both far and near
I'm gonna shine my light both bright and clear
If there's a dark corner in this land
I'm gonna let my little light shine!

Some say "It's dark, we cannot see"
But love lights up the world for me
Some say "Turn around and just go hide"
But we have the power to change the tide
Some call life a sad old story
But we see a world that's bound for glory
The real power is yours and mine
So let your little light shine!

This little light of mine, I'm gonna let it shine!
Let it shine, let it shine, let it shine!

The candle consists of two parts: the wick and the oil. The oil will not burn without the wick; a flame is extinguished if it falls directly into the oil. The wick is quickly consumed without the oil. To make

oil, we extract the essence from the
original substance; for this reason,
oil serves as an appropriate symbol
of spiritual Essence, the understanding and intention that transformed
us on Yom Kippur. However,
Essence cannot burn by itself; it
cannot create light in the darkness
of this world. The wick is denser
and provides a channel through
which the oil can flow.

Essence, similarly, needs to be channeled through action in the
world. It needs a material form. In the Torah, that spiritual Essence
is manifested through the *mitzvot,* biblical commandments that reg-
ulate and guide our behavior in relationship to God and others. They
include tasks such as lighting candles, placing a *mezuzah* on our
doorposts, wearing fringes on the corners of our garments, giving
charity, and keeping the Sabbath. The *Torah* includes 613 *mitzvot.*
In this same fashion, the understanding and good intentions that we
have developed during the fall Holy-Days cannot manifest without
specific action in the world. It must not remain a theory, idea, or
feeling but be translated into behavior. Specific actions, even though
they may seem trivial or unimportant, serve as a wick for the Spirit.
Like the wick, in and of themselves, they may be insignificant.
However, when they are connected with spiritual understanding and
intention, they serve as channels for bringing that understanding
into manifestation. They create a dwelling place on Earth for Spirit
in the same way as the Sanctuary provided a House for God. In this
way, we create light. The integration of wick and oil symbolizes the
synergy of intention, feeling, and action. In this respect, the candle
symbolizes the process by which we bring spiritual understanding
into our daily lives in the material world.

As the wick allows the oil to burn, spiritual truths are learned
through the intermediary of the material world. In the same way as
the oil cannot burn without the wick, spiritual truths cannot be
experienced except through a material form. Since the material

world is also God's creation, its truth can serve as a mirror reflecting Divine truth and light. The material world is not only darkness, a basis for our disconnection with our Higher Self, the source of false intelligence symbolized by the Greeks. It is also a source of truth and a vessel for spirit.

Shneur Zalman (*Likutei Torah*, 54) explains the relationship between the material world and spiritual realization using an analogy. If there is a very bright light, one cannot look at it directly because of its strength. One has to use a filter to see the light. Similarly, when one is trying to explain a matter of great wisdom, a profound truth, to a child, one can only do so through a garment. The garment is the metaphor. Then the child can understand the truth. The whole Torah is a metaphor for God's Presence through which we understand something that cannot be experienced directly. As God says to Moses, "No one can see my face and live." The *mitzvot* are metaphorical garments for archetypal truths. The ritual offers a foundation for discovering a personal meaning that gives focus and direction to our lives.

Right action raises us to a higher level than mystical experience. Action in the world causes a change in spirit, bringing down Divine light from above. The actions we take based on right behavior cause changes in our understanding, a deepening of learning. According to Shneur Zalman (*Likutei Torah,* 68), Yochanan ben Zakkai was the greatest of mystics, withdrawing from the world into contemplation for years. Yet he asked Rabbi Chanina ben Dosah to pray for him. Chanina's prayers were more potent because he was a man of action. In this spirit, the rabbis taught that anyone who focuses only on the mystical experience and rejects the material plane fails in the spiritual quest: One who says, "All I have is Torah" lacks even the Torah. If one has no deeds and actions, the light of the Torah cannot burn.

The miracle symbolized by Chanukah continues to this day. The light of a single candle is sufficient to enable us to see our way in the dark. The candle becomes a metaphor for lighting our way emotionally, behaviorally, and interpersonally.

Wick, Oil, Blue Flame, and Yellow Flame as Symbols of Four Motivators of Learning

There are four different parts of a candle: the oil, the wick, the blue flame, and the yellow flame. Shneur Zalman (*Likutei Torah,* 80-84) associates each of these parts with a different quality which energizes us in the process of growth. These include the following:

Oil	Yud	Yirah Eela'ah Higher Fear	Nitzotz—essence/ underlying need	Chaya	Essence of wisdom
Wick	Heh	Ahavah Eela'ah Higher love	One day's oil is sufficient for eight days; positive feedback from universe	Ruach	Heart; feeling; voice/tone
Yellow Flame	Vav	Ahavah Tata'ah Lower love	Impulse to change based on cognitive understanding	Neshama	Capacity to understand
Blue Flame	Heh	Yirah Tata'ah Lower fear	Impulse to change based on desire to avoid negative consequences	Nefesh	Words and letters; language

Lower Fear (*Yirah Tata'ah*) is comparable to aversive conditioning. We are motivated by a desire to avoid the pain that results from our dysfunctional and habitual coping response. At this level, our work is to subdue the old impulse, *Eetkafya.* As we do, this old habit burns in the fire of the blue flame. *Yirah Tata'ah* is associated with the final *heh* of God's name and with the aspect of soul known as *Nefesh. Yirah Tata'ah* is mediated through the words and letters that combine to form our language.

Lower Love (*Ahavah Tata'ah*) occurs when we are motivated not by fear but by the satisfaction we experience as self-knowledge deepens; we realize that our old ways of responding are no longer helpful to us. In this process, the old way of being burns with a yellow flame. *Ahavah Tata'ah* is associated with the *vav* of God's name and the aspect of soul known as *Neshama.*

Higher Love (*Ahavah Eela'ah*) is experienced when we are receptive to changes in outcome as a result of new ways of being in the world. Our efforts produce more light than seems logically possible. This quality is associated with the miracle of the oil that produced light for eight days when it was only expected to last for one. *Ahavah Eela'ah* is associated with the first *heh* in God's name. It refers to an experience that comes from outside ourselves in contrast to the Lower Love which comes from our own understanding. It is connected to the quality of soul known as *Ruach* and expressed through the heart in our feelings and voice. It is symbolized by the wick that burns and is not consumed, serving instead as a conduit for the oil.

Higher Fear (*Yirah Eela'ah*) refers to the experience of a larger perspective in which we view the original dysfunction as part of an evolutionary process in which we are inextricably bound, creating a sense of awe and respect. This connection with Essence, symbolized by the oil, is associated with the *yud* of God's name and the aspect of soul known as *Chaya*. This stage is associated with the experience of *Eethafcha* and represents the Essence of Wisdom.

Motivated by the Lower Fear and Lower Love, we are able to take steps to inhibit the old response, allowing ourselves to discover different ways for satisfying the underlying need. In so doing, we burn the material aspect and reconnect the essence of the oil to the light. That effort produces more positive results than we might imagine. Eventually, the old impulse becomes our ally; we can use it as a signal instead of being at its mercy. We no longer act on the basis of our impulse; instead, when we feel the impulse, we remind ourselves to shift to the new possibility for response.

PSYCHOTHERAPEUTIC THEMES ASSOCIATED WITH CHANUKAH

Chapter 1
I walk down a street
There is a deep hole in the sidewalk.
I fall in.
I am lost . . . I am hopeless.
It isn't my fault.
It takes forever to find a way out.

Chapter 2
I walk down the same street
There is a deep hole in the sidewalk.
I pretend I don't see it.
I fall in again.
I can't believe I'm in the same place.
But, it isn't my fault.
It still takes a long time to get out.

Chapter 3
I walk down the same street
There is a deep hole in the sidewalk.
I see it is there.
I still fall in . . . it's a habit.
My eyes are open
I know where I am.
It is my fault.
I get out immediately.

Chapter 4
I walk down the same street.
There is a deep hole in the sidewalk.
I walk around it.

Chapter 5
I walk down a different street.
            Portia Nelson, "Autobiography in Five Short Chapters"[3]

A Clinical Example of Therapeutic Process on Chanukah

The themes embedded in the ritual of Chanukah are illustrated by Don's work. Don, a lawyer in practice for himself, came for his first appointment in the midst of a career crisis. He had received an offer to join a firm. He needed to make a decision of critical importance to his career, and he was unsure what to do. On the one hand, he was struggling on his own, and the offer meant greater security and relief from the uncertainty; on the other hand, he liked the freedom of working for himself, the flexibility and independence of being able to set his own hours and to focus on the kind of legal work he most enjoyed. Moreover, even if he was very successful at the firm, he could never hope to achieve the level of income that would be generated in a successful private practice. Taking the new job meant giving up a dream. Afraid that he would make the wrong decision, he felt paralyzed, depressed, and tense. Moreover, the career struggle was creating tension with his wife, who felt angry at having to carry a disproportionate amount of the financial burden while his practice floundered.

After Don outlined the current difficulties, I asked him if his concerns for financial well-being were relatively recent or if they had been with him for a long time. He replied by talking about his father, whose career had been tumultuous and stressful. His father was a man of creativity and vision. At his best, he was energetic and courageous. When he had an idea, he enthusiastically moved forward to translate the idea into reality. Often, that enthusiasm paid off, bringing both material and emotional rewards. However, his father could also be grandiose, oblivious to realities, and impulsive. His blindness resulted in financial and emotional disasters that disrupted family life.

As Don worked to clarify the impact of his father's example on his own life, he discovered many important parallels. He appreciated his father's enthusiasm and vision but did not trust it. When he thought about taking the job at the firm, he felt depressed at the thought of giving up the vision. When he thought about remaining in private practice, he felt afraid that he might be falling into his father's obliviousness. Whatever he did, he would be making the wrong decision. As we continued to discuss the issues, Don realized the concern for security and realistic goals seemed to be irreconcilably opposed to the wish to honor his creativity and ambition.

I asked Don if he would be willing to enact a conversation between the two parts of himself, one of which he named the "Visionary" and the other of which he named the "Bookkeeper." He spoke first as the Visionary; he berated the Bookkeeper for being timid and for giving up. Then he spoke as the Bookkeeper, who

responded in kind, attacking the Visionary for his failure to acknowledge the precariousness of his financial situation.

As I listened to the discussion, I found myself becoming confused.
Each voice was extremely convincing. When I listened to the
Visionary, I found myself in agreement with him; it seemed a
tragedy for Don to give up the commitment to work he valued and
enjoyed for a job that allowed him to survive but which destroyed
his spirit. When I listened to the Bookkeeper, I found myself in
agreement with him. It would be foolhardy to pass up this opportunity and continue to pursue a dream that had already proved to be
unattainable. How could they both be right? How could they both
be wrong?

Gradually we realized the root of the problem: Don had set up a
rigid system in which one sub-personality had to be right and the
other subpersonality wrong. Both sub-personalities were partly
right, and both were partly wrong. Both perspectives needed to be
accepted and validated. Both needed to work together to create
solutions that satisfied both the Visionary and the Bookkeeper. Each
part needed to respect the unique understanding of the other part;
each needed to correct the other and accept one another's challenges.
Don needed to respect his dreams and ambition while also making
realistic assessments of his actual success.

Don experimented with a more collaborative dialogue between
the two voices. The Visionary acknowledged that the independent
practice was not financially successful and that the economic indica-
tors made it unlikely that it would turn around. The Bookkeeper
acknowledged that the job with the firm, while it offered security,
did not provide much professional or personal satisfaction; moreover,
while it provided some security, the possibilities for financial success
were limited.

Don began to brainstorm possibilities for integrating both perspectives. He realized he might be able to negotiate with the firm
both on financial and professional concerns. He also considered
options for making his independent practice more viable financially.
Don spent time exploring all these possibilities. The firm responded
positively to his initiatives, though not as fully as he wished. He

developed a business plan for remaining in independent practice. At the conclusion of this process, Don decided to close his independent practice and join the firm.

This was not the end of the therapeutic process. Don had successfully discovered the source of his problem: a split between two parts of himself that undermined and sabotaged one another rather than working together. He was able, with support, to engage in a more collaborative dialogue. However, a pattern that had operated for most of his life did not dissolve with only one experience, nor did it affect only one aspect of his life. He found himself trapped in this impasse again and again.

As part of his effort to take control of his finances, Don prepared an estimate of family expenses and income. He realized that his projected income would not cover the expenses of their current lifestyle. When he sat down with his wife and discussed the need to make adjustments by cutting back on vacations and plans to redecorate their house, she became depressed. She expressed concern that their lives would be severely constrained with no relief in sight. At first, Don felt trapped in her pessimism. Life again seemed to offer only two possibilities: an inadequate life living within one's means, or satisfying one's wishes in a manner that recklessly disregarded the financial realities.

Don and Lydia came to see me to discuss this impasse. As we talked, they realized they had fallen again into the trap of an "either/or" mentality. There were other possibilities. They planned vacations that did not require large expenditures of money, and they were able to budget for some new carpets even though they could not redecorate the entire house. Lydia took some time to express her anger and frustration for the years during which Don had been oblivious to his situation and failed to take charge. Don acknowledged his failures and expressed regret. He also asked to be acknowledged for the changes he had made.

His father suffered another financial crisis. In typical fashion, he had failed to put money away for real estate taxes and spent it instead on impulsive and unnecessary purchases. He turned to Don to bail him out. Don again felt stuck. He did not want to threaten his own fragile, financial stability, nor did he want to reinforce his father's recklessness. He also did not want to cut off from his father in a time of crisis. As Don discussed this impasse, he realized that he was trapped again into thinking that there could be only two possibilities: either jeopardizing his financial well-being while rescuing his father, or abandoning his father while protecting himself. He brainstormed alternatives. He refused simply to give his father the money, and he confronted him about his financial mismanagement. Then, he offered to purchase his father's second car. In this way, Don protected himself and helped his father; he obtained something he needed while also helping his father generate some cash.

As Don worked with his tendency to get stuck in an either/or mentality, he gained skill recognizing when he fell into the same trap and reorienting himself. We developed a shorthand between us. When I noticed either/or thinking, I would say, "The Bookkeeper and the Visionary are at it again." He would smile and make a shift. Then, he took a further step. He started to recognize the tendency himself. Sometimes, as he started to talk about something, he would stop himself and make a shift. He caught himself sooner and sooner. In time, I noticed that he no longer came into the sessions stuck. Instead, he spent time discussing how he had worked through an impasse on his own.

In his work, Don began to specialize. He developed a reputation as an excellent mediator. He was especially skillful in devising creative solutions for adversaries who were stuck in impasses. His own struggles to change either/or thinking eventually translated into greater competence and ability to help others with similar issues.

Eventually, Don cut back on his therapy from once a week, to once every other week, and then to once a month. After six months, we stopped with the understanding that Don would call if he found himself stuck and unable to work through the issues on his own.

Therapeutic Process on Chanukah

*Our worst fear is not that we are inadequate, our deepest fear
is that we are powerful beyond measure. It is our light, not our
darkness that most frightens us. We ask ourselves, "Who am I
to be brilliant, gorgeous, talented and fabulous?" Actually,
who are you not to be? You are a child of God; your playing
small doesn't serve the world. There is nothing enlightened
about shrinking so that other people won't feel insecure around
you. We were born to make manifest the glory of God within
us. It is not just in some of us, it is in everyone and as we let
our own light shine we unconsciously give other people permission to do the same. As we are liberated from our own fear
our presence automatically liberates others.*

Nelson Mandela

The exhilaration we experience in a breakthrough is vital to the
process of change, but that event does not mark the culmination of
our learning. In transforming life-long habits, we may be able to
change our responses in one synergistic moment—perhaps with help
and protection. However, as we cope with the day-to-day realities of
our lives, we are not always able to remember our new choices. In the
heat of the moment, we forget our insights and commitments, we
respond in the old way before we even realize what has happened. We
need time to practice, time to try our new way of being in different
situations with different people at different times. We need to practice the new way of being in more stressful and difficult moments.

This phase of therapy can be compared to creating a trail in the
woods. The first time a person takes a new path through the forest,
the journey is slowed by the need to struggle with the branches and
underbrush that impede the way. Time and effort is required to clear
away obstructions. The best route to the goal is not clearly identified. It may be necessary to backtrack and start again. The next time
is a little easier. The person has the benefit of the last attempt to
avoid pitfalls. The path is clearer, and there are footsteps from the
previous journey that help in finding the way. Each time the person

travels the route, the trail becomes a little clearer and easier to follow. Eventually, there is an unobstructed and easily traversed path.

Those who struggle with addiction understand this principle well. They know that alcohol is not a solution to stress. They know that alcohol abuse has negative side effects, that it is unhealthy, that it leads to avoidance of underlying issue, and that it does not resolve them. Nonetheless, when a person feels lonely, it is a battle to apply the learning. The pull of the old ways is great. The longing for the easy and familiar fix of the alcohol is strong. It is a battle not to succumb to the bodily pull and the old beliefs, that feed the addiction. For this reason, those who struggle with addiction often find it helpful to have the support of others in the form of twelve-step programs. Each day is a new beginning and a new struggle. The commitment to action eventually deepens one's understanding and commitment.

Through the course of the Days of Awe, we identified a rigid pattern of response that interfered with our capacity to respond effectively to our current life situation. On Sukkot, we experienced, in a protected environment, how we can respond in a new way. Now we work to integrate that new way of being into our daily life. As we enter the time of year when there is more darkness than light, we receive support through the Holy-Day of Chanukah. We work in the material world: the Holy-Day does not involve stopping work as we usually do at other times of the year. Our effort and initiative succeed even though the forces of long-engrained habits are strong. We work step-by-step, building new ways, and gradually extending our competence into more and more challenging situations. We feel a sense of victory even though our success is momentary as we fall back into our old ways of responding.

LIGHTING A CANDLE IN THE DARKNESS

- What are the old habitual tendencies that I am still impelled to repeat?

- What do I know I need to do instead of the old habit?

- What happens when I respond in the new way? What can I appreciate about my successes even if they are limited?

- What are the series of steps that take me to my goal?

- What is it that I need to repeat again and again in my efforts to integrate learning into daily life?

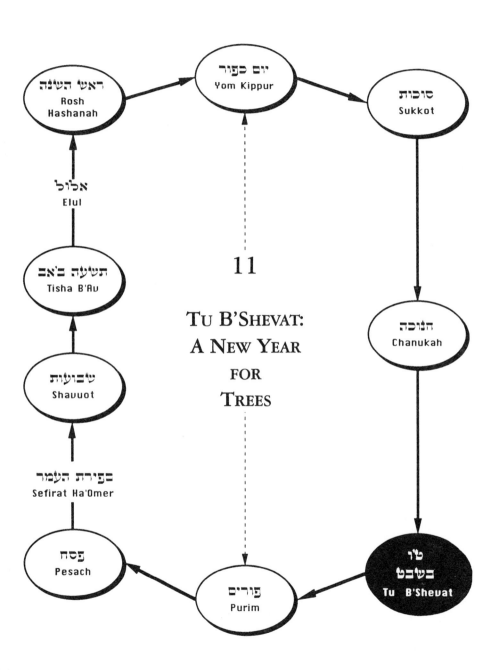

11

TU B'SHEVAT:
A NEW YEAR
FOR
TREES

Til this day, the trees live off the water of the past year; from this day on, they live off the water of this year.
[Jerusalem Talmud, Rosh Hashanah 1:2]

On the fifteenth day of the month of Shevat, we celebrate the new year for trees. In matters of ritual, fruit that matured before Tu B'Shevat belonged to the previous year; fruit maturing after that date belonged to the succeeding year. This categorization was important in computing tithes. It was also used in calculating the prohibition against eating the fruit of a tree during (1) the agricultural Sabbath year; (2) the *Shemitah,* which occurred every seven years; the jubilee year; (3) the *Yovail,* which occurred every fifty years; and (4) the *Orlah,* which applied to the first three years of the tree's growth.

On Tu B'Shevat, there are no restrictions on work or any obligations for additional prayers or rituals. There is a prohibition against fasting and recitation of penitential prayers. It is customary to eat many different kinds of fruits, especially the fruits grown in the land of Israel. Since the reestablishment of the state of Israel, Tu B'Shevat has also been a time for planting of trees.

In certain respects, Tu B'Shevat offers an experience similar to that

of Chanukah. The notion on Chanukah of lighting the darkness is expressed on Tu B'Shevat in the image of a plant slowly sprouting and growing, moving from seed to sprout to full maturation as it is nourished by water, soil, and sun. This image is also different; we make connection with an ecological, integrated, interdependent image of growth instead of the archetypal experience of a struggle embedded in the story of Chanukah.

THE MEANINGS OF THE TU B'SHEVAT *SEDER*

Inch by inch, row by row
Gonna make this garden grow.
All you need is a rake and a hoe
And a piece of fertile ground.
Inch by inch, row by row
Someone bless these seeds I sow.
Someone warm them from below
Til the rains come tumbling down.

Pulling weeds, picking stones
We are made of dreams and bones.
Need a place to call my own for the time is near at hand.
Grain for grain, sun and rain
Find my way thru nature's chain.
Tune my body and my brain to the music of the land.

Plant your rows straight and long,
Temper them with prayer and song,
Mother earth will make you strong if you give her love and care.
An old crow watching hungrily
From his perch in yonder tree.
In my garden I'm as free as that feathered thief up there!

Dave Mallet

These symbols serve as the focus for the kabbalistic tradition of a Tu B'Shevat *Seder*. Like the *Seder* on Pesach, the Tu B'Shevat *Seder* consists of a special ritual meal. There are four parts of the meal, each with special fruits and with special wine.

The first cup of wine is a white wine. Each successive cup is mixed with more red white. The fourth cup is a red wine. The wines of different colors symbolize the change of the seasons and the gradual return to color as spring comes. In the same way as the grapes are transformed over a period of time to become wine, each of us ferments in a unique process over the course of our lives. Shneur Zalman draws a parallel between the effects of consuming wine and mystical realization expressed in the aphorism "When the wine goes in, the secret comes out." This folk saying not only refers to indiscretions spoken while one is intoxicated; it also alludes to the process of mystical realization in which we experience the normally hidden consciousness of Spirit.

Different types of fruits are eaten in a specified manner during the Tu B'Shevat *Seder*. As we eat the fruits, we make a connection between our own development and the organic process of growth from seed to sprout to plant to fruit. No stage is regarded as evil or dysfunctional; each is vital to the process of growth. The four categories of growing things include (1): fruits with an inedible shell and an edible inside, (2) fruits with an edible outside and an inedible seed inside, (3) fruits that can be consumed in their entirety, and (4) sweet-smelling incense. Each of the categories represents a particular stage in our growth.

Type of Fruit	Wine	Season	Psychological Analogue
Inedible outside; edible inside	White	Winter	Outer defense, inner vulnerability
Edible outside, inedible seed	White with some red	Spring	External vulnerability, inner need
All edible	Red with some white	Summer	Conscious integration of protection and vulnerability
Scent	Red	Fall	Unconscious integration of protection and vulnerability

Fruit with an Inedible Protective Outside and Edible Inside

The Torah is like a tree to those who hold on to her.
                                                    from the Morning Prayers

These fruits include bananas, almonds, and oranges. The shell protects the fruit from external dangers—extremes in heat or cold, pests, and disease. Eventually, when the fruit is ripe, the shell rots, exposing the soft inside that contains seeds, allowing the plant to reproduce and continue in the cycle of life. In eating the fruit, we must also remove the hard, external layer so we can enjoy the sweetness and nourishment of our food.

In the same way, we develop a shell to protect from real and imagined assault. Perhaps we learned to stay silent to protect ourselves from shame or ridicule. Perhaps we learned never to ask for help for fear that someone might reject us or abandon us. At a later stage in our development, that protection no longer serves us. Instead, it seals us off from our environment in a way that inhibits our growth. In the same way as the shell rots so the seed can grow, we surrender the old defensive response, exposing the part of ourselves that has been hurt. At the time, this process is painful. We may attempt to resist it or deny it. However, now we can appreciate all the elements. We appreciate the creativity, resourcefulness, and determination with which we protected ourselves. We have compassion and understanding for the difficulty we experienced in surrendering that protection, and respect for our courage in allowing that process to occur.

Fruit with an Edible Outside and an Inedible Seed

God your Lord is bringing you to a good land—a land with flowing streams, and underground springs gushing out in valley and mountain. It is a land of wheat, barley, grapes, figs, and pomegranates—a land of oil, olives and dates.
                                                    [Deuteronomy 8:7–8]

The second set of fruits include dates, apricots, and olives. These fruits employ a different adaptation. The soft exterior protects the seed within. As it rots, it exposes the seed. The seed, in turn, rots, allowing a new sprout to emerge and grow. We can eat the soft exterior, but the seed cannot be eaten.

This type of fruit symbolizes the second stage of growth in which we expose the vulnerability, allowing ourselves to delve deeper until we free the seed within. The soft, sweet-tasting exterior symbolizes the soft, vulnerable part of ourselves. We feel the old vulnerability; we make connection with the part of ourselves that has been hurt. We feel the original pain that occurred when we were shamed or rejected. At the time, this process may have been painful and frightening. We might have wished we could return to our original protection, a time when we denied our need for support or connection. That which once was bitter now can be experienced as the sweetness of a tender, ripe fruit. We approach our vulnerability with the sweetness of compassion for the difficulty of our journey, appreciating our courage and persistence.

The seed within the fruit is analogous to the need underlying our vulnerability. As we experience our vulnerability, we gain awareness of the need that has been unsatisfied, a need, like the seed, that can be nurtured, allowing us to find new ways to respond and be fulfilled. The seed itself cannot be eaten. It must be planted, fertilized, tended, and given time to grow. It requires sun and water. In the same way, knowing the true need underneath the pain is only a beginning. We must attend to that need, learning more about what we require and how to respond to get what we need and satisfy the hunger. At an earlier stage, we might have found it difficult to tolerate having a need that we did not know how to satisfy. Now, we can tolerate feeling a need that we do not yet have the ability to satisfy. We can respect our persistence and our creativity.

Fruit That Can Be Completely Consumed

The righteous person will blossom like a date palm and will grow tall like a cedar.

Psalm 98

The third set of fruits includes apples and grapes. These fruits are completely edible; they can be consumed in their entirety. These fruits offer a third adaptation in which the protective function is fully integrated. Nothing has to be removed or changed. At this stage in our own growth, we experience a similar integration. We still need protection: the capacity to contain feelings, vulnerabilities, needs, and impulses when the environment around us may be unsupportive or hostile. However, we no longer need the primitive defenses of childhood that may have been harsh or extreme, such as repressing all feelings to prevent ourselves from expressing particular emotions. We contain feelings when we need to do so. We can express feelings and impulses appropriately and effectively to satisfy our needs. We are connected to our Essence, grounded and connected to everyday experience.

Incense

Among the works of man which human life is rightly employed in perfecting and beautifying, the first in importance surely is man himself. Human nature is not a machine to be built after a model, and set to do exactly the work prescribed for it, but a tree, which must grow and develop itself on all sides. It is not by wearing down into uniformity all that is individual in themselves, but by cultivating it, and calling it forth, within the limits imposed by the rights and interests of others, that human beings become a noble and beautiful object of contemplation. It is only the cultivation of individuality which produces, or can produce, well-developed human beings.

John Stuart Mill

The fourth set of growing things are fragrant spices and herbs. We no longer focus on material form but rather on smells that we experience but do not see or feel. Physiologically, the nerves associated with our sense of smell lead directly from the nose to the limbic system of the brain. Unlike other senses, they are not mediated by other cognitive processes: they directly affect our emotions. At the conclusion of the Sabbath in the *Havdalah* ritual, we directly nourish our souls by inhaling the invisible aroma of spices. Similarly on Tu B'Shevat, these essences connect us to the core of Spirit, the Essence within ourselves. As the process of integration is completed, all duality between material and spiritual dissolves. We experience what we cannot fully see, feel, conceptualize, or describe.

PSYCHOTHERAPEUTIC PROCESS ON TU B'SHEVAT

People enter therapy with problems. They leave therapy with issues.

Emily Ruppert

This integrated process of organic growth is exemplified by William, a successful architect who began therapy to cope with acute back pain. Will was creative and energetic. He never approached life half-heartedly. He was enthusiastic about everything he did. That enthusiasm was wonderful in many respects, but it also caused trouble. When he injured his back, he was advised to make a commitment to a program of regular exercise to strengthen his muscles and improve his flexibility. Initially, the program of exercise was helpful, but Will pushed himself too far. Each time he started to improve, he pushed himself to do more and reinjured himself. Consciously, Will realized that he needed to be more gentle. Nonetheless, he tended unconsciously to overdo it even when he thought he was being careful.

This tendency to overdo also occurred in other contexts; however, this trait had never caused him problems. In his work, the enthusiasm and ability to work hard was appreciated and rewarded. This tendency was reinforced by his father, who also tended toward hyperactivity. Will's father had been diagnosed as a manic-depressive. Through the course of Will's growing up, his dad had been hospitalized several times as a result of this illness. Will's father not only reinforced by example the pattern of hyperactivity and collapse, he also influenced Will more directly. He was enthusiastic about Will's career, always feeding the notion that he could do more and more. Similarly, he encouraged Will to buy a large home, promising to help with mortgage payments. He exacerbated Will's predisposition to believe that anything that could be imagined could be achieved.

Although Will was quite successful, he was overextended. Each month he struggled to cover the overhead costs of his own firm. His difficulties were compounded when his father was sometimes unable to provide the promised help with mortgage payments. Will worked under intense pressure. This pressure further exacerbated his health problems. Will understood that his tendency to do too much was not helpful. Nonetheless, he found it difficult to stop a lifelong pattern even though he knew that his body could no longer tolerate the continuing overload.

In the same way as the outer shell of a fruit protects the vulnerability within, Will's tendency to overdo also provided a protection. I asked Will to imagine how he would feel if he set limits, not just on exercise but also on work and spending. He sat silent for a few moments. Then he talked of feeling sad, angry, and frightened at the prospect of doing less. He did not want to abandon any of his dreams. He also did not want to disappoint his father.

Will recalled how his father had been hospitalized several times after episodes of hyperactivity. He was reluctant to set limits for fear that his father would become depressed and need to be hospitalized. Will's ability to work hard helped protect him from disappointing his father and risking a crisis. Beneath the shell lay the vulnerability that he had previously needed to protect. In the same way as the covering needs to be removed from the fruit, Will needed to set limits and take the risk to feel sad, angry, and frightened instead.

Will acted decisively and powerfully. He decided to scale back substantially in his lifestyle. He neither wanted nor needed such a large house. He rented the house for enough to cover expenses and found another place to live in a rural area that brought him closer to nature. He sold his business to one of his associates and took on work as a consultant with limited commitments. When his father objected, Will used the opportunity to initiate a discussion about the effects of manic episodes; he also set clear boundaries to protect himself from his father's grandiosity. Will developed some strategies to help him set better limits with his exercise by setting an alarm on his watch to remind him to stop and by wearing a bracelet on his left arm as a visual cue to pay attention to the beginnings of pain.

As he set better limits, feelings of sadness, rage, and fear did emerge. Will grieved not only the present losses but recalled the effects of excesses in his past, especially in childhood. As he did, Will also began to focus on the lack of an intimate relationship in his life. In many respects, the same pattern of grandiosity had plagued him in his relationships. He found himself often in love, overcome with the rush of a romance that then fell apart after a few months when the first conflicts led to a crash. With life less frantic and hectic, Will began to feel lonely.

Will became involved with a woman named Rachel whom he had known for many years. Built on a solid base of friendship, the relationship was very passionate and satisfying. However, after a few months, Will began to distance himself. He began fantasizing about other women; he started to spend more time alone. However, Will did not remain in his old pattern for coping with stress by ending a relationship when conflict emerged.

Will now resembled a fruit with a soft outside and a seed within. Able to sit with his vulnerable feelings, Will realized he needed to identify the conflicts and attempt to resolve them rather than end the relationship. By staying in the relationship and tolerating the feelings of vulnerability, he could nourish a seed that could bear fruit in his life. Will identified several areas of stress in the relationship. Will wanted time alone for travel, adventure, and creative expression, which sometimes conflicted with Rachel's desire to be more of a family and for Will to engage more with her daughter. Will wanted the freedom to explore other intimate relationships, while Rachel wanted to feel a sense of commitment. Will had not previously named the areas of distress, nor had he discussed them with Rachel.

When Will first discussed the areas of conflict with Rachel, they both felt hopeless. They could see no possible resolution except to end the relationship. They came for a session together. Rachel had also experienced difficulty in relationships. She tended not to speak up about what she wanted and tried to accommodate herself to her partner as much as possible. When it became unbearable, she ended the relationship.

Although both Will and Rachel felt hopeless, I did not share their despair. I raised another possibility. Would they both invest some time attempting to discuss the differences fully and work to resolve them? Instead of making compromises that felt unsatisfactory to everyone, they could work to develop creative agreements that addressed everyone's needs. They had not invested time and energy in discovering real solutions. Although the goal seemed impossible to achieve, they agreed to make the effort.

Although it appeared that their wants and needs conflicted, the areas of difference narrowed as we talked. Although Will wanted time alone, he enjoyed spending time with Rachel's daughter as well. He did resent expectations to participate in plans when he had no role in making decisions, and he sometimes felt excluded. Although Rachel wanted to be able to count on Will, she also felt comfortable with time on her own as well. She, like Will, experienced difficulty when she had no input regarding decision-making. They redefined the problem: they did not disagree about the desirability of time together and time apart, but they needed a better process for decision-making that allowed both to feel empowered and considered. They agreed to make decisions together. They structured some time to be together as a family, some time as a couple, and some time alone. Sometimes they could not reach agreement, but most of the time they worked out arrangements that felt mutually satisfying.

As they continued to practice making decisions together, Will and Rachel achieved the next stage in the process of growth, symbolized by the entirely edible fruit. At this stage, the protective mechanism is fully integrated. When Will experienced a conflict, he no longer felt impelled to withdraw. He recognized that impulse as a signal of a conflict. He could then clarify the issue, discuss it with Rachel, and search for a resolution. He no longer needed external support and structure of therapy to help him shift out of the old protective coping style. At this stage, Will no longer came to therapy with unresolved problems. He brought stories of success in which he caught himself beginning to withdraw and made the shift on his own.

Eventually, Will no longer felt the impulse to withdraw, nor did he consciously strive to identify, express, and work through conflict. Without thinking about it, he became aware of a conflict, discussed it, and worked toward a solution. In this final stage, the new style is fully integrated, symbolized by incense, which is invisible and needs no chewing or digesting to be consumed, by the aroma that enters directly into our being. At this stage, we have completely integrated the new way of responding. The old protective mechanism is no longer activated.

On Tu B'Shevat, we accept the entirety of this process of growth in each of its stages as steps in growth and development. We respect our constrictions as inevitable and necessary protective responses that allowed us to overcome difficulties. We accept the painful experiences that make us realize that those protective responses no longer serve us. We discipline ourselves to do the work needed to understand and make changes, persistent and patient as we strive to change habits ingrained through years of unconscious experience.

TU B'SHEVAT IN THE CYCLE OF THE YEAR

On one Tu B'Shevat during a visit to Jerusalem, I went to visit a Chasidic rabbi, the Amshinover Rebbe. Escorted by a friend, I arrived at the Rebbe's house of study late in the evening. We waited for hours with scores of others who sought the Rebbe's counsel. When my turn finally arrived, somewhere in the middle of the night, I was summoned to a small room where the Rebbe held court. Spontaneously, he began to lecture me about the importance of controlling desire. His words were not especially profound, especially to a young man in his early twenties. However, it was also Tu B'Shevat. On the table in front of the Rebbe sat a bowl with dates, figs, apples, bananas, and almonds, produce grown in the land of Israel. Beside the bowl was a large container filled with honey. As the Rebbe spoke, he selected an apple, carefully cut it into pieces, then spooned

a large gob of honey onto the slice and ate it. He offered me a piece
as well. Slowly, deliberately, steadily, and relentlessly, he spoke of
controlling desire while he continued to eat and eat and eat. His
hands became sticky with residues of honey and bits of fruit. The
counterpoint of his actions and his words confused me. Was he a
hypocrite who spoke one way and acted another? Was he simply out
of touch, unconsciously bingeing on food while controlling his other
appetites?

At the end of this encounter, I described what happened to my
friend. He was surprised. In the years he had known the Rebbe, he
had never observed him act in such a manner. He usually showed
restraint in his eating, consuming only the minimum needed to sustain himself. The only way to understand the Rebbe's actions was to
regard his behavior as a deliberate communication; the Rebbe was
telling me something by the way he ate. I thought, and continue to
think, about the meaning of that message. Although controlling
desire is important, it need not be understood as denial or repression.
Control means allowing, enjoying, and appreciating worldly pleasures, each in the proper context and time. Tu B'Shevat offers us
time to enjoy material pleasure because we have exercised control;
now we experience pleasure in the appropriate context.

On Pesach, we also encountered the archetypal image of the seed,
but it had not yet become a fruit. We were identified with our exterior shell, our defensive coping strategy that protected us from the
oppression in Egypt. We resisted surrendering that protection in the
unfriendly environment of the desert. We were helpless and needed
outside protection, guidance, and nourishment to survive and grow.
We tasted the first fruits on Shavuot, but it was not yet time to complete the harvest. We first experienced the drought of summer heat;
finding humility in our grief on Tisha B'Av, we painfully allowed the
old Identity to dissolve, to rot and return to the earth. As the seed
rotted, the new sprout grew through the Days of Awe. On Sukkot,
we finally completed the harvest, which nourished us through the
darkness of winter, giving way to new growth. Now, we can look

with appreciation at the process we have completed; we can look forward to our continued growth.

We are no longer caught in the immediacy of a painful and often difficult struggle. We can appreciate and value each stage in our development: how we had to protect an inner vulnerability with a tough shell, a defensive behavior that sealed us off from others and perhaps even from ourselves; how we exposed that vulnerability, like a fruit with a soft, edible exterior; how we encountered the seed within, that Essence that needed to be nourished; how we nourished that seed; and how we grew to become the fruit that can be completely consumed and enjoyed. In so doing, we make connection with the universal Essence represented by the sweet smell of incense that has no material form.

BEARING FRUIT: STAGES OF GROWTH

- *Fruit with an inedible protective outside and edible inside*— What was the shell which protected you from hurt? What was the vulnerability within which needed protection?

- *Fruit with an edible outside and an inedible seed*—What was your experience as the inner vulnerability surfaced? What was the seed hidden underneath the vulnerability? How did you access that seed?

- *Fruit which can be completely consumed*—How did you nurture that seed within? What was your experience as you completed that process? How did you experience the growth and maturation of that seed into a fruit?

- *Incense*—Surrendering concepts and words for a moment, allow yourself to breathe, to sense, to receive, and to appreciate the experience of your self, your growth, and your transformation, a new identity emerged from the old.

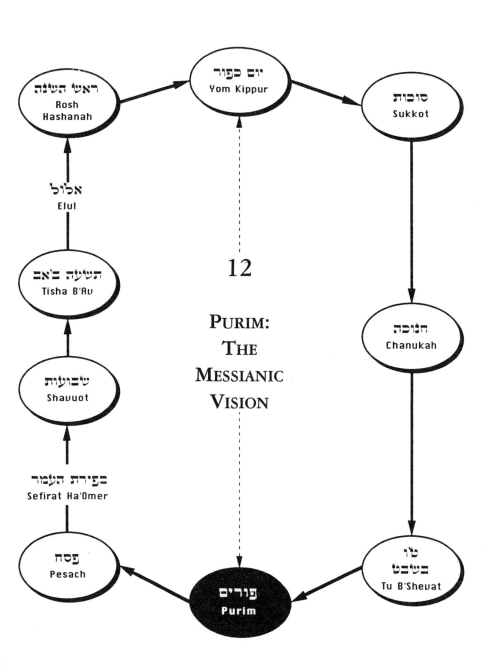

ראש השנה
Rosh
Hashanah

יום כפור
Yom Kippur

סוכות
Sukkot

אלול
Elul

תשעה באב
Tisha B'Av

12

חנוכה
Chanukah

שבועות
Shavuot

PURIM:
THE
MESSIANIC
VISION

ספירת העמר
Sefirat Ha'Omer

פסח
Pesach

פורים
Purim

טו
בשבט
Tu B'Shevat

And Mordecai wrote these things, and sent letters to all the Jews that were in all the provinces of the King Achashveros, both near and far, reminding them to keep the fourteenth day of the month Adar, and the fifteenth day of the same, yearly, the days when the Jews had rest from their enemies, and the month which was turned from sorrow to gladness and from mourning into a good day; that they should make these days of feasting and gladness, and of sending portions one to another, and gifts to the poor.

[Book of Esther 9:20–22]

Purim, an early spring festival that occurs on the fifteenth of the month of Adar, commemorates the deliverance of the Jews of Persia from a plot to kill them. King Achashveros's villainous minister, Haman, planned the destruction of the Jews but was stopped by Queen Esther and her uncle, Mordecai.

Purim marks the culmination of the Holy-Day cycle of the year, the process that began the preceding Pesach. We began our journey dependent, stumbling, unconfident, and ineffective; we left our personal Egypt, gained understanding on Shavuot, confronted denial and grieved the discrepancy between the dream and the reality on Tisha B'Av, looked inward to see how we need to change during the month of Elul, worked diligently to identify that change during the Days of Awe, and struggled to manifest a new way of being into the world on Sukkot, Chanukah, and Tu B'Shevat. On Purim, we finally experience the triumph and the payoff for that work.

293

Pesach through Tisha B'Av	Unconscious dysfunctional responses	Identification with old Ego structure
Elul through Yom Kippur	Conscious dysfunctional responses	Disidentification with old Ego structure
Sukkot through Chanukah	Conscious effective responses	Manifestation of new Ego structure
Purim	Unconscious effective responses	Identification with new Ego structure

On Purim, we celebrate our maturation. The symptoms that propelled us out of our habitual responses may not have disappeared. However, our insight about how to cope has not only translated into understanding and insight, has not only led us to experiment or struggle with new ways of being, but has also become fully integrated into our lives. We experience a sense of autonomy. We are able to take initiative to resolve difficulties rather than being powerless, passive, or dependent on others to facilitate the changes. We are able to look back on our journey with perspective and humor. What once was the stimulus for tears can now be approached with laughter. The darkness of our pain is lightened by our current success and appreciation of our learning and growth.

THE DEVELOPMENTAL PROCESS FROM PESACH TO PURIM

Shneur Zalman interprets the story of Purim as an archetypal representation of this stage in our development. Each incident in the story is not only a historic event but a step in the evolution of consciousness, creating a dwelling place in the human spirit for God's Presence.

The story of Purim takes place in the court of Achashveros, the king of Persia. The Jews live in exile under the rule of a foreign nation: they do not live in their own land. In many respects, their situation parallels the slavery in Egypt, when they also lived in exile and under the rule of the Pharaoh rather than in Israel. Haman, like Pharaoh, was angered by the Jews allegiance to God and their spiritual mission, their refusal to accept the hegemony of the earthly rulers. In the same way as Pharaoh initially took reprisals against the Israelites when his authority was challenged, killing the firstborn sons and increasing their work, Haman planned to kill all the Jews and take their property after Mordecai refuses to bow down to him.

However, there are many differences in the story of Purim and the events in Egypt. In Egypt, the Israelites are aware of their slavery, they experience the pain of oppression, but, like infants, all they can do is cry for help. Moses, in spite of his adoption by the daughter of Pharaoh, is forced to flee Egypt when he takes a stand in support of the Jews. God intervenes, selecting Moses, Aaron, and Miriam to lead the people. Pharaoh's power is overcome only with Divine intervention in the form of the miracles of the plagues and the splitting of the sea. Even with all this support, the Israelites are skeptical; they do not believe they can escape their slavery. They repeatedly resist their leaders and rebel against their authority. Eventually, the Israelites leave Egypt and begin their journey to the land promised by God. After leaving Egypt, the Israelites are dependent on God for nurturance and guidance. They are led by the pillar of smoke and the pillar of fire; they are fed by the manna. They do experience Revelation, a moment of face-to-face connection with God. They commit with the words "We will do, and we will hear," but they are unable to sustain that commitment in action: as soon as Moses leaves them and ascends the mountain, they lose faith and build the golden calf.

In contrast, in the story of Purim, the Jews are aware of Haman's plot and mobilize to defeat their oppressors. God does not intervene directly in the events; God's name is not even mentioned in the Book of Esther, which chronicles the history. Moreover, the Book of Esther was not written by God, as was the Torah, which tells the story of Egypt—it was written by Mordecai. The Jews do not require the outside guidance and nurturance that was necessary after leaving Egypt. Mordecai and Esther are not explicitly selected by God as leaders; there is no burning bush and no face-to-face dialogue with God. Mordecai and Esther naturally emerge as leaders as a result of their autonomous, self-initiated, and freely chosen responses to the crisis.

The Jews do not resist their leadership as occurred in the time of the slavery in Egypt: when they are told of the plot against them, they support Esther with three days of prayer and fasting as requested. They fight to stop their oppressors rather than hold back, but they fight within the limits imposed on them by their leaders. They nourish one another, celebrating their victory with gifts to the poor and presents of food for one another. In contrast to Pharaoh, who resists the call for an end to oppression, the king of Persia responds when Esther makes him aware of the threat by Haman. Consequently, the Jews do not need to leave Persia. They can accomplish their mission of manifesting God's Presence on earth even in exile; they do not need to live in the land of Israel to do so.

Both Pharaoh and Achashveros symbolize the forces of nature. At Pesach, we are not strong enough to fight the natural forces that bind us to our old way of being, thinking, and doing. Outside intervention is required to escape the oppression. In contrast to the time of Revelation when we were unable to translate our words into action, on Purim we are able to act more autonomously and effectively to counter that threat. God is still present but acts through the forces of nature rather than in opposition to them; we are connected to God and able to manifest Essence into the activity of daily life.

For the kabbalists, the Purim story provides an archetypal description of the Messianic era. We do not envision a universe in which the material world ceases to exist and all returns to Spirit but one in which the material and spiritual domains are integrated. God's will is manifest on earth, and God's dwelling place is secured in the material world. In this sense, there is an acceptance of life's journey; we trust, we are competent, and we can work through difficulties.

Pesach		Purim	
Image	Psychological Theme	Image	Psychological Theme
Exile in Egypt	Formation of Ego	Exile in Persia	Formation of Ego
Slavery in Egypt	Ego structure becomes dysfunctional; symptoms	Haman's plot to kill the Jews	Ego structure becomes dysfunctional; symptoms
Ruled by Pharaoh who opposes Israelites	Natural world & fate resist change	Ruled by King Achashveros who responds to Jews	Natural world & fate accept change
Moses, Aaron & Miriam selected by God	Emerging leadership by spiritually attuned aspect of Self	Mordecai & Esther autonomously respond	Integrated leadership by spiritually attuned aspect of Self
Israelites resist leaders & unable to fight oppressors	Spiritual aspect of personality unable to fight old Ego structure	Jews collaboratively struggle to overcome oppression	Spiritual aspect of personality able to fight old Ego structure
Miracles required for redemption	External support necessary for change	Human activity brings redemption	Inner strength to make changes in responses
Escape slavery by leaving Egypt for Israel	Change possible only in protected environment	Overcome threat while remaining in Persia	Change integrated in all environments

DIFFERENT PATHS TO AT-ONE-MENT:
YOM KIPPUR AND PURIM

Life is not a problem—Life is the closest God has yet come to a solution.

© Ashleigh Brilliant

Shneur Zalman compares Purim to Yom Kippur. The holiest day of the Jewish year is also referred to as *Yom Kippurim*. The name suggests the connection. *Yom Kippurim* literally means "a day like Purim." On both Holy-Days, we find the concept of fate. The name of the Holy-Day, Purim, comes from *pur*, the lots Haman threw to determine the day for the slaughter of the Jews. Similarly, on *Yom Kippurim*, the high priest throws lots to determine which of the two sheep will be thrown into the valley of Azazel and which will be sacrificed at the Sanctuary (*Torah Or*, 184).

On *Yom Kippurim* we return to One-ness. We are face-to-face with the Divine Presence. The image of being face-to-face with God is not taken literally. It provides a vivid image for describing a direct encounter with God's Presence in which we separate ourselves from all material needs and concerns. Although we do not abhor the world of material existence, bodily needs are not our primary focus.

On Yom Kippur, we achieve this experience by dissociating from the world through fasting and abstinence from earthly pleasures. As a result, adversity ceases to matter because we function at a different level. We make connection with the Essence of life. The material plane no longer matters. Pain and struggle dissolves because we maintain a spiritual perspective in which current life issues no longer become overly significant. We understand life's difficulties as the consequences of negative actions in the past. We learn from our history, take responsibility for choices we have made, and change our responses accordingly. In this way, the difficulties of life inform us rather than oppress us; they lose their negative quality. Darkness is transformed into light.

On Purim, we do not disconnect, disidentify, and transcend the material world, nor do we focus on our own dysfunctional responses. We do not deny bodily needs like sexuality and hunger. Instead, we integrate these human needs; our needs can then serve as a vehicle for manifestation of Spirit. On Purim, we also return to One-ness, face-to-face with God, but we do so in the context of daily activity rather than by separating ourselves from everyday reality.

Shneur Zalman uses an analogy to explain this experience. Our heads contain our brain, the center of understanding; our heads also contain our sense organs related to seeing, hearing, and taste. If we turn our backs to God, we focus on self as separate and become disconnected. When we turn our heads, we reorient our understanding and perception. If we orient ourselves toward God, wherever we turn, even in the material world, we remain connected with God's Presence. As we manifesting our awareness and understanding in our actions, we change darkness into light.

The nullification of self on Yom Kippur is symbolically enacted by the High Priest when he casts lots and surrenders his own preferences to fate. Haman casts lots much as the high priest casts lots. Although Haman also appears to nullify himself, Shneur Zalman suggests that the similarity is comparable to that of "a monkey imitating a person." Haman's intent was not spiritual, not selfless. Haman wanted power. He wanted to destroy Mordecai and take his possessions. Consequently, Haman and his sons do not triumph: they are hung on a gallows fifty cubits in height. The fifty cubits represent Essence, paralleling the fiftieth day of the *omer,* the moment of Revelation on Shavuot. For Shneur Zalman, the image of Haman on the gallows suggests elevating and subsuming material needs to the needs of Essence and Spirit. On Purim, this process occurs in the context of human activity rather than through the sacrificial service in the Sanctuary.

The experience on Purim represents a more complete integration of change than on Yom Kippur. In the *Megillah,* we read that the Jews "took upon themselves to do as they had begun" (Esther 9:23). Shneur Zalman interprets this verse as an indication that the Jews received the Torah fully and completely. At other times in the year, we have been motivated by avoidance of pain. On Pesach, we are driven by the pain of our slavery. At the time of Sinai on Shavuot, according to the *Midrash,* the Jews were reluctant: they received the Torah with God holding the mountain above their heads. During the Days of Awe, we are also driven by desire to stop a dysfunctional coping pattern that undermines our effectiveness. However, at Purim, the Torah was received freely and independently; the Jews were willing and able to practice their religion in daily life. What was achieved through fasting and abstinence on Yom Kippur is achieved through celebration and feasting on Purim. Purim is more than a day for drunkenness and fun; it represents a fulfillment of the Divine vision.

INTEGRATED SPIRITUALITY: MORDECAI RIDING
THE KING'S HORSE ESCORTED BY HAMAN

As long as you have your feet on the ground, your head is perfectly safe in the clouds.

© Ashleigh Brilliant

Integrated manifestation of Spirit in the material world is described by Shneur Zalman (*Torah Or,* 179) in his interpretation of how King Achashveros honors Mordecai. Overhearing two servants plotting to kill the king, Mordecai reveals the plot and saves the king's life. Initially, the king forgets to reward Mordecai. Late one night, the king is reminded of Mordecai's deed and decides to reward him. Haman had been waiting to see the king, hoping for the king's permission to hang Mordecai and eliminate his hated enemy. King Achashveros, learning of Haman's presence, seeks his adviser's counsel:

> And the King said to him: "What shall be done for the man whom the King desires to honor?" Haman said in his heart, "Whom would the King desire to honor besides myself?" And Haman said to the King: "For the man whom the King desires to honor, let royal apparel be brought which the King used to wear, and the horse the King rides, and whose head a royal crown is set. And, let the clothes and the horse be delivered to the hand of one of the King's most noble princes, that they may dress the man whom the King desires to honor, and parade him through the streets of the city on horseback, and proclaim, 'So shall it be done to the man whom the King desires to honor'"
>
> [Book of Esther 6:6–9]

According to Shneur Zalman, the story serves as a metaphorical description of the manifestation of Essence into material form, the creation of a dwelling place on earth for Spirit through human activity. The garment of the King symbolizes the experience of God as immanent, *Memaleh Kol Almin*. All of the created universe is a garment that God has made. The natural world allows for an indirect experience of Spirit. Just as a garment covers the person, creation clothes and hides God's Presence. A person's dress indirectly allows us to know something about the human being we cannot see. In the same way, Essence, which is also not directly seen, is made visible through the garment of creation.

The crown symbolizes the direct connection between Essence and the material level. The crown refers to the mystical experience of One-ness in which we merge with the transcendent aspect of God's Being, *Sovev Kol Almin*. The garment of the king—God as immanent—and the crown—God as transcendent—are carried by the third element—the horse on which the king rides, a symbol for the process of revelation through the *Torah.*

Mordecai is honored for his service to the king by dressing in the king's garments and wearing the royal crown. Seated on the king's horse, he is escorted through the streets by Haman. This image symbolically expresses the integration of the personality and the spiritual connection experienced at this time of year. Mordecai symbolizes self-nullification and humility. He represents the aspect of the person connected to Essence for whom material concerns are subservient to a sense of spiritual purpose.

Mordecai, the symbol of humility and self-nullification, is raised up and crowned; he is now served by Haman, the symbol of self-centeredness, who squires the horse. Haman represents the aspect of oneself tied to material reality, concerned only with individual needs, disconnected from relationship with others, and lacking a sense of spiritual purpose. This aspect of ourselves that is isolated and inflated is not denied or excised, but integrated into the personality. According to Shneur Zalman, we need an element of self-preservation. One-sixteenth portion of ourselves needs to be prideful and self-centered. To accomplish our spiritual task, we need to preserve and respect our unique individuality. However, our respect and pride in that individuality is integrated into our personality, so we are neither inflated nor diminished, in the balance necessary for a grounded spirituality. This same idea was expressed by the Kotzker Rebbe who advised his students to maintain a proper perspective by writing two notes to themselves and placing one in each pocket. One note reminded them of their vulnerability and limits with the verse "Ashes to ashes, and dust to dust." The other note carried the message "The whole world was created to enable me to complete my task."

Story Element	Archetypal Meaning
King	God
Royal garments	*Memaleh Kol Almin,* Creation, God as Immanent
Crown	*Sovev Kol Almin,* God as Transcendent
Horse	*Torah,* Revelation
Mordecai	Humility, lowered eyes self-nullification
Haman	Pride, heart, self-inflation

Shneur Zalman suggests that the balance between Mordecai and Haman, between humility and pride, is also present within ourselves at this time of year. Our eyes symbolize our capacity to "see," to sustain awareness of a larger perspective in which our own individuality is subsumed and becomes part of the infinite universe of Spirit. When we "see" in this way, according to Shneur Zalman, we walk with lowered eyes. In contrast, the heart burns with love. The heart longs to ascend and be joined to the One. The heart is prideful enough to believe that such a mystical experience is possible. We learn to live in balance between these two forces.

At this time of year, we find ourselves in the image of Mordecai, led through the streets, wearing the king's garments, riding the king's horse, and wearing the crown of the king, led by Haman. For each of us, vulnerabilities that are acknowledged and nurtured become our strengths. The ego and its habits of personality becomes a superficial exterior that protects the true core of Self. We are connected to God's immanence and God's transcendence, allowing that experience to carry us into the world empowered by the imprint of Revelation. Haman, the symbol of selfishness and inflated grandiosity, is joined with Holiness. A reversal occurs in which the paradox of these polarities is integrated. We have attained the state which Rabbi Nahman describes in his allegory about the garden. When the parts of the statue are restored to their rightful places, the garden again becomes a place of beauty and nourishment. This theme is also expressed in Rabbi Nahman's allegorical description of the relationship between the spiritual and material aspects of ourselves using the image of a lame man and a blind man who help each other find their way out of the forest.

ESTHER AS A SYMBOL OF SPIRITUALITY EXPRESSED THROUGH THE MATERIAL WORLD

"What is REAL?" asked the Rabbit one day, when they were lying side by side near the nursery fender, before Nana came to tidy the room. "Does it mean having things that buzz inside you and a stick-out handle?"

"Real isn't how you are made," said the Skin Horse. "It's a thing that happens to you. When a child loves you for a long, long time, not just to play with, but REALLY loves you, then you become Real."

"Does it hurt?" asked the Rabbit.

"Sometimes," said the Skin Horse, for he was always truthful. "When you are Real, you don't mind being hurt."

"Does it happen all at once, like being wound up," he asked, "or bit by bit?"

"It doesn't happen all at once," said the Skin Horse. "You become. It takes a long time. That's why it doesn't happen to people who break easily, or have sharp edges, or who have to be carefully kept. Generally, by the time you are Real, most of your hair has been loved off, and your eyes drop out, and you

> *get loose in the joints and very shabby. But these things don't matter at all, because once you are Real you can't be ugly, except to people who don't understand."*
>
> *"I suppose you are real?" said the Rabbit. And then he wished he had not said it, for he thought the Skin Horse might be sensitive. But the Skin Horse only smiled.*
>
> *"The Boy's Uncle made me Real," he said. " That was a great many years ago; but once you are Real you can't become unreal again. It lasts for always."*
>
> from *The Velveteen Rabbit*

Esther's name in Hebrew is associated with the root *astir*, which means "hidden." Esther symbolizes the quality of God's Essence hidden in the material world. The miracle of Purim is hidden in human activity. It does not require an aberration of nature to provide salvation. Esther's ability to influence the king is the agent of salvation rather than any external miracle.

For Shneur Zalman, Esther's ability to manifest spirituality through natural forces is greater than the power of all other prophets who could not operate through the material world, who had to rely on visions and miracles. In this sense, the miracles of Purim are at a higher level. God's will was manifested even in the natural process of human activity; moreover, the results are just as powerful as if God had intervened directly to foil Haman's plot. This integration of Spirit into creation is suggested by *gematria*, mystical interpretation through discovery of numerological connections between words. The numerical value of *ELoHeeM*, the name for God as revealed in Creation, equals the numerical value of *HaTeVa*, the word for nature.

$$\aleph = 1$$
$$\lamed = 30$$
$$\he = 5$$
$$\yod = 10$$
$$\mem = 40$$
$$= 86$$

$$\he = 5$$
$$\tet = 9$$
$$\bet = 2$$
$$\ayin = 70$$
$$= 86$$

Mordecai learns of Haman's plan. He asks Esther for help. She asks him to mobilize the community to support her with three days of fasting and prayer. Then she takes the risk to speak. Her words are heard, and the plot is foiled. No miracles occur, only autonomous human activity. Esther begins her efforts to save the Jews by inviting the king and Haman to a banquet. She does not immediately push away the symbol of evil and materiality. The source of evil is in separation and isolation rather than connectedness. Esther brings the evil closer, so as to elevate and transform it. The power of evil dissolves with connectedness.

Esther does not immediately confront the king with Haman's plans. She twice approaches the king before revealing Haman's plot. She takes a chance when she initiates contact without being invited. If the king is angered by her assertiveness, he may have her killed. However, the king responds favorably. The first time Esther approaches him, he extends his golden scepter, the symbol of his monarchy, for her to touch. On the second encounter, he hands her the scepter.

Shneur Zalman interprets these two events as symbolic representations of our experience of spirituality as it develops through the Holy-Day celebrations of the year. Esther's initial separation from the king is a metaphorical representation of our own separation from Essence. The duality between the spiritual and material domains is not a battle between "Good" and "Evil." The material world is also God's creation. The difficulty arises when the material world is disconnected from Spirit. Insofar as our own thoughts, expression, and actions are disconnected from Spirit, they can be compared to a desert that is fertile but not yet cultivated.

Paralleling Esther's actions to approach the king as a result of the threat from Haman, we are propelled by the pain and suffering of our disconnection to regain the closeness with Spirit. The king's favorable response in stretching out his scepter to Esther symbolizes the connection we feel with Spirit in celebrating the Holy-Days of the year.

In the same way that Esther's connection is fleeting and limited, our connection through the Holy-Days is also momentary and incomplete. Approaching God through the joy of the Holy-Days is equivalent to touching the head of the golden staff. The gold of the staff is the vehicle for God's light. The staff remains in God's hand, but we are energized and nourished even by connection to the tip.

The Spirit within us is strengthened, and we are energized for our
next encounter. The joy of the
Holy-Days enters our bodies, facilitates our ability to overcome
obstacles, and brings us closer to
God.

When Esther approaches the
king for the second time, he gives
her the staff. This act suggests a
moment of full and complete reconnection. The darkness turns into
light. At the end of days, in the Messianic era, we will attain this
higher level. The light of God's Presence will be so strong that all of
God's light will be manifest, below as above. There will be no difference between Spirit and matter, darkness and light, upper or
lower realms of creation.

For this reason, the kabbalists' suggest that all of the scriptures
will be unnecessary in the Messianic era except for the *megillah* of
Purim. Similarly, all Holy-Days will be abolished except for Purim,
as suggested by the text:

> *The Jews ordained, and took upon themselves, and upon all*
> *their progeny, and upon all those who joined themselves to the*
> *community, that they would keep these two days according to*
> *the appointed time every year. And these days shall be remem-*
> *bered and kept throughout every generation, every family,*
> *every province, and every city; and these days of Purim shall*
> *not fail from among the Jews, nor the memorial of them per-*
> *ish from their seed.*
>
> [Book of Esther 9:27–28]

At the Messianic era, this light will be fully revealed and will
manifest itself in the thoughts, expression, and actions of each person and be seen by others. Although the Messiah has not yet arrived
and we have not yet realized a permanent integration, each of us has
the quality of Esther at this time of year. The inner spark of Spirit
manifests through the garments of our thought, expression, and
action in the material world.

This theme is also suggested in another aspect of the Purim story when a contest is held to find a new queen after the removal of Vashti. We are told that each candidate spends six months in preparation, anointed with special oils. Then each spends six months immersed in incense made from myrrh (*mor*), after which she is received by the king.

The women who approach the king are symbols of the feminine principle in each of us as we approach God. *Mor* comes from the same root as the word *mereerut,* which means "suffering." The six months' immersion in *mor* symbolizes suffering associated with conscious awareness of our disconnection from Spirit. Incense, like Essence, is experienced in the core of our being even though it cannot be seen. Mordecai's name, which can be read as *Mar Dachya,* also comes from the same root. The source of Mordecai's power is willingness to experience the bitterness. As a result of that consciousness, we are able to approach the king. As a result of our willingness to sit with our pain, we attain a capacity for purity and connection.

RITUAL ENACTMENT OF ARCHETYPAL THEMES ON PURIM

At-One-Ment

The ritual celebration of Purim allows us to experience the story as we enact the archetypal themes expressed in it. The day before Purim is a day of fasting, helping us make a visceral connection to the three days of prayer and fasting as Esther prepared to approach the king. The fasting also helps connect us to the experience of at-one-ment that occurs at the time of Yom Kippur.

Celebrating Success

We not only read the Book of Esther; we retell the story in a spirit of celebration. Listeners interrupt the reading with noisemakers each time Haman's name is mentioned to fulfill the biblical injunction to "blot out the name of Amalek." We eat a festive meal in the afternoon of Purim. As we celebrate the success of the Jews, we can also appreciate and enjoy the success of our own efforts to overcome adversity and make changes in how we respond.

Connectedness with Others

The ritual of Purim occurs in community. We read the Book of Esther in the synagogue. We eat the Purim meal in community. It is customary to dress up in costumes, masquerading as one of the protagonists in the story or as a modern-day counterpart. We give charity to the poor and send portions of food to friends in the same spirit that the Jews of Persia celebrated their victory. In these ways, Purim allows us to enjoy the varied connections with others.

Transformation of Evil

The transformation of evil and negativity that occurs on Purim is not simply an intellectual exercise. The ritual helps us experience this theme directly. Haman's triangular hat provides the geometry for special Purim pastry. The mention of his name becomes the occasion for our celebration. According to Rava, one of the rabbis of the Talmudic era, the obligation is to drink so much wine on Purim that we become confused as to whether we are cursing Haman or blessing Mordecai. We can do so because Haman is no longer a negative force. We view his plot as a vehicle through which God's plan ultimately unfolds. We use Haman's energy to fuel our lives.

In wearing masks and costumes, we have the opportunity to play with different identities. We can become Mordecai, Haman, Esther, the king, or any of their modern-day counterparts. Initially, we rigidly and unconsciously enacted dysfunctional ways of being that exacerbated our suffering. Now, these roles are simply masks and costumes that we can consciously wear or remove, a source of fun rather than a cause of pain. The experience of Essence in the material world is also enacted

Even our spiritual identities can become rigid, dysfunctional identities. For this reason, it is also customary to parody sacred literature. In Hasidic communities, even the spiritual leaders are included: a *Purim Rebbe* takes over to lead the festivities, functioning as jester and satirist.

The *Shabbat* before Purim is known as *Shabbat Zachor*, the "Sabbath of Remembrance." We recall Amalek, Haman's ancestor, who attacked the Israelites as they wandered in the desert. Amalek viciously pursued the elderly and the sick who traveled at the rear of the tribe. In the battle, the Israelites won as long as Moses held up his arms. When Moses tired and lowered his arms, the Amalekites began to win. Eventually, Moses allowed Aaron and Chur to help support his arms. After the battle, God asks the Israelites to remember the lesson of this battle:

> *Remember what Amalek did to you as you came out of Egypt. He met you on the way and attacked you from the rear, all those who were weak, at a time when you were faint and weary, and he did not fear God. Therefore, it shall be when the Lord your God has given you rest from all your enemies in the land which the Lord your God gives you for an inheritance, you shall blot out the remembrance of Amalek from under heaven; you shall not forget.*
>
> [Deuteronomy 25:17–19]

The descendants of Amalek continue to attack us from generation to generation. Amalek sometimes manifests in the form of external adversity and oppression; sometimes he appears as an inner attacker when we are self-abusive. In identifying the enemies and challenging them, we fulfill the commandment of remembering to fight that worthy battle.

PSYCHOLOGICAL THEMES ASSOCIATED WITH PURIM

The themes associated with Purim are illustrated by the experience of the Isaacs family. I worked with them, together with a colleague, for more than three years. There were six children in a blended family, ranging in age from 7 to 18, four from the husband's first marriage and two from the wife's first marriage. When we first began to meet, all of the children were in major crises. One was suicidal, another anorexic, a third was not performing in school, two others hated one another, and one struggled with a drug problem. The father was consumed with work as an attorney and was often absent from home even on evenings and weekends. The mother struggled to hold everything together while coping with one crisis after another. The noncustodial father was very critical and angry. He had moved away from the community. The noncustodial mother suffered from chronic depression and was dysfunctional as a parent.

We all worked effectively and diligently to make changes. The mother learned to be assertive as well as nurturing. Dad committed himself to taking an active role with parenting. Together they tackled the difficult problems. When we found ourselves, at one session, with apparently nothing to discuss, I suspected that the time was approaching to end the therapy. We sat staring at one another, sitting in an awkward silence. We had confronted many problems together, but we never had a problem with silence. There was always too much to talk about. I wondered if there was some awful crisis, a secret that everyone feared discussing, but there was no crisis; we simply did not seem to have anything to say to one another.

Something, however, seemed missing; the silence felt uncomfortable. While this family knew how to be together in pain and to struggle through crisis, they did not know how to celebrate with one another. How would they have contact if they had no problems? We were almost ready to end our work together, but there was one more step. We needed to fill the vacuum that had been created by our success. We discussed what the family might do with the time and energy that was freed up since they no longer needed to focus on pain. They talked about planning a vacation together, a river-rafting vacation, to celebrate their success. They talked about what they might do on evenings and weekends.

Most of the family was animated, but Gary, the father, had withdrawn. I was reminded of how he often had sat silent in our very first sessions, failing to interact at all. I thought about challenging him. However, before I could do so, I noticed that the 7-year-old, sitting across from his father, had slumped in his chair, pulling on his ear, obviously imitating his father. The other children noticed and began to giggle. Eventually, Gary looked up from his reverie to see everyone laughing. He creased his brow in a moment of anger as he realized what was happening, but then the crease dissolved, his face relaxed, and he joined the laughter.

At the early stages of our work together, Gary's response would have been very different. He would have remained stuck in his anger, shaming the children, lecturing them on respect. Then he would have withdrawn again, leaving his wife to pick up the pieces. I could see the impulse of the old pattern still remained—in the momentary crease of his brow. Humor replaced anger as a vehicle of communication. Gary was able to receive his son's challenge and change. He was able to shift gears. The family no longer needed my help. The old patterns were present but no longer tormented and ruled the family as once they did.

When we ended our work together, the family decided to celebrate the completion of the therapy with a formal dinner party. We arranged for a caterer to prepare a gourmet meal. We were able to use a meeting room at Gary's office for our celebration. Everyone contributed to the party in some way. We marked our ending with celebration of our success, an unusual and appropriate ending for our work.

The therapeutic tasks illustrated by the Isaacs family clarifies the process that occurs at the time of Purim as a completion of the developmental cycle of the year. When we enter therapy, we tend to be dependent and helpless; we are unable to cope with a problem or symptom. The therapist provides support, guidance, and encouragement for the client to discover and transform dysfunctional coping habits. In ending therapy, the person is once more able to cope.

The therapeutic process involves more than simply the ability to cope; at its best, we seek to realize our fullest potential. In the language of Abraham Maslow (1974), the goal is self-actualization. Maslow identified several stages of autonomy. The first stage is the ability to satisfy needs for material and economic survival in the complex web of twentieth-century life. After these needs are achieved, we can identify social needs for connection, intimacy, and affection. Then we can work to satisfy needs for self-actualization, clarifying a unique identity, purpose, and task for our life.

As children, we are dependent and unable to function economically. We cannot provide food, clothing, and shelter for ourselves. We require the assistance of adults. In achieving autonomy in relationship to survival, we are able to function independently as economic beings, to work and receive enough reward to be able to support ourselves in terms of basics. When survival needs are unmet, social satisfaction is irrelevant. However, once survival needs are met, we begin to focus on social needs. Do we like others? Do they like us? Is there a sense of mutuality and connectedness? If survival needs and social needs are met, the focus changes; we can then think about needs for self-actualization. What is the meaning of work? Is it intrinsically rewarding in terms of basic values such as the need for expressiveness, to make a contribution, to create? The task is to manifest our Essence in daily life.

This notion of self-actualization parallels Jung's description of the Ego-Self Axis. At this time of year, we have fully integrated the new Ego structure based on the new experience of Essence. In Assagioli's model, we have succeeded in reorganizing the personality, subsuming the old parts under the authority of the Higher Self. Our responses in the world are based on a clarified sense of purpose and a deepened understanding of ourselves and our environment. This stage of the therapeutic process is characterized by the experience of satisfaction, the transformation of negativity, and the experience of interdependence.

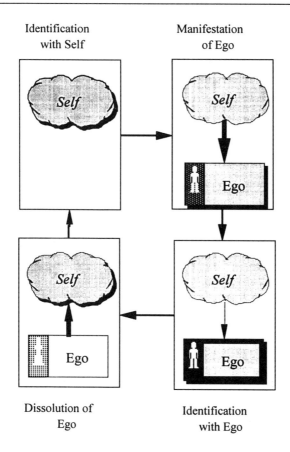

Identification
with Self

Manifestation
of Ego

Dissolution of
Ego

Identification
with Ego

Experiencing Satisfaction

The experience of satisfaction and completion is vital to the process of therapy. Our hunger motivates us to prepare food, eat, and digest it. As we do, the gnawing emptiness associated with hunger disappears, replaced with the fullness that registers as satisfaction. If we fail to recognize when we are full, if we fail to experience our satisfaction, we may continue to eat when we are not really hungry. If we fail to recognize our success, we may mistakenly act as if nothing has changed. One client, after losing fifty pounds, began to think about taking a dance class. Week after week, she returned to the therapy having failed to register for the class. As we discussed her difficulty, she realized that she still thought of herself as overweight and unable to move. Even when she looked in a mirror, she continued to see herself as carrying extra pounds. She needed to experience her success so she could move on to her next task.

Transformation of Negativity

In Jung's perspective, each of us has a "shadow," undeveloped, disowned parts of ourselves. In therapy, we begin to acknowledge and accept these parts that have previously been disowned—our fear, sadness, vulnerability, anger, and other 'negative' feelings. In respecting and acknowledging those parts, we gain control, we honor their positive essence, and we harness the energy to serve the Self. In this sense, even death does not imply loss, failure, or catastrophe. We ultimately triumph when we carry on the work of Esther and Mordecai by taking the risk to respond to the difficulties of life informed by our sense of the true Self.

After a successful struggle, we can accept the whole of ourselves. The rigidity that we viewed as an impediment no longer seems so difficult. It becomes a mask, something we can use to add to our sense of play. It no longer threatens or controls us. It is a mask that can be removed when it is unnecessary. The core of Spirit within can always shine through. Shneur Zalman expressed this understanding in comparing a person to a diamond. A diamond's beauty results from tiny imperfections within the crystal that reflect the light in each of the gem's facets. In the same way, the imperfections within each of us also become the source of our beauty as they are reflected through the crystal of our souls.

A similar perspective is described by Milton Erickson (1958) in his model of utilization. In this view, negative life events are not our fault, nor is it helpful to dissociate from them. Instead, we work to utilize what happens to us to strengthen our lives. Erickson developed this perspective as a result of his own struggles with polio, which nearly killed him and left him paralyzed. His great skill as a hypnotherapist began as a result of his particular condition. For a period of time, he was totally paralyzed, able only to exercise his senses. In this state, he had opportunity to develop great perceptive skills in picking up visual and auditory stimuli. He also gained awareness of physiological processes and learned to use a variety of techniques to manage pain and regain motor functioning. All of these discoveries provided the foundation for his skill as a hypnotherapist. Erickson did not make himself have polio, nor was polio a gift. Erickson was eminently successful in making lemonade from the lemons of life.

Victor Frankl (1975), a psychiatrist who survived the Holocaust, developed a similar perspective. While Frankl was imprisoned in a concentration camp, he decided to study human behavior under oppression, to explore how people responded to adversity. He discovered that people who coped successfully with oppression did so by finding a personal meaning for the experience that allowed them to live with hope. Based on his discoveries, Frankl developed a model for psychotherapy known as logotherapy, in which clients are helped to find a positive meaning and positive responses to the adversity in their lives.

When we succeed in this effort, we do not simply accept the difficulty, we find a way to utilize the adversity as a way to nourish and strengthen us. We make it a positive force in our lives. For example, Etty Hillesum, a woman in her twenties who perished in the Holocaust, describes, in her diaries, her struggles to overcome the impact of the Nazi threat. Etty lived in Amsterdam during the war. She describes how she gradually became aware of the Nazis' oppression. Initially depressed and scared, she gradually finds courage. She eventually gives up an opportunity to escape, deciding to go to the camps to care for children. Although she is killed, she finds meaning in her determination to live from love and compassion rather than to be destroyed spiritually:

> I am reminded daily of the fact that a human being has a body too. I had thought that my spirit and heart alone would be able to sustain me through everything. But now my body has spoken up for itself and called a halt. I now realise [sic], God, how much You have given me. So much that was beautiful and so much that was hard to bear. Yet whenever I showed myself ready to bear it, the hard was directly transformed into the beautiful. And

the beautiful was sometimes much harder to bear, so overpow-
ering did it seem. To think that one small human heart can expe-
rience so much, oh God, so much suffering and so much love. I
am grateful to You, God, for having chosen my heart, in these
times, to experience all the things it has experienced.[1]

At the age of twenty, Marta had been hit by a car while riding a
bicycle. Marta lay in a coma for more than a month before she
regained consciousness. Even as she recovered, she was virtually
unable to move and barely able to speak. She was, however, painfully aware of her predicament. Her father, who had been a workaholic
businessman, completely shifted his priorities so as to be available for
her care. Marta felt extremely guilty for all the trouble she had
caused her family. In a session with her father, she cried as she told
him how terrible she felt to be so dependent. Her father responded
by describing to her how much his life had changed in positive ways
as a result of her illness. His marriage had been on the verge of disaster, and he had been unhappy in his work life. Although he was
tremendously saddened by her tragedy, he felt grateful because the
crisis has served as a catalyst for positive changes in his life.

On the Purim when I first drafted this chapter, my wife suffered
an ectopic pregnancy. Her blood pressure dropped as a result of
internal bleeding. The day before Purim, we found ourselves in the
emergency room. By the afternoon, she was stabilized but weak. We
had lost the baby whom we had hoped to welcome into our family.
It was odd to sit in the synagogue that night and hear the Megillah.
Had this happened at Pesach or Tisha B'Av, perhaps I would have
focused more on my loss or helplessness. But, it was Purim, and I
found myself not grieving but relieved and at peace. I was oddly
focused on the positives. My wife had not died; she would be able to
get pregnant again; I was surrounded by a community of friends
who generously offered support and help. My 4-year-old stepson
came to the hospital in a costume hastily made by his grandmother,
as Max the Doctor. The spirit of Purim helped us find humor when
we were faced with loss.

Interdependence and Cocreation

Dreams are created out of reality, and reality is shaped by dreams.

© Ashleigh Brilliant

In the same way as the Jews of Persia worked together to overcome Haman's threat, we also need to involve others to help us. Our connection with others at this stage is not the passive, uninformed dependency of the child who lacks understanding and who is powerless. At this stage, we are active and empowered. If we do lack understanding or power, we know how to make use of help from others. We stay in charge of the process, not surrendering our ability to make choices about how to proceed. For example, when Mordecai challenges Esther to see the king, she does not simply comply nor does she refuse. She accepts the challenge, but first asks for help. Through the dialogue with Mordecai, they collaboratively develop a plan.

At this stage, we also experience a capacity for being in relationship in many different ways—able to give and receive, tease and be teased, follow and lead, win and lose. This capacity reflects an inner comfort with the full range of feeling within ourselves as well as the wisdom to know how and when to express those feelings appropriately.

PERSONAL APPLICATION OF THEMES FROM PURIM

A man doesn't have time
to have time for everything;
He doesn't have seasons enough to have
a season for every purpose.
Ecclesiastes was wrong about that.

A man needs to love and to hate at the same moment,
to laugh and cry with the same eyes,
with the same hands
to cast away stones and to gather them,
to make love in war and war in love.

And to hate and forgive and remember and forget,
to set in order and confuse, to eat and to digest
what history takes years and years to do.

A man doesn't have time.
When he loses he seeks,
when he finds he forgets,
when he forgets he loves,
when he loves he begins to forget.

And his soul is experienced,
his soul is very professional.
Only his body remains forever an amateur.
It tries and it misses,
gets muddled, doesn't learn a thing,
drunk and blind in its pleasures
and in its pains.

He will die as figs die in autumn
shriveled and full of himself and sweet,
the leaves growing dry on the ground,
the bare branches already pointing to the place
where there's time for everything.

Yehudah Amichai[2]

At the time of Pesach, we began a journey of transformation. We were pulled out of a womb that constricted instead of nourishing us. Through the course of the year, we worked to cope with the new reality, to gain insight about how to function, to realize the discrepancies between ideals and reality, to turn inward and make the commitment to change patterns of coping that no longer served us. Now, at the time of Purim, we are able to integrate the new identity. We not only know what to do, we are able to do it, and we can do so easily and fully. Instead of being rigidly identified with one way of being, thinking, feeling, and acting, we are capable of a full range of responses, so that we have the choice, moment to moment, to meet the world in ways that most effectively help create a dwelling place on earth for Spirit. At this stage, we recognize in ourselves the qualities of Esther and Mordecai: no longer dependent, able to find support within ourselves and from one another.

THE MESSIANIC VISION

- What are the masks of the new and old identity that you can freely wear and remove?

- What do you appreciate about your old way of being? Your old self?

13

THE CIRCLE BECOMES A SPIRAL

The serious problems in life, however, are never fully solved. If ever they should appear to be so, it is a sure sign that something has been lost. The meaning and purpose of a problem seems to lie not in its solution, but in our working at it incessantly.

Carl Jung

We have come full circle. A year later, we find ourselves at the end of our journey. We have given birth to a new aspect of Self and nurtured this new identity through all the stages of development and maturation. A year ago, at the time of Pesach, we were propelled out of slavery, pushed into a new universe, one in which old patterns of coping no longer served us. Dependent upon external support and struggling to understand our new universe, we wandered in the desert during the time of the counting of the *omer*. On Shavuot, we experienced Revelation, a flash of intuitive realization clarifying where we were and what we must do. We grieved our inability to manifest that vision at the time of Tisha B'Av. Then, during the Days of Awe, we worked to heighten awareness of our dysfunctional responses and to commit to developing new choices for response. Through the winter months we worked to integrate that new way of being, marked by Chanukah and Tu B'Shevat. Finally, on Purim, we celebrated the completion of that process.

Although we have completed our circle, we have not completed our journey. Another Pesach approaches just four weeks after Purim. The process of development does not stop. Each year, a new aspect of self develops in response to continuing changes in ourselves and in the world around us. Each step prepares us for the next. Each year has a unique energy and focus.

Each year, as we experience the Holy-Days, we find ourselves at a different point in the journey. Another year has passed. We stand at a different point in the life cycle. We cope with new changes in our lives—birth, sickness, and death; relationships beginning, evolving, and ending; problems and opportunities in our work. We face new issues and concerns. We struggle with new crises. We build on past achievements. We look toward the future.

Each year, the circle returns us, again and again, to the same Holy-Days, the same rituals, the same stories, the same images. However, we are not the same. We see with different eyes and hear with different ears. We may focus on a different element of the story, a different symbol, or even a different understanding of the same event. One year, at Pesach, we might focus on the importance of taking the first step as Nachshon did when he entered the sea; another year, we might make connection with the quality of powerlessness in which we can only cry out for help; the year after, we might identify with the experience of resistance by not wanting to leave the place of slavery. We might clarify our path even if we find ourselves resisting the image of the Holy-Day by realizing that we do not think of ourselves as enslaved; the contrast between the archetypal story and our personal experience may help us realize how we feel ourselves empowered and free.

The crises of life are difficult, overwhelming, and unending. The rigid habits are persistent and pervasive. It is not easy to change. Sometimes we think we have let go of an old way but discover instead that we have regressed and not even been aware of it.

It takes work to sustain the dialogue, to encounter the tradition. We have to invest time and energy in finding personal meaning in the ritual, stories, and images. We have to learn from our ancestors from previous generations who have left us their writings and their oral traditions. Sometimes their communication is difficult to understand and requires translation from a foreign language. We have to make sense of images and terminology of a culture that is also foreign to us. We have to find truths that are sometimes contaminated by misunderstanding, imperfection, or prejudice, both personal and cultural.

We not only have to listen to the voices from our past, but we also have to listen to ourselves, to the truth of the light within ourselves that is also a manifestation of God's Presence. We have to clarify when our truth is contaminated by our own imperfections, biases, and misunderstandings. We have to add our own revelation to the revelation of the past.

In this process, we have to strike a balance so that we remain open to the wisdom of the past while respecting our own personal understanding. As Martin Buber suggests, we need to be in dialogue:

> One must, however, take care not to understand this conversation with God . . . as something happening solely alongside or above the everyday. God's speech penetrates what happens in the life of each one of us, and all that happens in the world around us, biographical and historical, and makes it for you and me into instruction, message, demand. Happening upon happening, situation upon situation, are enabled and empowered by the personal speech of God to demand of the human person that he take his stand and make his decision. Often enough we think there is nothing to hear, but long before we have ourselves put wax in our ears.

> The existence of mutuality between God and man cannot be proved, just as God's existence cannot be proved. Yet he who dares to speak of it, bears witness, and calls to witness him to whom he speaks—whether that witness is now or in the future.[1]

Through the course of each year, a new aspect of self is born, develops, and matures. Each year builds on the past so as to continue the course of development through adult life. The circle of the year becomes a spiral. The chambered nautilus, a sea animal with a partitioned, spiral shell, offers a graphic, natural symbol of the spiral in time. When first hatched, the tiny creature fills its shell. When the soft body and shell covering both grow a size larger, it seals off a small empty chamber and lives only in the forward part of the shell, in front of the pearly partition. From that empty chamber, it builds a delicate tube called the siphuncle, connecting it with the front-occupied chamber. Each time the chambered nautilus grows another size larger, it seals off another empty chamber, extends the siphuncle tube, and moves another space forward in the enlarging shell. This process is repeated over and over as growth continues. The spiral of the shell follows a logarithmic curve; it is the simplest of all known curves. The diameter of the coil grows in exact proportion to its length; each new coil is exactly three times that of the coil preceding it.

The shell of the nautilus offers a graphic representation of our own development in the spiral through time. The nautilus outgrows its shell, builds a new chamber, and migrates into its new home. The shell provides a visible testimony to the changes through the course of life, a delicate image in which forms of the past are not discarded, imperfect residues but a source of beauty and balance. We resemble that nautilus. We also migrate, year after year. As we build new ways to live, we leave behind us old, constricting ways of being. We also leave behind us a spiral of past identities that give us unique depth, balance, and beauty. This notion is expressed in Oliver Wendell Holmes's poem, "The Chambered Nautilus":

> *This is the ship of pearl, which, poets feign,*
> *Sails the unshadowed main,*
> *The venturous bark that flings*
> *On the sweet summer wind its purpled wings*
> *In gulfs enchanted, where the Siren sings,*
> *And the coral reefs lie bare,*
> *Where the cold sea-maids rise to sun their streaming hair.*
>
> *Its web of living gauze no more unfurl;*
> *Wrecked is this ship of pearl*
> *And every chambered cell,*
> *Where its dim dreaming life was wont to dwell,*
> *As the frail tenant shaped his growing shell,*
> *Before thee lies revealed,*
> *Its irised ceiling rent, its sunless crypt unsealed.*

Year after year beheld the silent toil
That spread his lustrous coil;
Still, as the spiral grew,
He left the past year's dwelling for the new,
Stole with soft step its shining archway through,
Built up its idle door,
Stretched in his last-found home, and knew the old no more.

Thanks for the heavenly message brought by thee,
Child of the wandering sea,
Cast from her lap, forlorn!
From thy dead lips a clearer note is born
Than ever Triton blew from wreathed horn!
While on my ear it rings,
Through the deep caves of thought I hear a voice that sings.

Build thee more stately mansions, O my soul,
Leave thy low-vaulted past!
Let each new temple, nobler than the last,
Shut thee from heaven with a dome more vast,
Till thou at length are free,
Leaving thine outgrown shell by life's unresting sea.

That spiral extends beyond our personal life journey, widening to include the journeys of those around us. Each generation also has a particular task and focus. That task and purpose may only be understood years later. When Etty Hillesum wrote her diary, it was a private document. Her diary was discovered fifty years after her death. Etty never knew the impact her diaries would have two generations later. The spiral extends beyond the time frame of our own lives and widens to include the evolution of consciousness from generation to generation.

In 1972, I made a journey to India. In a suburb of Agra, home of the Taj Mahal, I visited a construction site for a shrine honoring a religious leader. The shrine was being built of marble. The plan was to decorate the building with representations of all the native flowers known in India. The shrine was being built only with hand tools. I saw workmen sawing large slabs of marble; two men each held one end of a six-foot-long saw. A young boy poured water into the crevice to cool the metal as they worked. In one day, they sawed through an inch. One man worked for a month to carve a flower. Construction had begun forty-five years ago. Plans called for completion of the shrine in another ninety years. No one working on the building on that day would be alive to see its completion.

In our culture, we have become impatient for completion and change. In an era of sound bites and immediate gratification, it is especially important to view our lives in the context of generations past and future; we need to understand our task as part of an effort that began years before we were born and extends years into the future after we are no longer alive.

Scientific theories regarding the creation of the universe hypothesize that there was an original moment of creation, a "big bang" that was the source of our universe. Studies by astrophysicists indicate that, in the beginning, all matter was once unified and that the universe is ever expanding from its original state. Two forces govern this expansion: on the one hand, there is a centrifugal force that creates expansion as objects move away from one another; on the other hand, there is a gravitational force that pulls matter back together. Interestingly, the balance of these forces is quite close. Scientists are not able to predict whether the universe will continue expanding indefinitely as centrifugal forces overcome gravity's pull or whether gravitational force will, in the end, pull the universe back to Oneness. Perhaps the balance is such that what we do with our lives may help determine whether the universe will return to Unity or continue to expand infinitely into separateness.

Understanding the larger purpose gives significance and meaning to the present moment in our lives, to the crises we face and the suffering we experience. Our determination and hard work make light in the darkness for ourselves and those around us. That light shines into the future, illuminating the path of those who will follow. In this sense, it is not only we who grow and develop. God also evolves as the depth of our understanding and comprehension matures.

יהיו לרצון אמרי פי והגיון לבי לפניך ה' צורי וגואלי'

OTHER PUBLISHED WORK BY
JOEL ZIFF

Ziff, J (1980). "Establishing guidelines for differential processing of structured experiences based on self-knowledge stage theory." *Group & Organization Studies* 5:234–246.

Ziff, J. (1994). "Faces of Light." In *The Psychology of Health, Immunity, and Disease*, vol. 2, pp. 473–498. Mansfield, CT: National Institute for the Clinical Application of Behavioral Medicine.

Ziff, J. (1989–1990). "I & Thou: The Client-practitioner Relationship in Somatic Education." *Somatics* Autumn/Winter: 28–34.

Ziff, J. (1996). "Partzufim—Faces of Light: On the Evolving Relationship with God." In *The Fifty-Eighth Century*, p. 33. Northvale, NJ: Jason Aronson.

Ziff, J. (1988). "Playing The Blues: case study of a remorseful patient." *The Psychotherapy Patient* 5:291–299.

Ziff, J. (1983). "Shabbat As Therapy." *Journal of Psychology and Judaism* 7:118–132.

Ziff, J., and Ruppert, E. "The Mind, Body, & Soul of Violence." *Transactional Analysis Journal* 24:161–177.

PSYCHOTHERAPY REFERENCES

Alexander, F. M. (1985). *Constructive Conscious Control of the Individual.* Downey, CA: Centerline.

———— (1971). *The Resurrection of the Body.* New York: Dell.

———— (1984). *The Use of the Self.* Downey, CA: Centerline.

Alon, R. (1990). *Mindful Spontaneity.* Dorset, England: Prism Press.

Assagioli, R. (1976). *Psychosynthesis.* New York: Penguin.

Benjamin, B. (1984). *Listen to Your Pain.* New York: Penguin Books.

Berne E. (1985). *Games People Play.* New York: Ballantine.

Borysenko, J. (1988). *Minding the Body, Mending the Mind.* New York: Bantam.

Bradshaw, J. (1990). *Homecoming.* New York: Bantam.

Brennan, B. (1993). *Light Emerging.* New York: Bantam.

Brooks, C. (1982). *Sensory Awareness.* Santa Barbara, CA: Ross Erikson.

Buzan, T. (1974). *Use Both Sides of Your Brain.* New York: Dutton.

Campbell, J., with Moyers, Bill (1988). *The Power of Myth.* New York: Doubleday.

Canter, R. (1980). *And a Time to Live.* New York: HarperCollins.

Cheek, D. (1994). *Hypnosis.* Boston: Allyn & Bacon.

Combs, G., and Freedman, J. (1990). *Symbol, Story and Ceremony.* New York: Norton.

Cousins, N. (1983). *Anatomy of an Illness.* New York: Bantam.

Davis, M., and Eshelman, E. (1982). *The Relaxation and Stress Reduction Workbook.* Oakland, CA: New Harbinger.

Dossey, L. (1989). *Recovering the Soul.* New York: Bantam.

Dychtwald, K. (1977). *Body-Mind.* New York: Jove.

Edinger, E. (1986). *The Bible and the Psyche.* Toronto: Inner City.

———— (1972). *Ego and Archetype.* New York: Penguin.

———— (1986). *Encounter with the Self.* Toronto: Inner City.

Erickson, M. (1958). Hypnosis. *Encyclopedia Britanica.* pp. 995–997.

Feldenkrais, M. (1972). *Awareness through Movement.* New York: Harper & Row.

———— (1977). *The Case of Nora.* New York: Harper & Row.

———— (1981). *The Elusive Obvious.* Cupertino, CA: Meta.

———— (1984). *The Master Moves.* Cupertino, CA: Meta.

———— (1985). *The Potent Self.* San Francisco: Harper & Row.

Ferrucci, P. (1982). *What We May Be.* Los Angeles: Tarcher.

Fisher, R., and Ury, W. (1981). *Getting to Yes.* New York: Penguin.

Frankl, V. (1975). *The Unconscious God.* New York: Simon & Schuster.

Freud, S. (1950). The dynamics of the transference. In *Collected Papers,* vol. 2, pp. 312–333. London: Hogarth.

Fromm, E. (1986). *You Shall Be as Gods.* Greenwich, CT: Fawcett.

Gendlin, E. (1980). *Focusing.* New York: Bantam.

Gordon, D. (1978). *Therapeutic Metaphors.* Cupertino, CA: Meta.

Gorman, D. (1981). *The Body Moveable.* Guelph, Ontario: Ampersand.

Green, B. (1984). *The Holistic Body Therapy Textbook.* San Diego, CA: Body-Mind Enterprises.

Haley, J. (1984). *Ordeal Therapy.* San Francisco: Jossey-Bass.

———— (1973). *Uncommon Therapy.* New York: Norton.

Hammond, D. C. (1990). *Handbook of Hypnotic Suggestions and Metaphors.* New York: Norton.

Hampden-Turner, C. (1988). *Maps of the Mind.* New York: Macmillan.

Hanna, T. (1980). *The Body of Life.* New York: Knopf.

———— (1988). *Somatics.* Boston: Addison-Wesley.

Harris, T. (1973). *I'm OK—You're OK.* New York: Avon.

Hendricks, G., and Hendricks, K. (1994). *At the Speed of Light.* New York: Bantam.

Herman, J. L. (1992). *Trauma and Recovery.* New York: Harper-Collins.

Holtz, B. W. (1990). *Finding Our Way.* New York: Schocken.

Jaffe, D. (1986). *Healing From Within.* New York: Simon & Schuster.

Jevne, D. F., and Levitan, A. (1989). *No Time for Nonsense.* San Diego, CA: Lura Media.

Jones, F. P. (1976). *Body Awareness in Action.* New York: Schoken.

Juhan, D. (1987). *Job's Body.* South Barrytown, NY: Station Hill.

Kabat-Zinn, J. (1990). *Full Catastrophe Living.* New York: Dell.

———— (1994). *Wherever You Go There You Are.* New York: Hyperion.

Keene, S. (1990). *Fire in the Belly.* New York: Bantam.

Keleman, S. (1987). *Embodying Experience.* Berkeley, CA: Center Press.

———— (1985). *Emotional Anatomy.* Berkeley, CA: Center Press.

Kepner, J. (1987). *Body Process.* New York: Gestalt Institute of Cleveland.

Krieger, D. (1979). *The Therapeutic Touch.* Upper Saddle River, NJ: Prentice Hall.

Kurtz, R. (1984). *Hakomi Therapy.* Boulder, CO: Hakomi Institute.

Kurtz, R., and Prestera, H. (1976). *The Body Reveals.* New York: Harper & Row.

Lankton, S. and C. (1983). *The Answer Within.* New York: Brunner/ Mazel.

LeShan, L. (1989). *Cancer as a Turning Point.* New York: Dutton.

Locke, S., and Colligan, D. (1987). *The Healer Within.* New York: New American Library.

Lowen, A. (1972). *Depression and the Body.* Baltimore, MD: Penguin.

———— (1958). *The Language of the Body.* New York: Macmillan.

Malott, R., et al. (1973). *An Introduction to Behavior Modification.* Kalamazoo, MI: Behaviordelia.

Markova, D. (1991). *The Art of the Possible.* Emeryville, CA: Conari.

Marrone, R. (1990). *Body of Knowledge.* Albany: State University of New York Press.

Maslow, A. (1974). *Religions, Values, and Peak Experiences.* New York: Viking.

Masters, R., and Houston J. (1978). *Listening to the Body.* New York: Dell.

McKay, M., et al. (1988). *Messages.* Oakland, CA: New Harbinger.

Miller, A (1990). *The Untouched Key.* New York: Doubleday.

———— (1986). *Thou Shalt Not Be Aware.* New York: New American Library.

Miller, S., et al. (1986). *Life Span Plus.* New York: Macmillan.

Morris, D. (1977). *Man Watching.* New York: Harry Abrams.

Moustakas, C. (1961). *Loneliness.* Upper Saddle River, NJ: Prentice-Hall.

Murphy, M. (1982). *The Future of the Body.* Los Angeles: Tarcher.

Myers, I. B. (1980). *Introduction to Type.* Palo Alto, CA: Consulting Psychologists Press.

Nichols, M., and Zax, M. (1977). *Catharsis in Psychotherapy.* New York: Gardner.

O'Hanlon, W. and Hexum, A. (1990). *An Uncommon Casebook.* New York: Norton.

Okun, B. (1990). *Seeking Connections in Psychotherapy.* San Francisco: Jossey-Bass.

Olsen, A. (1993). *Body Stories.* Barrytown, NY: Station Hill Press.

Peck, M. S. (1977). *The Road Less Traveled,* New York: Touchstone.

Perls, F. (1973). *The Gestalt Approach.* Ben Lomond, CA: Science and Behavior Books.

Pesso, A. (1969). *Movement in Psychotherapy.* New York: New York University Press.

Polster, E. and M. (1974). *Gestalt Therapy Integrated.* New York: Vintage.

Rogers, C. (1972). *On Becoming a Person.* Boston: Houghton-Mifflin.

Rolf, I. P (1978). *Rolfing.* New York: Harper & Row.

Rossi, E. (1985). *Dreams and the Growth of Personality.* New York: Brunner/Mazel.

———— (1993). *The Psychobiology of Mind-Body Healing.* New York: Norton.

———— (1991). *The Twenty Minute Break.* Los Angeles: Tarcher.

Rossi, E. and Cheek, D. (1988). *Mind-Body Therapy.* New York: Norton.

Rywernt, Y. (1983). *The Feldenkrais Method: Teaching By Handling.* San Francisco: Harper & Row.

Saltzman, N., and Norcross, J., eds. (1990). *Therapy Wars.* San Francisco: Jossey-Bass.

Sarno, J. (1986). *Mind over Back Pain.* New York: Berkeley Books.

Satir, V. (1967). *Conjoint Family Therapy.* Palo Alto, CA: Science & Behavior Books.

Seligman, M. (1990). *Learned Optimism.* New York: Random House.

Siegel, B. (1988). *Love, Medicine & Miracles.* New York: Harper & Row.

——— (1990). *Peace, Love, & Healing.* New York: Harper Collins.

Simonton, S. M. (1984). *The Healing Family.* New York: Bantam.

Simonton, S. M., and Simonton, O. C. (1984). *Getting Well Again,* New York: Bantam.

Skynner, R., and Cleese, J. (1984). *Families and How to Survive Them.* New York: Oxford University Press.

Smith, E. W .L. (1985). *The Body in Psychotherapy.* Jefferson, NC: McFarland.

Sobel, D., and Ornstein, R. (1990). *Healthy Pleasures.* Boston: Addison-Wesley.

Steere, D. (1982). *Bodily Expressions in Psychotherapy.* New York: Brunner/Mazel.

Steiner, C. (1982). *Scripts People Live.* New York: Bantam.

Stewart, I., and Joines, V. (1987). *TA Today.* Chapel Hill, NC: Lifespace.

Tannen, D. (1990). *You Just Don't Understand.* New York: Ballantine.

Tate, D. (1989). *Health, Hope, & Healing.* New York: Evans.

Thie, J. (1979). *Touch for Health.* Marina Del Ray, CA: DeVorss.

Tohei, K. (1978). *Book of Ki.* New York: Japan Publications.

——— (1983). *Ki in Daily Life.* New York: Harper & Row.

Ury, W. (1991). *Getting Past No.* New York: Bantam.

Watzlawick, P., et al. (1974). *Change.* New York: Norton.

Weil, A. (1987). *Health and Healing.* Boston: Houghton Mifflin.

Weltner, J. (1988). Different strokes. *Family Therapy Networker.* May–June: pp. 53–57.

——— (1985). Matchmaking: Choosing the Appropriate Therapy for Families at Various Levels of Pathology. *Family Therapy Networker.* Oct.: pp. 23–37.

White, M., and Epston, D. (1990). *Narrative Means to Therapeutic Ends.* New York: Norton.

Whitfield, C. (1987). *Healing the Child Within.* Deerfield Beach, FL: Health Communications.

Whittaker, C., and Napier, A. (1978). *The Family Crucible.* New York: Bantam.

Wilber, K. (1984). *A Sociable God.* Boulder, CO: Shambhala.

Wilber, K. and T. (1988). Do we make ourselves sick? *New Age Journal* Sept.–Oct., pp. 50–54, 88–91.

Williams, W. (1990). *The Power Within.* New York: Harper & Row.

Wulff, D. (1990). *Psychology of Religion.* New York: Wiley.

Yalom, I. (1985). *Theory and Practice of Group Psychotherapy.* New York: Basic Books.

——— (1992). *When Nietzsche Wept.* New York: Basic Books.

Zemach-Bersin, D., et al. (1990). *Relaxercise.* New York: HarperCollins.

Zinker, J. (1994). *In Search of Good Form.* San Francisco: Jossey-Bass.

Zukav, G. (1989). *The Seat of the Soul.* New York: Simon & Schuster.

JEWISH REFERENCES

Agnon, S.Y. (1975). *Days of Awe.* New York: Schocken.

Bakan, D. (1975). *Sigmund Freud and the Jewish Mystical Tradition.* Boston: Beacon Press.

Bedford, S. (1983). *Prayer Power.* Chico, CA: A & S.

Berg, P. (1983). *The Kabbalah Connection.* Jerusalem: Research Centre of Kabbalah.

——— (1983). *Kabbalah for the Layman.* Jerusalem: Research Centre of Kabbalah.

Blumenthal, D. (1988). *God at the Center.* San Francisco: Harper & Row.

——— (1978). *Understanding Jewish Mysticism.* New York: Ktav.

——— (1982). *Understanding Jewish Mysticism. Vol. II.* New York: Ktav.

Breslov, Rabbi Nahman of. (1972). *Likuetei Maharan.* B'nei Brak, Israel: Yeshiva Breslov.

Buber, M. (1965). *Between Man and Man.* New York: Macmillan.

——— (1953). *Good and Evil.* New York: Scribner's.

——— (1958). *I and Thou.* New York: Scribner's.

——— (1982). *On the Bible.* New York: Schocken.

——— (1961). *Tales of the Hasidim: Early Masters.* New York: Schocken.

——— (1961). *Tales of the Hasidim: Later Masters.* New York: Schocken.

——— (1961). *Two Types of Faith.* New York: Harper & Row.

Bulka, R. (1979). *Mystics and Medics.* New York: Human Sciences Press.

Buxbaum, Y. (1990). *Jewish Spiritual Practices.* Northvale, NJ: Jason Aronson.

Fishbane, M. (1979). *Text and Texture.* New York: Schocken.

Foxbrunner, R. (1993). *Habad.* Northvale, NJ: Jason Aronson.

Frankel, E. (1993). *The Classic Tales.* Northvale, NJ: Jason Aronson.

Frankl, V. (1966). *Man's Search for Meaning.* New York: Washington Square Press.

Green, A. (1992). *Seek My Face, Speak My Name.* Northvale, NJ: Jason Aronson.

———— (1981). *Tormented Master.* New York: Schocken.

Green, A., and Holtz, B. (1977). *Your Word is Fire.* New York: Paulist.

Greenberg, I. (1988). *The Jewish Way.* New York: Summit.

Grishaver, J. (1993). *And You Shall Be a Blessing.* Northvale, NJ: Jason Aronson.

Halevi, Zev ben Shimon (1985). *Adam and the Kabbalistic Tree.* York Beach, ME: Samuel Weiser.

———— (1979). *Kabbalah.* London: Thames and Hudson.

———— (1987). *Kabbalah and Psychology.* York Beach, ME: Samuel Weiser.

———— (1984). *The Work of the Kabbalist.* York Beach, ME: Samuel Weiser.

Hareuveni, N. (1980). *Nature in Our Biblical Heritage.* Kiryat Ono, Israel: Neot Kedumim.

———— (1984). *Tree and Shrub in Our Biblical Heritage.* Kiryat Ono, Israel: Neot Kedumim.

Heifetz, H. (1978). *Zen and Hasidism.* Wheaton, IL: Theosophical Publishing House.

Hillesum, E. (1985). *An Interrupted Life.* New York: Washington Square.

Hoffman, E. (1985). *The Heavenly Ladder.* New York: Harper & Row.

Holtz, B. (1984). *Back to the Sources.* New York: Summit.

———— (1990). *Finding Our Way.* New York: Schocken.

Ishbitz, Rabbi Tzvi Elimelech of. *B'nai Yisaschar.*

Jacob, L. (1976). *Hasidic Thought.* New York: Behrman House.

———— (1977). *Jewish Mystical Testimonies.* New York: Schocken.

———— (1966). *Seeker of Unity.* New York: Basic Books.

Jung, C. (1938). *Psychology and Religion.* New Haven, CT: Yale University Press.

Kaplan, A. (1986). *A Call to the Infinite.* New York: Maznaim.

———— (1984). *The Chasidic Masters.* New York: Moznaim.

———— (1985). *Jewish Meditation.* New York: Schocken.

———— (1973). *Rabbi Nachman's Wisdom.* Jerusalem: Breslov Research Institute.

Kitov, E. (1978). *The Book of our Heritage.* Jerusalem: Feldheim.

Kramer, C. (1989). *Crossing the Narrow Bridge.* Jerusalem: Breslov Research Institute.

Kushner, L. (1975). *The Book of Letters.* New York: Harper & Row.

————— (1991). *God Was in this Place and I Did Not know.* Woodstock, VT: Jewish Lights.

————— (1977). *Honey from the Rock.* New York: Harper & Row.

————— (1981). *The River of Light.* Chappaqua, New York: Rossel.

L'Heureux, C. (1986). *Life Journey and the Old Testament.* New York: Paulist.

Langer, U. (1976). *Nine Gates to the Chassidic Mysteries.* New York: Behrman House.

Lyady, Shneur Zalman of. (1980a). *Likuetei Torah.* Brooklyn: Kehot

————— (1980b). *Siddur.* Brooklyn: Kehot.

————— (1975). *Torah Or.* Brooklyn: Kehot.

Midrash Rabbah (1966). Jerusalem.

Minkin, J. (1955). *The Romance of Hassidism.* New York: Thomas Yoseloff.

Polsky, H., and Wozner, Y. (1989). *Everyday Miracles: The Healing Wisdom of Hasidic Stories.* Northvale, NJ: Jason Aronson.

Rosenfeld, A. (1983). *Tisha B'Av Compendium.* New York: Judaica Press.

Sanford, J. (1981). *The Man Who Wrestled with God.* New York: Paulist.

Schachter-Shalomi, Z. (1983). *The First Step.* Toronto: Bantam.

————— (1993). *Paradigm Shift.* Northvale, NJ: Jason Aronson.

Schachter, Z. (1991). *Spiritual Intimacy.* Northvale, NJ: Jason Aronson.

————— (1975). *Fragments of a Future Scroll.* Germantown, PA: Leaves of Grass Press.

Schneerson, Rabbi Menachem. (1994). *Timeless Patterns in Time.* Brooklyn: Kehot.

Scholem, G. (1961). *Major Trends in Jewish Mysticism.* New York: Schocken.

Steinsaltz, A. (1984). *Biblical Images.* New York: Basic Books.

————— (1992). *In the Beginning.* Northvale, NJ: Jason Aronson.

————— (1995). *On Being Free.* Northvale, NJ: Jason Aronson.

———— (1988). *The Long Shorter Way.* Northvale, NJ: Jason Aronson.

———— (1988). *The Strife of the Spirit.* Northvale, NJ: Jason Aronson.

———— (1989). *The Sustaining Utterance.* Northvale, NJ: Jason Aronson.

———— (1993). *The Tales of Rabbi Nachman of Bratslav.* Northvale, NJ: Jason Aronson.

———— (1996). *Teshuvah.* Northvale, NJ: Jason Aronson.

———— (1980). *The Thirteen Petaled Rose.* New York: Basic Books.

Strassfeld, M. (1985). *The Jewish Holidays.* New York: Harper & Row.

Torah (1981). Trans. Aryeh Kaplan. New York: Maznaim.

Waskow, A. (1982). *Seasons of Our Joy.* New York: Bantam.

Wiener, S. H., and Omer-Man, J. (1993). *Worlds of Jewish Prayer.* Northvale, NJ: Jason Aronson.

Wiesel, E. (1981). *Somewhere a Master.* New York: Summit.

Zevin, Rabbi Shlomo (1956). *Sipurei Chasidim.* Jerusalem: Beit Hillel.

Zohar (1983). Ed. and trans. D. Matt. New York: Paulist Press.

NOTES

Preface

[1] Erving & Miriam Polster, *Gestalt Therapy Integrated* (New York, Vintage, 1974), pp. 57–58.

Chapter 1

[1] Yehuda Amichai, *Sheat Hachesed* (Tel Aviv: Shocken, 1982), pp. 50–51.

[2] Joseph Campbell with Bill Moyers, *The Power of Myth* (New York: Doubleday, 1988), p. 5.

[3] Zelda, *Shirai Zelda* (Tel Aviv: Kibbutz Hameuchad, 1985), p. 117.

Chapter 5

[1] Abraham Rosenfeld, *Tisha B'Av Compendium* (New York: Judaica Press, 1983), p. 363.

[2] Clark Moustakas, *Loneliness* (Upper Saddle River, NJ: Prentice Hall, 1961), pp. 5–8.

[3] Abraham Rosenfeld, *Tisha B'Av Compendium* (New York: Judaica Press, 1983), p. 211.

Chapter 9

[1] Eliyahu Kitov, *The Book of Our Heritage* (Jerusalem: Feldheim, 1978), p. 140.

[2] Eliyahu Kitov, *The Book of Our Heritage* (Jerusalem: Feldheim, 1978), p. 138.

[3] Eliyahu Kitov, *The Book of Our Heritage* (Jerusalem: Feldheim, 1978), p. 154.

Chapter 10

[1] Eliyahu Kitov, *The Book of Our Heritage* (Jerusalem: Feldheim, 1978), pp. 272–273.

[2] Eliyahu Kitov, *The Book of Our Heritage* (Jerusalem: Feldheim, 1978), pp. 272–273.

[3] Charles Whitfield, *Healing the Child Within* (Deerfield Beach, FL: Health Communications, 1987), p. 125.

Chapter 12

[1] Etty Hillesum, *An Interrupted Life* (New York: Washington Square, 1985), p. 207.

[2] Yehudah Amichai, *Sheat Hachesed* (Tel Aviv: Shocken, 1982), pp. 50–51.

Chapter 13

[1] Martin Buber, *I and Thou* (New York: Schribner's, 1958), pp. 136–137.

INDEX

Accountability
  clinical example, Rosh
    HaShanah, 187–190
  God-human relationship, Rosh
    HaShanah, 185–187
  psychological perspective,
    Rosh HaShanah,
    191–192
  Rosh HaShanah, 185–192
Action
  mystical union, Yom Kippur,
    225–227
  revelation, Shavuot, 112
Active principle *(eetkafya)*, Rosh
  HaShanah, 195–198
Adult developmental processes,
  habituation and dehabitua-
  tion, 8–12
Alexander, M. F., 216
Alexander technique, transforma-
  tion of evil into good, Yom
  Kippur, 216
Alter, Yehudah Aryeh Leib, xviii

Amichai, Yehudah, 24
Animus and *Anima,* archetypes
  and, 25
Archetypes
  Chanukah, 253–258
  Jewish tradition and, 26–28
  Jungian analysis and, 25
  Purim, 302
  ritual enactment of, Purim,
    307–309
Assagioli, R., 14, 15, 17, 118,
  156, 197, 215
At-one-ment. *See* Mystical union
Autonomy
  developmental factors, 43–53
  Sefirat Ha'Omer, 96–97

Barley
  day-by-day learning, Sefirat
    Ha'Omer, 94–95
  Shavuot, Sefirat Ha'Omer and,
    115

Beauty *(tiferet)*, Sefirat Ha'Omer,
    personal applications, 105
Behavioral modality
    holy-day celebrations, healing,
        37
    psychotherapy, healing, 31–32
    state-dependent learning,
        memory, and behavior
        (SDLMB), 18–19
Behavior therapy, Sukkot,
    245–246
Berne, E., 174, 191, 198
Birth, symbol of transformation,
    Pesach, 64–66
Brain
    left-brain learning, Sefirat
        Ha'Omer, 100–102
    right-brain learning, Shavuot,
        117–121
Brilliant, A., 12, 15, 18, 19, 21,
    45, 52, 71, 73, 76, 80, 97,
    100, 112, 129, 147, 170,
    175, 185, 187, 191, 255,
    256, 257, 297, 300, 316
Buber, M., 323

Campbell, J., 25
Candle, as symbol, Chanukah,
    258–266
Change, tools for, 24–28. *See also*
    Healing
Chanukah, 253–274
    as archetypal event, 253–258
    candle as symbol, 258–266
    descriptive summary of, 7
    developmental stages, 51
    overview of, 253
    personal applications, 273–274
    psychotherapy, 266–273

Chasidism, Jewish developmental
    model, 15–17
Childhood
    developmental factors, Sefirat
        Ha'Omer, 96–99
    developmental stages, 44–45
Chol, state-dependent learning,
    memory, and behavior
    (SDLMB), 21–24
Chuppah, revelation, Shavuot,
    113
Cocreation, Purim, 316 317
Cognitive modality
    developmental factors, Sefirat
        Ha'Omer, 98
    holy-day celebrations, healing,
        38–39
    psychotherapy, healing, 33–34
Commitment
    psychological perspective,
        Shavuot, 120–121
    revelation, Shavuot, 112–113
Compassion
    self-reflection and, Elul,
        164–166
    therapeutic process and, Elul,
        170–174
Compassionate self reflection
    forgiveness and, personal
        applications, Elul,
        179–180
    personal applications, Elul,
        174–176
Conflict
    intrapersonal, xx–xxi
    Judaism and, xviii–xx
Consciousness, 18–24
    redemption process, Pesach, 71

Consciousness *(continued)*
  state-dependent learning,
    memory, and behavior
    (SDLMB)
    described, 18–19
    Jewish theory of, 21–24
    psychotherapeutic implica-
      tions of, 19–21
    transformation of, revelation,
      Shavuot, 111–112
Consolation, grieving process,
  Tisha B'Av, 143–146
Constructive guilt, self abusive
  guilt versus, Tisha B'Av,
  147–159

Days of Awe, developmental
  stages, 50–51
Dehabituation. *See* Habituation
  and dehabituation
Dependency
  developmental factors, 43–53
  Sefirat Ha'Omer, 92–93,
    96–97
Developmental factors
  adult, 8–12
  Jewish developmental model,
    15–17
  psychological developmental
    model, 12–15
  Sefirat Ha'Omer, 96–99
  stages, 43–53
    childhood, 44–45
    God-human relationship,
      52–53
    Holy-Day cycle, 48–52
    psychotherapy, 45–48
DNA, body and, 13

Ego
  redemption process, Pesach,
    68–75
  self and, psychological devel-
    opmental model, 12–15
Elul, 163–180
  compassion, therapeutic
    process and, 170–174
  descriptive summary of, 6
  developmental stages, 51
  overview of, 163–164
  personal applications,
    174–181
    compassionate self-reflec-
      tion, 174–176
    forgiveness and compassion-
      ate self-reflection,
      179–180
    relationships, 175–179
  self–reflection
    compassion and, 164–166
    therapeutic process and,
      165–170
Emotional modality
  grieving process, Tisha B'Av,
    135–136
  holy-day celebrations, healing,
    38
  psychotherapy, healing, 32–33
Erickson, M., 18, 119
Essence
  Chanukah, 263
  manifestation and, Yom
    Kippur, 219–220
Evil. *See* Good and evil

Father, God as archetypal,
  Shavuot, Sefirat Ha'Omer
  and, 116

Feldenkrais, M., 246–247

Feldenkrais method, Sukkot, 246–247

Forgiveness
  compassionate self reflection and, personal applications, Elul, 179–180
  relationships, Elul, 175–179

Foundation (yesod), Sefirat Ha'Omer, personal applications, 105

Frankl, V., 314 315

Freud, S., 155

Frost, R., 226

Gestalt therapy, xviii, xx
  self-reflection, Elul, 168–169
  state-dependent consciousness, 21
  Sukkot, 247–248

Glasser, W., 156

Glory (hod), Sefirat Ha'Omer, personal applications, 105

God-human relationship
  accountability, Rosh HaShanah, 185–187
  archetypes and, 26–28
  Chanukah, 256, 260, 262–266
  developmental stages, 52–53
  father archetype, Shavuot, Sefirat Ha'Omer and, 116
  grieving process, Tisha B'Av, 137–138
  holidays and, 4
  Jewish developmental model, 15–17

mother archetype, developmental factors, Sefirat Ha'Omer, 99

mystical union, Yom Kippur, 221–227

Purim, 308–309

receptive principle (eethafcha), Rosh HaShanah, 198–201, 203–204

state-dependent learning, memory, and behavior (SDLMB), 21–24

Sukkot, 235–243

teshuvah, Rosh HaShanah, 192–194

Yom Kippur, 229

Goethe, 120

Golden Calf
  grieving process, Tisha B'Av, 131–132
  guilt, constructive versus self-abusive, Tisha B'Av, 150–151

Good and evil
  Purim, 308–309
  Yom Kippur, 207–216
    clinical example, 208–214

Grieving process
  consolation, Tisha B'Av, 143–146
  guilt, constructive versus self-abusive, Tisha B'Av, 147–159
  healing response, Tisha B'Av, 140–143
  psychological perspective, Tisha B'Av, 138–140
  ritual, Tisha B'Av, 129–138

Guilt, constructive versus self-
    abusive, Tisha B'Av,
    147–159

Habituation and dehabituation,
    8–17
  adult developmental processes,
    8–12
  Jewish developmental model,
    15–17
  psychological developmental
    model, 12–15
Harris, T., 191
Healing, 28–43. See also Change;
    Learning
  grieving process, Tisha B'Av,
    140–143
  holy-day celebrations, 35–43
    behavioral, 37
    cognitive, 38–39
    emotional, 38
    focus of holiday, 39–43
    interpersonal, 37–38
    psychophysical, 38
    spiritual, 39
  psychotherapeutic modalities,
    30–35
    behavioral, 31–32
    cognitive, 33–34
    emotional, 32–33
    interpersonal, 32
    psychophysical, 33
    spiritual, 34–35
  transformation and, Yom
    Kippur, 217–219
Herzl, T., 219
Hillesum, E., 325
Holidays
  connection with, 4

Holidays (continued)
  descriptive summary of, 6–7
  psychotherapeutic function of,
    4–5, 7–8
  purpose of, 3–4
  state-dependent learning,
    memory, and behavior
    (SDLMB), 22–23
  summary chart of, xxiii
Holmes, O. W., 324
Holocaust
  guilt, Tisha B'Av, 156
  Purim, 314–315
Holy-Day celebrations
  healing, 35–43
    behavioral, 37
    cognitive, 38–39
    emotional, 38
    focus of holiday, 39–43
    interpersonal, 37–38
    psychophysical, 38
    spiritual, 39
  ritual, structure and spontane-
    ity, 53–57
Holy-Day cycle
  developmental stages, 48–52
  meaning of, 321–326
  Purim, 294–296
  Tu B'Shevat, 287–289
Holzer, J., 70
Hope, initiative and receptivity,
    integration of, Pesach,
    76–79
Hypnosis, state-dependent con-
    sciousness, 21

Imagery, change and, 24–28
Infancy, developmental factors,
    Sefirat Ha'Omer, 96–99

Initiative, receptivity and, inte-
    gration of, Pesach, 75–79
Interdependence
    God-human relationship,
        developmental stages,
        52–53
    Purim, 316–317
Interpersonal modality
    holy day celebrations, healing,
        37–38
    psychotherapy, healing, 32
I-Thou relationship, God-human
    relationship, developmental
    stages, 52–53

Jewish mysticism, psychology
    and, xxi–xxii
Jewish tradition, archetypes and,
    26–28
Judaism, conflict and, xviii–xx
Jung, C. G., 12, 14, 25, 62, 167,
    313, 321
Jungian analysis
    archetypes and, 25
    transformation of evil into
        good, Yom Kippur,
        214–215

Kalir, 134–135
Kavanah (spontaneity), structure
    and, ritual, 53–57
Kelippah, Jewish developmental
    model, 15–17
Keva (structure), spontaneity
    and, ritual, 53–57
Kodesh, state-ependent learning,
    memory, and behavior
    (SDLMB), 21–24
Kohlberg, L., 97

Language, developmental factors,
    Sefirat Ha'Omer, 99
Learning. See also Healing
    Chanukah, 257, 260–262
    day-by-day, Sefirat Ha'Omer,
        93–96
    left-brain, Sefirat Ha'Omer,
        100–102
    right-brain, Shavuot, 117–121
    state-dependent learning,
        memory, and behavior
        (SDLMB), 18–19
Left-brain learning, Sefirat
    Ha'Omer, 100–102
Levi Yitzchak of Berditchev, 55
Love, Chanukah, 265–266
Loving kindness (chesed), Sefirat
    Ha'Omer, personal applica-
    tions, 104

Maimonides, M., 254, 255
Malchut (kingdom), Sefirat
    Ha'Omer, personal applica-
    tions, 105
Mallet, D., 278
Mandela, Nelson, 272
Manifestation, essence and, Yom
    Kippur, 219–220
Marriage, revelation, Shavuot,
    113
Maslow, A., 311
Matzah, symbol of transforma-
    tion, Pesach, 68
McBroom, Amanda, 66
Memory, state-dependent learn-
    ing, memory, and behavior
    (SDLMB), 18–19
Mental modality. See Cognitive
    modality

Messianism, Purim, 318
Mill, J. S., 282
Miller, A., 155, 157
Miracles
    Chanukah, 256
    redemption process, Pesach, 73
Mitchell, Joni, 43
Moses, redemption process,
    Pesach, 72–73
Mother, God as archetypal,
    developmental factors,
    Sefirat Ha'Omer, 99
Moustakas, C., 140
Mystical union
    Purim and Yom Kippur,
        297–299
    ritual enactment of archetypes,
        Purim, 307
    Yom Kippur, 221–227
Mysticism, psychology and,
    xxi–xxii

Nahman, 303
Nebuchadnezzar II (k. of
    Babylon), 128
Negativity, transformation of,
    Purim, 313–316
Ninth of Av. See Tisha B'Av
Nitzotz, Jewish developmental
    model, 15–17
Nullification, revelation, Shavuot,
    111

Perls, F., xviii, xx, 169, 203, 247
Personal applications
    Chanukah, 273–274
    compassionate self-reflection,
        Elul, 174–176
    Elul, 174–181

Personal applications (continued)
    forgiveness and compassionate
        self-reflection, Elul,
        179–180
    Pesach, 83–85
    Purim, 317–318
    relationships, Elul, 175–179
    Rosh HaShanah, 204
    Sefirat Ha'Omer, 102–106
    Shavuot, 120–121
    Sukkot, 248–249
    Tisha B'Av, 159
    Tu B'Shevat, 289
    Yom Kippur, 227–230
Pesach, 61–85
    descriptive summary of, 6
    developmental stages, 49–50
    initiative and receptivity, inte-
        gration of, 75–79
    overview of, 61–62
    personal applications of,
        83–85
    psychotherapeutic process
        associated with, 80–83
    redemption process, 68–75
    slavery as positive transforma-
        tive experience, 62–63
    symbols of transformation,
        64–68
Piaget, J., 98
Placebo effect, state-dependent
    consciousness, 20
Plato, 221
Powerlessness
    acknowledgment of, Rosh
        HaShanah, 203–204
    grieving process, Tisha B'Av,
        140–143

Powerlessness *(continued)*
  initiative and receptivity, inte-
      gration of, Pesach,
      76–79
  redemption process, Pesach, 71
Projective tests, change and, 24
Psychology
  accountability, Rosh
      HaShanah, 191–192
  guilt, Tisha B'Av, 153–159
  Jewish mysticism and, xxi–xxii
  Purim, 309–317
  relationships, Elul, 179
  Sefirat Ha'Omer, 100–102
  Shavuot, 117–121
  spirituality and, xvii–xviii
  Tisha B'Av, 138–140
Psychophysical modality
  holy-day celebrations, healing,
      38
  psychotherapy, healing, 33
Psychosynthesis, transformation
      of evil into good, Yom
      Kippur, 215-216
Psychotherapy
  accountability, Rosh
      HaShanah, 187–190
  active principle *(eetkafya)*, Rosh
      HaShanah, 196–198
  Chanukah, 266 273
  compassion, Elul, 170 174
  developmental stages, 45 48
  healing, 30 35
      behavioral, 31–32
      cognitive, 33–34
      emotional, 32–33
      interpersonal, 32
      psychophysical, 33
      spiritual, 34–35

Psychotherapy *(continued)*
  Pesach and, 80–83
  receptive principle *(eethafcha)*,
      Rosh HaShanah,
      201–203
  religious ritual and, 4–5, 7–8
  self-reflection, Elul, 165–170
  state-dependent learning,
      memory, and behavior
      (SDLMB), 19–21
  Sukkot, 243–248
  transformation of evil into
      good, Yom Kippur,
      214–216
  Tu B'Shevat, 283–287
Purim, 293–318
  archetypal themes, ritual
      enactment of, 307–309
  descriptive summary of, 7
  developmental stages, 51
  Esther as symbol of spirituali-
      ty, 303–307
  Holy-Day cycle, 294–296
  integrated spirituality,
      300–303
  overview of, 293–294
  personal applications,
      317–318
  psychology, 309–317
  Yom Kippur, mystical union,
      297–299

Rationality, developmental fac-
      tors, Sefirat Ha'Omer, 97
Receptive principle, Rosh
      HaShanah, 198–204
  clinical example, 201–203
  God-human relationship,
      198–201
  powerlessness, acknowledg-
      ment of, 203–204

Receptivity
    initiative and, integration of,
        Pesach, 75–79
    mystical union, Yom Kippur,
        224–225
Redemption process, Pesach,
    68–75
Red Sea, splitting of, redemption
    process, Pesach, 74
Relationships, personal applica-
    tions, Elul, 175–179
Relaxation, state-dependent con-
    sciousness, 20–21
Religious ritual, psychotherapy
    and, 4–5
Revelation, 109–113
    action, 112
    commitment, 112–113
    consciousness, transformation
        of, 111–112
    nullification, 111
    personal experience of, 110
    transcendent experience of,
        110–111
Right-brain learning, Shavuot,
    117–121
Rilke, R. M., 217
Ritual
    archetypes, Purim, 307–309
    change and, 24–28
    grieving process, Tisha B'Av,
        130–131
    state-dependent learning,
        memory, and behavior
        (SDLMB), 22
    structure and spontaneity,
        53–57
    transformation of evil into
        good, Yom Kippur,
        207–208

Rogers, C., 173
Rosh HaShanah, 185–204
    accountability, 185–192
        clinical example, 187–190
        God-human relationship,
            185–187
        psychological perspective,
            191–192
    active principle (eetkafya),
        195–198
    descriptive summary of, 7
    developmental stages, 51
    overview of, 185
    receptive principle (eethafcha),
        198–204
        clinical example, 201–203
        God human relationship,
            198–201
        powerlessness, acknowledg-
            ment of, 203–204
    teshuvah, 192–194
Rossi, E., 18, 19, 20, 119, 149

Sanctuaries, destruction of
    grieving process, Tisha B'Av,
        133–138
    guilt, constructive versus self-
        abusive, Tisha B'Av,
        152–153
Sartre, J. P., 83
Satisfaction, Purim, 313
Seder, of Tu B'Shevat, meaning
    of, 278–283
Sefirat Ha'Omer, 89–106
    day-by-day learning, 93–96
    dependency and, 92–93
    descriptive summary of, 6
    developmental factors and,
        96–99

Sefirat Ha'Omer *(continued)*
  developmental stages, 50
  overview of, 89–90
  personal applications,
    102–106
  psychological perspective,
    100–102
  Shavuot and, 114–117
  turmoil and, 91–92
Self
  archetypes and, 25
  ego and, psychological devel-
    opmental model, 12–15
  redemption process, Pesach,
    68–75
Self-abusive guilt, constructive
  guilt versus, Tisha B'Av,
  147–159
Self-reflection
  compassion and, Elul,
    164–166
  compassionate, personal appli-
    cations, Elul, 174–176
  therapeutic process and, Elul,
    165–170
Shavuot, 109–121
  descriptive summary of, 6
  developmental stages, 50
  overview of, 109
  personal applications,
    120–121
  psychological perspective,
    117–121
  revelation, 109–113
    action, 112
    commitment, 112 113
    consciousness, transforma-
      tion of, 111–112
    nullification, 111

Shavuot, revelation *(continued)*
    personal experience of, 110
    transcendent experience of,
      110–111
  Sefirat Ha'Omer and,
    114–117
Shemer, N., 259
Slavery
  positive transformative experi-
    ence
    Pesach, 62–63
  symbols of, 64 –68
  redemption process, Pesach,
    68–75
Smelting furnace, symbol of
  transformation, Pesach,
  67–68
Soul
  Jewish developmental model,
    15–17
  redemption process, Pesach,
    68–75
Spirituality
  Esther as symbol of, Purim,
    303–307
  integrated, Purim, 300–303
  psychology and, xvii–xviii
Spiritual modality
  holy-day celebrations, healing,
    39
  psychotherapy, healing, 34–35
Splitting of the sea, redemption
  process, Pesach, 74
Spontaneity, structure and, ritual,
  53 57
Sprouting seed, symbol of transformation, Pesach, 66 67
State-dependent learning, memory, and behavior (SDLMB)
  described, 18–19

State-dependent learning, memo-
    ry, and behavior *(continued)*
    Jewish theory of, 21–24
    psychotherapeutic implications
        of, 19–21
Stories, change and, 24–28
Strength *(gevurah),* Sefirat
    Ha'Omer, personal applica-
    ·tions, 104
Structure, spontaneity and, ritual,
    53–57
Sukkot, 233–249
    descriptive summary of, 7
    developmental stages, 51
    meaning of, 235–239
    overview of, 233–235
    personal applications,
        248–249
    psychotherapy, 243–248
    Yom Kippur and, 239–243
Symbol
    candle as, Chanukah, 258–266
    change and, 24–28
    Esther as, Purim, 303–307
    Seder of Tu B'Shevat, 278–283
    of transformation, slavery as
        transformative experi-
        ence, Pesach, 64–68

Ten Commandments, Golden
    Calf, grieving process, Tisha
    B'Av, 131–132
Ten Plagues, redemption process,
    Pesach, 73
Teshuvah, Rosh HaShanah,
    192–194
Tikkun, day-by-day learning,
    Sefirat Ha'Omer, 96,
    102–103

Tisha B'Av, 125–159
    descriptive summary of, 6
    developmental stages, 50
    grief as healing response,
        140–143
    grief to consolation, 143–146
    grieving process, 129–138
    guilt, constructive versus self-
        abusive, 147–159
    overview of, 125–129
    personal applications, 159
    psychological perspective,
        138–140
Titus (e. of Rome), 128
Transactional analysis, account-
    ability, Rosh HaShanah,
    191–192
Tu B'Shevat, 277–289
    descriptive summary of, 7
    Holy-Day cycle, 287–289
    meaning of *seder,* 278–283
    overview of, 277–278
    personal applications of, 289
    psychotherapy, 283–287
Turmoil, Sefirat Ha'Omer and,
    91–92

Victory *(netzach),* Sefirat
    Ha'Omer, personal applica-
    tions, 105

Wheat, Shavuot, Sefirat
    Ha'Omer and, 115
Williamson, C., 254
Working through, self-destructive
    abuse, guilt, Tisha B'Av,
    153–155

Yalom, I., 173

Yochanan ben Zakkai, 264
Yom Kippur, 207 230
    descriptive summary of, 7
    developmental stages, 51
    essence and manifestation,
        219–220
    mystical union, 221–227
    overview of, 207
    personal applications,
        227–230
    Purim, mystical union,
        297–299
    Sukkot and, 239–243
    transformation and healing,
        217–219

Yom Kippur *(continued)*
    transformation of evil into
        good, 207–216
    clinical example, 208–214
    psychotherapy, 214–216
    ritual, 207–208

Zalman, Shneur, xxi, 16, 23, 26,
    64, 66, 68, 94, 96, 97, 98,
    99, 110, 112, 114, 116,
    138, 165, 166, 174, 175,
    193, 194, 195, 199, 200,
    203, 223, 224, 229, 237,
    238, 239, 240, 241, 242,
    255, 257, 263, 265, 294,
    297, 298, 299, 300, 301,
    302, 304, 305, 314

CREDITS

The author would like to express his gratitude to the parties listed below for permission to use their material:

"The Rose" by Amanda McBroom, © Warner-Tamerlane Publishing Corp. (BMI) and Third Story Music Inc. (BMI). All rights administered by Warner-Tamerlane Publishing Corp.(BMI). All rights reserved. Used by permission from Warner Bros. Publications US Inc., Miami FL 33014.

"The Circle Game" words and music by Joni Mitchell, © 1966 (Renewed 1994) Crazy Crow Music (BMI). All rights reserved. Used by permission from Warner Bros. Publications U.S. Inc., Miami FL 33014.

Various Aphorisms by Ashleigh Brilliant. © Ashleigh Brilliant.

"Loneliness" Reprinted with the permission of Simon & Schuster from *Loneliness* by Clark E. Moustakas. Copyright © 1961 and renewed 1989 by Clark E. Moustakas.

"Song of the Soul" by Cris Williamson. Copyright © Cris Williamson.

"The Garden Song" written by Dave Mallett. Copyright © 1975 Cherry Lane Music Publishing Company, Inc. (ASCAP). All rights reserved, used by permission.

"If I Only Had A Brain," words by E.Y. Harburg, music by Harold Arlen. © 1938 (Renewed) Metro-Goldwyn-Mayer, Inc. © 1939 (Renewed) EMI Feist Catalog Inc. All rights reserved. Used by permission from Warner Bros. Publications U.S. Inc., Miami FL 33014.

"You Darkness that I come from...", by Rainer Maria Rilke, translated by Robert Bly from *Selected Poems of Rainer Maria Rilke*, edited and translated by Robert Bly. Copyright 1981 by Robert Bly. Reprinted by permission of HarperCollins Publishers Inc.

"Each Man Has a Name" by Zelda. Copyright © Zelda. Used by permission of ACUM, Israel.

Two songs from *Sheat Hachesed* by Yehuda Amichai. Copyright © Yehuda Amichai. Used by permission of ACUM, Israel.

"Who Will Light a Candle" from *Book Four* by Naomi Shemer. Copyright © Naomi Shemer. Used by permission of ACUM, Israel.

ABOUT THE AUTHOR

Joel Ziff, Ed.D. is a psychologist, consultant and trainer in private practice in Newtown, Massachusetts, and a teacher at Lesley College and the Interfaith Foundation. He also offers workshops on the application of psychotherapeutic process to Jewish practice. Ziff has developed a multidimensional perspective integrating work with behavior, body process, emotion, mind, relationship, and spirit. His background is in gestalt, family systems, classical and Eriksonian hypnosis, developmental theory, transpersonal psychology, transactional analysis, group process, and the Rubenfeld Synergy method of body-oriented psychotherapy. Ziff lives with his wife Elizabeth Rosenzweig and their two children, Max and Lev Samuel.